Cambodia Calling

Cambodia Calling

A Memoir from the Frontlines of Humanitarian Aid

Richard Heinzl

Founder of Médecins Sans Frontières/Doctors Without Borders Canada

John Wiley & Sons Canada, Ltd.

Library and Archives Canada Cataloguing in Publication Data

Heinzl, Richard
    Cambodia calling : a memoir from the frontlines of humanitarian aid / Richard Heinzl.

ISBN 978-0-470-15325-3

    1. Heinzl, Richard. 2. Cambodian-Vietnamese Conflict, 1977–1991—Medical care. 3. Doctors Without Borders (Association)—Biography. 4. Medical assistance, Canadian—Cambodia. 5. Physicians—Canada—Biography. 6. Physicians—Cambodia—Biography. I. Title.
RA390.C3H43 2008   610.92   C2008-900456-6

Production Credits
Cover design: Ian Koo
Interior text design: Tegan Wallace
Typesetter: Thomson Digital
Printer: Friesens

John Wiley & Sons Canada, Ltd.
6045 Freemont Blvd.
Mississauga, Ontario
L5R 4J3

This book is printed with biodegradable vegetable-based inks. Text pages are printed on 55lb 100% PCW Hi-Bulk Natural by Friesens Corp., an FSC certified printer.

Printed in Canada

1 2 3 4 5 FP 12 11 10 09 08

*Dedicated with reverence to the
people of Combodia
and
To Carrie Heilbron, and Ryan and Carson Heinzl*

On Pembroke Road look out for my ghost,
Dishevelled with shoes untied,
Playing through the railings with little children
Whose children have long since died.

Patrick Kavanagh,
If Ever You Go To Dublin Town (Extract)

Contents

Contents

Author Note

In recalling the facts presented in *Cambodia Calling*, the author relied upon journal notes, correspondence, interviews with individuals, review of literary and journalistic information, and simply memory. Every attempt has been made to present a truthful recollection of events. Names have been changed in a very few instances to protect the identity of patients and others who, because of time and events, I would not want to jeopardize. It is not for us to judge those who were doing their best given their resources and training, and in such an extreme situation.

Inaccuracies in spelling may have occurred as some names and facts were recalled phonetically, and others may have been unintentionally altered due to these events occurring quite a few years ago. Where dialogue has been recreated, it was done with the full intent to impart to the reader the most accurate rendition of what was said and what occurred.

List of Characters

(in order of appearance)

Drs. Don and Liz Hillman—Canadian pediatricians working in Kampala, Uganda

Dave—a Ugandan artist in Jinja, Uganda

Malcolm Lowry—a traveler from New Zealand

Dr. James E. Anderson (Jim)—a professor and founder of McMaster University Medical School

Bosch—a local acquaintance in Grenada

Jim Lane—friend and co-founder of MSF Canada

Jacques de Milliano—founder of MSF Holland

Rob Overtoom—a Dutch physician working in Sisophon, Cambodia

Chuon—driver

Smiles—a young girl in Sisophon

Monsieur Mogiath—director of the Sisophon Hospital

Madame Boran—hospital midwife

Dr. Sann—hospital physician

Sok Samuth—hospital nurse

Dr. Bun Thoeun—hospital physician

Rhee—cook and housekeeper

Sao Sim—government official in Sisophon

Maurits van Pelt—MSF country director, Cambodia

Dr. Nhean—hospital physician

Madame Somath and Madame Jewn—housekeepers/cook

Wi—driver

Ian Small—Canadian MSF volunteer

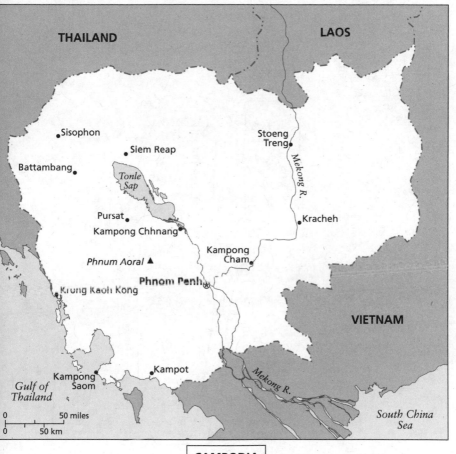

THAILAND

LAOS

Sisophon

Siem Reap

Battambang

*Tonle
Sap*

Stoeng
Treng

Mekong R.

Pursat

Kampong Chhnang

Kracheh

Phnum Aoral ▲

Kampong
Cham

Krong Kaoh Kong

Phnom Penh

VIETNAM

Kampong
Saom

Kampot

Mekong R.

*Gulf of
Thailand*

*South China
Sea*

0   50 miles

0   50 km

CAMBODIA

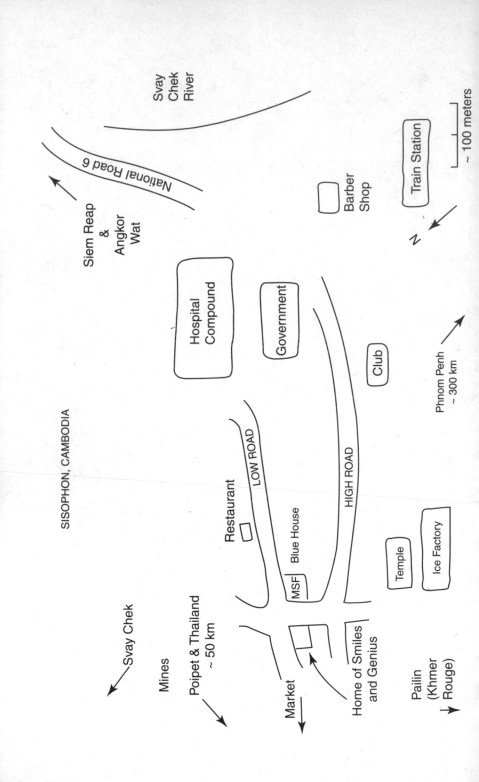

PART I

1

Kenya-Uganda Border
near Tororo

May 1985

Ahead is a border compound with a wooden tower and a long barbed-wire fence that tracks a river bank until it dives into the green tropical forests of Uganda where the war is on. There is no shadow and very little mid-day wind. I feel the intense African sun through my cap, and, looking up, see a white-edged thundercloud, dark at its center, readying for an equatorial deluge. No one seems to notice me, other than some shirtless kids hiding in the roadside thickets. They appear self-absorbed, as if possessed. It's the way their blunted eyes hold you, not letting go. One long stare at the curious foreigner, the mzungu or blanc, whatever they call you here.

I thought the wooden gate in front of me would make a creaking noise as I pushed on the splintered frame, but a gust of wind springs it open wide. That's how storms begin over here—a solitary gust pierces the calm and the mile-high clouds split, letting loose a torrent of rain. The open gate leaves a gap in the perimeter fence. It's saying the thing you're looking for is over here. Come through.

So I walk through unchecked, into a foreign country in plain view, a twenty-two-year-old medical student from the other side of the world on elective in Africa. I lay my pack down by the cracked white wall of the main office and expect to see a border official sleeping away in the torrid heat, his chair tilted back in a corner of the room. Yet there is no one present. Nobody to ask who I am and why I'm here. There are just indecipherable letters spray-painted on the cinder block, a framed picture of President Milton Obote, and splintered shelving that in some remote time had held official papers. I

3

keep hearing a crying sound off in the forest—some kind of bird or monkey. Or perhaps an insect. Even beetles make fierce sounds here.

In the middle of the compound is a mess of heavy machine parts and the metal carcasses of army trucks and jeeps. The parts might rust for another fifty years, before someone decides to drag them away. I am reminded of Paul Nash's painting "Totes Meer," or "Dead Sea," with all that war wreckage piled high. I wander over to the unmanned border tower. Fifty feet high, it overlooks emptiness. No binoculars, no radio or military gun position. No one up there to signal the arrival of an intruder to the rest of the country.

I feel my pockets. Nothing missing. Still have the 800 Kenyan shillings wrapped in a wad around a US fifty and, sewn into my pants, more US cash, my passport, the visa and the all-important letter of introduction for two Canadian pediatricians working at Makerere University in Kampala. If I were to be questioned, I would explain that the good doctors are expecting me, that all is arranged. I am simply hitching a ride across the country to join my compatriots in Kampala.

Out past the border tower and the barbed-wire fence, there is one road leading into Uganda, lined with banana trees and tall grasses. About a kilometer away I can make out a collection of olive green trucks and some men milling around. They are Ugandans and I am certain they are military. Still no border guards or customs people between me and them, just signs with emblems saying "Republic of Uganda" and "By Order of the Constabulary, Uganda Police Force." There are more posters of Obote—one as big as a billboard where he is surrounded by adoring, uniformed children holding school books. It has a Stalinist feel to it.

As I wander down the road, people begin to emerge from the tall grass and scrub. They're not a border foot patrol or military types, but simply a family coming out of the bush onto the road. There are six of them, the adults carrying vinyl suitcases and burlap sacks. The mother is wearing a citrus-colored Busuti dress with puffed-up, exaggerated shoulders. Each child has a box to carry, tied up neatly with string. In a swoop, the mother lowers an enormous demijohn of gasoline from her head onto the road and rests momentarily close beside me, calling me a name which I guess means white person or English man. Everyone seems to have different names for foreigners. I sling my navy blue Lowe Alpine backpack over my shoulder and we all march down the road.

"Kampala?"

The father nods and points to the east. He is wearing a 1950s Stetson type of hat and a pin-striped suit too small for his tall frame. He walks with purpose and grumbles when he talks. I help one of the kids pick up a box. The kids joke with me, trying to open the zippers on my pack to see what's inside.

"How are you getting to Kampala?"

"No Kampala," he says, shaking his head, and then I couldn't follow him until I hear him say "Jinja."

Jinja is good. It's on the way.

Once the olive green trucks down the road see the family and me, they do very fast three-point turns and speed toward us. But they aren't green at all. The canopy shade had darkened their true colors—yellows and reds. I feel my thigh again for my passport. It's a nervous habit, now automatic. Better to keep the passport sewn into a thigh pocket and keep a small amount of spending cash in a lap pouch in case I'm confronted by a thief. Let him have the twenty bucks and get on with the day.

I get ready to report to the border police or the military or whoever is screeching towards us in those vehicles. Not my fault there was no one to report to at the border crossing. And the family I am with hadn't followed any kind of border protocol either. We all just wandered in. But as the cars dart closer to us, it turns out they are just taxis, jalopies in worse shape than the ones I'd ridden in Kenya. The drivers pull up and bid for our business. They lobby to take us deeper into the country.

One of the drivers appears to know the father of the family, even though they don't actually say anything to each other. Some invisible communication gets everybody's luggage, including mine, loaded into and onto the car, a yellow Toyota with no front windshield. It's got mismatched hub caps and a red passenger door borrowed from some other car. The other drivers make faces and start yelling at us; one of them tries to take my pack into his car until our driver raises his voice and slams a door to secure my bag and keep him away. We all marshal into his car as the driver ties down the last of our luggage.

After a moment, the taxi pulls away and the wind rushes through the open space where the windshield used to be to dry our sweat. The mother and her daughters start clapping a beat and serenade us with a resplendent traditional song. The father turns to me and after a moment speaks haltingly, "First I tell you about my people and then you tell me about yours."

He says his people are very magical in their ways, born with a power called nyama and they wield it with skill and control all things in the universe. Nyama is a potent, wild energy present in all the rocks, trees, people, and animals that inhabit the earth. But it's more than that. It's a kind of soul. It controls nature, the stars, and the motions of the sea.

We lumber down the road, occasionally hitting a stretch of asphalt that soon gives way to hard-packed earth. Our driver is often forced to swing off the road into the scrub to get around some of the bigger pot holes, which look like craters left by detonated landmines. This was Uganda's main route to the capital, the Tororo-Jinja Highway. It's lined with lush forest. Through a clearing I can see sunshine lighting up a rain shower in a green valley.

After a while, the family's mother falls asleep on my shoulder. I must have slept too because the next thing I know we are in a rainstorm. Those mile-high clouds have turned black. The deluge is doing its best to turn the mud into soup. The craters begin to fill with rainwater. Tiny rivers crisscross the road, but in an hour the dazzling white sun burns through the clouds and forest cover. Magically everything is soon dry again.

We travel for four hours and, around five, the sun begins to yield, relinquishing its radiant warmth. The taxi has delivered us through another day in Africa and the cool night is on its way. We get out at a crossroads to urinate. The mother and her daughters find a latrine behind a thatched hut. The men just stand at the roadside. People come out of the bush to sell us mangos and cashews. There is a cluster of bamboo huts, the first village we've come to. Still no military anywhere, no border officials, not even any flags.

That's when we hear shouting down the road and gunfire. Some trucks come our way. Our driver unstraps the suitcases, jugs, and boxes and throws them to the ground. It only takes a few seconds for the family to pick everything up and steal away into the trees and tall grass. They simply vanish.

The driver motions me to get into the car and he says something about shillings. I suggest maybe I should go off into the bush too, but when I ask for my pack, the trucks pull up and he just waves the idea away. Two soldiers get out. Totally scary soldiers wearing sunglasses, Kalashnikovs strapped to their shoulders. I have my passport ready but they concentrate on the driver. I have no idea what they are saying. The soldiers tower over him as he offers explanations. It is the Luganda language, and when they're not speaking the soldiers are chewing something, spitting at the ground. I open the car door to get out, but they yell at me to stay put. I try to look as casual as possible, like nothing at all is the matter, like I am an ignorant foreigner who doesn't understand the commotion. After a few minutes my driver puts some money in a cigarette pack and hands the pack to one of the soldiers. Then the soldiers begin laughing, flashing their teeth at everyone. Everybody laughs along with the soldiers until they pile into their truck and drive away.

I ask my driver what had happened. I want to know if the money he paid them means we could now go freely to Kampala, but his English is muddled. He draws a map instead, though I have no idea what the lines represent or which way is west. He writes down some figures, no doubt the amount of the bribe he paid the soldiers or the portion I am expected to contribute. And in the end he just waves the whole conversation away, offering a universal gesture to say that he can't explain but I should come with him. I look around. There's nowhere to sleep or get food, no other taxis, so I just recline in the back seat. I didn't have to be anywhere. No one knows I am in Uganda.

We drive for another hour, the wind blasting us. Maybe it is the fading sun, but the roads do seem to be getting better and there are more cars as we go farther west. The driver tries to tell me something about where we are going and what is going to happen. We can't be far from Lake Victoria and the head of the White Nile, but things don't get any clearer for me until a sign says "Jinja, 20 miles." As we enter the city's outskirts, it is nearing six, the day darkening quickly as it always does at zero latitude. The imperfections of the slums and shantytowns are hidden by the failing light of dusk. This is what Uganda must have looked like before the wars. Paradise.

The driver takes me to a building with barred windows. It's dark inside and there again are the same government-issued pictures of President Obote. The building resembles a police station, only it is empty. We rest against the car. I pull out my wallet to pay something for the ride but the driver motions me to wait. What is it going to be now? Twenty US for the police, ten for the driver, an extra ten for gas? Or was fifty more like the price for a Ugandan "get out of jail free" card? He motions me to wait, saying, "Okay, okay, no problem," and I think, What do I do if this is bad news? Run down an alley, and then?

But instead, a young man in Buddy Holly glasses wearing an ill-fitting maroon suit jacket and flood pants comes running up the street with books under one arm and a large artist's portfolio slung over his shoulder. He is waving at me as he runs.

"Hello, English. How are you today?" A lot of smiling and hand-shaking and he slaps me on the back like we are old friends. He seems to know the driver well. This fellow is definitely not some kind of official.

"This is Jinja, right? I'm not sure why I'm here. I was trying to go to Kampala."

"Yes, English, you are in Jinja. Jinja is the great capital of the Kingdom of Busoga. Me, I am Dave." There is quite a bit of laughter and hand-holding going on between Dave and the driver, and Dave says there is absolutely nothing to worry about, that he will take care of me personally. On his honor.

"I need to get to the capital. Isn't it possible to go to Kampala? Maybe take a different taxi?"

"No, no. There is no taxi at night, actually. No one goes after dark. Not a bit."

"No bus or something? I'm already a couple of days behind and there are people waiting for me at the university," I lie.

"Very bad at nights." He shakes his head. "No cars." The driver, too, shakes his head.

"Well, what do people do in Jinja? I guess I need a room and something to eat."

"Okay, okay, no problem. Don't worry, really. I have a very nice room in the hotel. They are great friends of mine."

"Is it far?"

"No, English. That's it over there." He says "there" like "they-ah."

"What about the war? Is it safe here in Jinja?"

Dave laughs at that. "No war in Jinja. They leave Jinja alone."

The taxi driver taps Dave on the back. There is some unfinished business so the two step back behind his taxi and talk. I watch them go through some kind of negotiation, then Dave ambles over to me, his head down.

"You have to pay two thousand shillings."

"That's way too much." I have no idea how much a shilling is worth, but I make it seem like two thousand was some kind of joke. They go behind the taxi again. Dave stabs at the air. Then the driver stabs at the air.

Dave looks at me. "How much can you pay?"

"How much is five hundred shillings in dollars?"

Dave thinks. He says five hundred is less than one British pound. Actually maybe a third of a pound. Not even a dollar for a full day's drive.

"Okay, five hundred."

They confer again. This time they don't bother to go behind the car. The driver protests. He waves his arms around until Dave raises his voice. Then they shake hands.

"Yes, yes, five hundred for today." They both smile.

I tell them I will pay on the condition that I can exchange money at the hotel and pay with my leftover Kenyan shillings, the banknotes I wasn't going to use anyway, except maybe for bookmarks. And I demand that the driver take me to Kampala in the morning, at first light. I make it clear I want to go all the way to the capital in one day, no overnight stops.

The driver says that going west to the capital is different than the trip I made today, that the price is very much higher because of the scarcity of gasoline farther inland from the border. Plus he needs money to pay the soldiers. "Money for cigarettes," he calls it. He also says the price will be much higher again because I'll be the only one in the car and he will have to pay his half-brother something for accommodation and food in the capital. But he does emphasize I will be the sole passenger. The whole car to myself.

Dave says, "Three thousand shillings. He takes you to the university in Kampala. That's all. Three thousand."

"How about two thousand?" I ask, but immediately they turn the offer down. Their turn to laugh at my indignant proposition. Something is different. The tone of the negotiations has changed. Something about going all the way to Kampala through all those checkpoints. Not even twenty-five hundred will do it. It is going to be three thousand, final. No negotiating.

2

The Grand Hotel

Jinja, Uganda / May 1985

Jinja is motionless in the dark, too quiet. Long rows of brick buildings line the squared-off streets. Sad, sagging wooden structures,
each with an ad-libbed thatched or corrugated metal roof. No electric lights, just an occasional glimpse of a cooking fire down an alley.
All the telephone polls are naked of wires, and we walk over badly
crumpled concrete sidewalks. Plants and trees grow out of the cracks
and rubble. We pass several stripped-out rusting carcasses of cars.

We step into to what Dave calls the "Grand Hotel." The dark
building looks to be six or seven stories tall. Dave is holding my hand
as is the custom between men. I have my heavy Lowe backpack slung
over my shoulder and Dave is still carrying his artist's portfolio and a
clutch of books. A couple of street kids follow us to the door but they
aren't allowed inside. Dave yells at them to go away. He delights in demonstrating his authority, asserting his role as my protector, and doesn't
want anyone interfering with his business. He reassures me that I'll be
on my way to Kampala and the Canadian pediatricians in the morning.

In the lobby, I can make out a large woman sleeping at a desk by
the light of a single candle. Dave barks something to her like, "What
are you doing, woman? Why are they paying you to sleep?" and as she
comes to life some lights blink on and a ceiling fan starts whirling.
The hotel actually isn't too run-down at all. Nice old wood décor,
probably mahogany, a bar room with a rail off to one side. A classic
colonial hotel.

"Passport," the woman says. "You sign." She pushes a form in
triplicate over to me, each page separated by black carbon paper that

has been used so many times it will never manage another copy. And there are other forms. One to exchange money, one for my pack—which I refuse to leave behind—one for the bathroom key down the hall, and a final form to sign before I'm given the room key. You couldn't make out my name or passport number on any of the copies. I wait in silence while she stamps and signs them all.

Another woman emerges from the bar, bringing tea. Steaming hot, sweet milky tea. Dave tells me it's a local commodity and points north to the tea plantations.

The woman behind the desk opens a wall cabinet that houses the room keys. Every hook holds a key. I wonder if I'm the only guest. She pulls a key labelled 108 off its hook.

"Higher up, if okay—up high? Top floor." I point up.

She reaches for key 201.

"Seven, seven," Dave scolds the woman, turning to me laughing and shaking his head. "She is a gross incompetence, actually. Believe me, my friend. I am sorry."

"Am I the only guest?"

"There is one more British."

Dave says he will make arrangements for me to meet the "British," but I reply that all I want is a newspaper, something to eat, and a beer. He apologizes for the kitchen being closed. He says it has been locked up for weeks on account of the war. But, of course, he can find food and beer for me in the city, for an excellent price, at virtually no trouble to himself. He says the beer will be delivered to my room. He will take care of everything.

He is animated and a bit loud with his opinions, just the kind of person I imagine the authorities don't like. Dave reminds me of the refugees whom I saw hanging around the Nairobi markets when I'd been in Kenya: student types, intellectuals, who were persecuted for having opinions. That was their crime. They disappeared for their ideas and they all had that spooked look in their eyes. The fidgeting hands. The constant habit of looking over their shoulder as they talked.

Dave avoids answering my questions about the war. He waves them away. He doesn't want to talk about Idi Amin and Milton Obote, so I ask him what he's carrying in the portfolio and what all the books are for. At this he holds his chin up and says, "Really," rolling the "r," "I am a paint-ah," and as he says it, he looks directly at me through the Buddy Holly glasses, waiting for a response. But before I say anything, he starts pulling sketches from his portfolio, spreading them on the table. One is a drawing of a tractor he has rendered in charcoal. It has a wheel missing. Another is of a little boy and girl, but it is hard to tell them apart. There is a pencil sketch of water buffalo, each animal tilting oddly. All are minimalist images, a bit like the great Caribbean primitive artist Canute Caliste from Grenada. Each sketch is signed with a bold flourish—"Dave." He describes his plan to finish his technical training and then devote his life to painting. He looks skyward, confessing he can't afford much in the way of acrylic paints any more. Down to three colors now, two browns and a blue. He was forced to leave blank spots on the last few canvasses where the green grass and yellow sun should go.

Dave walks me around the hotel lobby, showing me his paintings displayed on the walls, each one for sale and all showing the same tan cow and a sugar palm. Five dollars a painting. One canvas has an extra feature: a group of children, each holding a milk bowl. The shadows from the tree and cow aren't in perspective and for some reason he gave the cows a squint. Each eye stares off in a different direction. It looks like a cartoon.

We sit down. A man arrives and joins us at the table. It's the other "British" Dave had mentioned. Actually, it turns out he is a Kiwi. His name is Malcolm Laurie and he has been doing the sub-Saharan route from Senegal to Kenya on motorcycle. He had crashed his bike and was now pausing in town, trying to get a fuel pump and lifter combo. He calls it a "stupid fuelling pump and lifter combo" and reviles Jinja as the "worst bloody city" he's ever seen. The three of us sit at the barroom table looking at Dave's paintings until Dave excuses himself to find beer and food out in the city for us. As soon as he is gone, Malcolm starts going on acidly about how brilliant the paintings are. He pretends to hug one of them. He thinks it imperative to acquire a "Dave." These original works of art, he opines, could be worth untold sums one day. He throws some worthless black copper pennies on the table. Wise to invest in a "Dave" as soon as possible. We'll soon be witnessing an entire new art movement, the "Dave-ists."

Malcolm certainly is not enjoying his trip through Africa. He has been robbed three times, so everyone is a "stupid fucking thief" here. He can't stand taking the anti-malarials and the "chloroquin head" he gets from it. He couldn't put his finger on how the drugs bothered him but he doesn't like the feeling; when he stopped taking them, within a month, he came down with malaria. He had been sick, he says, "constantly." The local medics "don't know a fucking thing" and he hopes they all "get their own stupid disease." He also says it's impossible to find a local girlfriend without having to pay something.

I notice a kid hanging around the hotel doorway trying to get Malcolm's attention. Not a word of English from the boy, only whispers in Luganda. Malcolm finally sees the boy and waves him over. He lets the boy know we are hungry and thirsty. Then, to make things perfectly clear, on a napkin, Malcolm sketches a bottle of Nile Brewery lager, the local beer, pretends to drink it and feel cold. "Baridi," says the boy.

Malcolm wants something to smoke as well. He inhales from an imaginary cigarette and then makes a gesture with his hands around his head to make it seem like the imaginary smoke had put him into a state of total happiness, nirvana after a long day. The boy exited immediately and was back in twenty minutes, all smiles, with bread, bananas and six beers on ice so cold all the labels had slipped off. And wrapped up in newsprint, he hands Malcolm what he calls kag, a local weed, black-brown against the newsprint. And with it is some kind of a cured tobacco leaf to wrap and smoke the weed in. Smiling broadly, the boy uses his hands to show how the smoke will make Malcolm's head light and happy. Malcolm pats him on the back, slips him some shillings and tells him he is a very, very good boy.

We retire to Malcolm's room, on the sixth floor.

"I dunno, man. Should you really spark that up here?" I ask.

"Awe, don't fucking worry about it. We're on the sixth floor. They all smoke."

"I dunno."

"Look, I've smoked in every fucking country in West Africa."

"This is East Africa, man."

"We smoked so much in Nigeria I lost a week. Up in Kano they have a way of rolling it up in a newspaper and the men from the village stand in a circle in the clearing. They keep passing it around until every last one of them is on the ground looking up at the stars. You wake up like that the next day."

There's a knock at the door. Malcolm idles over to it, wanting to know, "Who the fuck is there?" It's Dave and he's alone, so Malcolm lets him in.

Dave gives us a smile. He calls me Doctari now, knowing why I am passing through East Africa. But as he scans the room, he takes a deep breath in through his nose and starts to freak out. No other way of putting it. He just freaks out, waving his hands around trying to clear the smoke. He shuts the door behind him and stares at us.

"You're smoking bhang? You're smoking bhang in the hotel?"

Malcolm says, "So?"

Dave says, "The police will get you much trouble. They will take you for this. I have seen it."

He runs over to the open window, sees that it is open pretty much to the top already, tries to open it wider, fails, then cranes his neck out the window and looks down to the street to see if anyone is out there.

"You are crazy to do this, actually. This is very bad, really."

"Sit down, Dave," says Malcolm. "No one knows. No one has to know."

"You are crazy. Actually a great risk."

"Now, no one's going to find out anything. We're up here in our private fucking room on the fifth floor and it's our little secret."

"Sixth floor," I tell him.

"Sixth floor," says Malcolm "and it's a private party and let's just forget about it. It's all gone now anyway."

"Oh, you can still smell it. Do you know what they can do to you for this?"

Malcolm was patting Dave's back, and Dave was shaking his head at the floor when there was more knocking at the door. Dave goes rigid.

15

Malcolm prances over. A man we didn't know is standing there. He's got six more bottles of cold beer.

"Who are you?"

He points to the beer.

"Who told you we needed more beer? The kid?"

The man makes the universal I don't know gesture with his hands. Malcolm feels how cold the beers are, pays up and tips the man, giving him one of the beers as a bonus. The man disappears. Dave is sitting on the bed with his head in his hands.

"Please don't do any more of that. I advise you to get rid of it. It's all gone?" asks Dave.

"All gone," reassures Malcolm.

"True?"

"Honest," says Malcolm winking at me. "What were you here for anyway?"

"I don't remember," says Dave.

"You must have come for a reason."

Dave picks himself off the bed and quietly shakes his head at Malcolm. "I came to say I have taken a room here in the hotel tonight."

"That's a boy. Have a beer."

"Maybe it was a mistake. You may get us in great trouble."

"Come on, have a beer."

"I cannot, really." he says, again rolling the R. "I will retire now."

Malcolm pats him on the back and tells him to come back if he wants a beer. Dave says thank you.

"Or a smoke," says Malcolm, at which point Dave goes stiff again and Malcolm has to calm him down one last time before he sends him on his way to his room somewhere in the dark hotel. Soon Malcolm leaves, too.

Then it seems wearyingly late, maybe midnight already. I'm thinking I'm the only guest on the seventh floor. There's no noise from the neighboring rooms. Way better than the night I spent earlier in the week, waiting for a ride into Uganda from Kakamega, where, in the adjacent rooms, the prostitutes kept their business affairs going all night. Not easy sleeping with that going on in stereo.

I lie on the bed and listen to the BBC on my Czech shortwave radio, which comes in on the 5900 band. The "Africa Report" is just beginning, drifting in and out with the cosmic buzz of the ionosphere. The fourth news item is a report on Uganda. Obote's faction is threatening to give up on negotiations with the Tanzanians. Key rebels and the Tanzanians apparently are not willing to wait much longer. The people are behind him. Their troops are amassing at the border and stockpiling arms. We are maybe a hundred miles from the action.

With the window open all the way, the African air floats into my room. I crack another bottle of beer but am slow to finish it. My map points to where I am—sure enough, a long hundred miles inside Uganda and there are many more to Kampala.

3

The Jinja-Kampala Highway

May 1985

I'm standing in the doorway of the Grand Hotel listening to the city noises. It is something to see Jinja in the morning, lit up by an equatorial sun. There are hundreds of people in motion, pushing and pulling carts, pedaling bicycles, and quite a decent number of cars and bouncy trucks lumbering around corners, some with people crouched up on the roof and hanging onto the back. And if you look a little closer, every third man is barefoot and every T-shirt has holes.

Some women in those citrus-colored Busuti dresses pass by a group of barefoot, muttering men gathered around a doorway. The women march by in dignified silence but one of the men must have said something. When the last woman passes, she gives a sudden display of indignity, scowls at them, and presses her gold cross to her chest.

Dave appears in the lobby, behind his Buddy Holly glasses, talking it up with some of the hotel staff. No big smile this morning. He approaches me with his head down.

"Yes, there is a problem, Doctari. That driver, he is only taking you tomorrow. Not today."

"What do you mean? The deal was we're going today."

"Yes. He has a problem with his car. The engine has a great problem."

"There must be another way to Kampala. I need to go to Kampala today. To—day."

"Yes, it is very sad."

"It isn't sad. It is stupid."

"That driver is stupid. Yes. I will tell him."

"Call him whatever you like. I have to go now. Isn't there another way to Kampala?"

Malcolm comes into the lobby, all cheery. He's had a peaceful night's sleep and decides, what the hell, he's going to start the day with a beer. We pull up to the bar on wicker chairs in front of the Dave originals. Malcolm and the hotel manager know about some buses that could take me to Kampala, as well as private cars. Not too expensive either. I start planning my getaway with them. Malcolm says he would have taken me there on his bike if he had the "stupid fuelling pump and lifter combo." He says I haven't lived until I've seen Africa from a Kawasaki.

"Okay, okay, English," says Dave, "I will find that man. You wait here. I will get him."

"The driver?"

"Yes, I will find him."

"What's the point? His car is broken."

"You wait here."

I pull a three-day-old *International Herald Tribune* from my pack and slide it over to Malcolm.

"Going-away present."

"Bloody brilliant, man! That does it, you're having another beer."

Dave shows up about fifteen minutes later.

"Everything is arranged. That driver will take you to the capital."

I go outside. There is a new driver standing by the same yellow Toyota with the red door and missing windshield. This driver is younger than yesterday's, maybe twenty, and he's wearing a Haile Selassie T-shirt. He has ceremonial scars on each cheek and he's all smiles.

"How's the car?" I ask him.

"It okay."

"No problem with the car?"

"No. Fine."

"Wasn't there a problem with the engine? Why we couldn't go?"

"No."

"Okay. Three thousand, right?"

He is smiling and nodding. All systems go for the run to Kampala. I pay the driver. Dave and the driver do some secondary exchange with my money. The driver opens the car door.

"Keep working on your paintings," I tell Dave. "I will look for your paintings in the galleries of Europe."

He said that would be his great honor.

"Sure," says Malcolm. "They need more African art hanging there."

"Really?"

"Sure," he says, patting him on the back, telling him that it's just a question of time before his art becomes famous.

As we pull away, I can't tell where the driver is taking us but I keep saying "Kampala" and he keeps nodding. I ask him about the car problem and why we almost didn't go.

"There is no problem," says the driver.

"What was Dave saying then?"

"I don't know. The car is fine."

"Wasn't there a problem this morning? Dave was saying there was a great problem. Something wrong with the engine?"

"No. It okay."

But as we leave Jinja, we don't seem to be going the right way. The streets are getting narrower and narrower, the houses more dense. Then we stop at a residence. The front door opens and someone is getting in my car. It is an old woman with glasses and a scarf wrapped around her upper body and head. The scarf keeps her face hidden. She adjusts herself in the front seat and purposely looks out the window ignoring me. I try to address her directly, but she keeps looking away.

"Who is she?"

"This Majanan."

"Who's Majanan?"

The driver shrugs his shoulders.

I ask where she is going and remind the driver that this is supposed to be my car all the way to Kampala for the three thousand. Not a bus run for him to make extra fares. No answer from up front. I keep asking what the plan is. I don't want to be stopping for extra rides. I remember telling him it wasn't a mutatu taxi. It was already going to be many hours to the capital and I absolutely had to be there by night, which wasn't true. He puts his hand in the air to say he doesn't really understand anything I'm saying. Suddenly the driver has forgotten how to speak English. Later I ask if the woman is his mother. He says it's his aunt.

We drive and drive. It doesn't seem possible but the Jinja-Kampala Highway is even worse between Jinja and Kampala. I go over the Rand McNally map of East Africa, but trying to estimate hours on the road from distances on a map is a hopeless task in Africa.

I pull out Stevenson and Fanshawe's *Birds of East Africa* but there aren't any birds in the sky. I don't have any other books with me. I'd given away the three novels I had already read, something I don't usually do. They were heavy to carry—and Graham Greene's *The Heart of the Matter*, a book about expatriate love in West Africa, had been soaked in a puddle of gin one night in Kisumu.

Up ahead of us there is a military checkpoint. Army trucks blaze past us. Our car stops. I hold up my passport for the soldiers to see. Most of them are standing on a Russian flatbed truck, each with automatic weapons. They are wearing improvised uniforms, some with camouflage pants and a T-shirt, others with no shirt at all. A few have machine gun bullet-belts crisscrossing their chests, and one of them is leaning against a bazooka. They stop every car, sticking their heads inside the vehicles one at a time. A quick interrogation for each. I'm wondering how much a bribe would be out here in the scrubland. When are they going to nudge me and start asking for an explanation? Ask me why there is no stamp in my passport? But the amazing thing is, they just wave us on. In fact, none of them really look at me. No eye contact. Not even the ones who look to be fourteen or fifteen years old. Just spooked kids, cigarettes in their mouths and wide eyes sweeping the scene, like they were on something.

We got the car going and every so often we'd be passed by a four by four, usually a Land Cruiser or a Land Rover, nice machines for these roads. Each has its organization's logo emblazoned on the door and some have flags of the International Committee of the Red Cross and Red Crescent. There was another flag too, and I don't recognize it at first. It is like a red-on-white cross but the reverse of it, like a color negative: it is the flag of Médecins Sans Frontières.

Most of what I know about MSF came from a rambling conversation I had during the fall of '83 with an acquaintance named Al Kewley, a man who looked a little like George Orwell. Kewley was well-read and traveled, and had been following MSF's growth. We used to talk for hours in a café he ran called Delectables on Danforth Avenue in Toronto. He called MSF the French Foreign Legion of medicine and said if you really want to prove yourself as a humanitarian, you had to work with them.

The boxy white Toyota Land Cruiser with that MSF flag pulls in, rather fast, and when it stops, a low cloud of brown road dust eases away from the truck and floats to where I am standing. It floats right through me. The passengers exit and stand stretching in the knee-deep brown cloud: two women and two men, expats speaking French and Flemish. They all light up Gitanes, while the driver goes to the hut to get cold beers from an ice box for all of them. He calls out "Bbiya," which I surmise is Lugandan for beer.

One of the MSF men is quite tall and bearded and he has an odd way of walking with his mouth cocked to one side, as if he was about to confide in you. I watch him ask the café owner if he can play his cassette on the café's ghetto blaster. Not allowed, he is told. So the tall man puts his arms around the owner and pretends to plead. Still no. Then he gets down on one knee and asks again until the owner acquiesces. In a minute they have his music playing, he is dancing and asking the owner to turn it up. The two women from the truck go off to the far end of the café and sit on a log. They sit there smoking, letting the African sun warm their faces, taking no notice of their dancing colleague. I gather they've seen this before.

The other man comes up to me. "Avec qui travaille-tu? Ah, you are English. Who are you working with?"

I am in the country illegally; some kind of medical-student-gone-AWOL trying to see what war was like. So I just say, "I'm traveling on my own. You?"

He sticks his thumb out at the MSF emblem on the Land Cruiser. "We're going up north on an explo."

"What's up there?"

"Merde. The war has made it bad." Then he tells me all the hellish details: everything has been busted up since Idi Amin, measles is now rampant; people are disappearing. He explains how factions are warring and trying to take charge and how gangs are moving through the villages. He tells me their team had been in Kampala to buy supplies. The back of their car was crammed with boxes of food, cases of beer, pharmaceuticals, and other equipment like IV fluids and mosquito coils, whatever they could squeeze in, plus they had a dozen other boxes secured to the roof racks. All the things you couldn't get up north, not even at extortionate prices.

The tall man with the beard comes over and hands us beers, sweeps his hair back and shakes my hand. He has his head cocked to the side and is half dancing to the West African music he has going on the box. Wants to know if I want a Gitanes.

"You like my music? Ali Farka Touré? I don't care if you like it. I'm just asking."

"Yeah, Senegal," I say.

"Non, mon ami, Mali. Mali." He has his hands around my back, trying to get me to dance with him, but I point to the women and say I'd rather dance with them. So he yells to them, telling them to come over and dance, but they ignore us. He says they better come over and meet the traveler or he will not give them any beer. They ignore him so he cranks his head back to me and says the women are completely rude. He decides he won't give them any beer and wants to know how to pronounce "bitch" correctly. He yells over to them again and points to me, calling me "Voyageur, complètement fou!"

Finally the women offer muted, polite gestures to say hello: gestures just obvious enough to acknowledge my existence and just minimal enough to serve as a snub. Even when we walk over to them, they only manage a stingy "Oui, oui, bonjour."

It is ten a.m., the sun already high up and we are drinking beer in the shade. The tall Belgian dances over to the hut and helps himself to the volume knob, grabs two more bottles of beer and then spins around in the sun. The African kids are laughing at this. Out comes the owner to tell everyone the music is too loud. A bus pulls in covering all of us in another cloud of brown dust. People spill out and laugh at the dancing foreigner and his music. A few of the younger ones begin to dance along with him. More beers are passed around for the expats and the Belgian man hands out cigars. Even the women on the log start smoking them. We are all smoking Romeo y Julietas from Cuba when the driver revs up the Land Cruiser and signals it is time to go. The tall one retrieves his cassette from the owner and cranes his neck one last time to find me before climbing inside the truck. The women get up from the log, offering only, "C'est dommage nous avons manqué de temps pour parler, mais bonne chance quand même."

It sounded like, "Charmed, I'm sure."

The Land Cruiser dips down into a pot hole before popping up amongst the palm fronds and onto the hard-packed mud that passes for a road. As it picks up speed, the limp flag on the truck's flagpole comes to life and the trail of brown dust floats into the bush. The MSF team is gone but it was as if I'd just seen something beautiful. A chance encounter on a bombed-out roadside watching them drink beer and smoke Cuban cigars under the morning's radiant sun, recharging themselves before speeding way up north to some desecrated place caught up in war.

4

Makerere University

Kampala, Uganda / May 1985

My driver leaves me and my backpack on a cracked patch of cement at the east campus gates of Mulago Hospital just as the sun drops into the forest. The façade of Uganda's greatest hospital looks white and clean, like it might be the equal of the Nairobi Hospital in Kenya where the wealthy and the diplomats go. But war has a way of ruining things and now, even though it looks pristine on the outside, I am to discover that very little works inside the grand building. Everything is dark in there.

I walk past several medium-size white brick buildings that appear empty and choose to enter one that has the words "Casualty" and "Mess" painted on the same entrance sign. In an adjoining foyer, a few nurses in blue uniforms chat under a solitary light bulb but I see no patients. I remember thinking, Where is everyone?

A man in a short white smock is standing by a service entrance muttering while he tosses the contents from boxes onto a large pile. He is shaking his head at the mess. In the pile I recognize x-ray films and parts for incubators. There are electric switches and many different kinds of fuses and sample jars. The man has a pile six feet high in front of him.

"These things don't work, my friend. You see? We have no machines to run them in. There is no technician so they are useless. What can we do?"

He says his name is Mr. Mabwe. He has several gold-capped teeth, and faded tattoos on his neck. When he finds out I am a medical student, he asks if I know how to fix an x-ray machine. He shows me a circuit board and then he throws it into the pile as if he is mad at the object. He says I had come to his country at a very bad time. He says this and then hurls a box of light bulbs onto the pile.

I spend the next while shuffling around the wards and offices peeking in on people and patients. Nobody appears to mind. I'm obviously a foreigner and have a free pass to anywhere in the hospital. I recall the same thing happened in Nairobi at the Kenyatta National Hospital. I ventured into that dark and cavernous building with no introduction or contact name and stopped at the dressing station to ask a rotund nurse in a white uniform if I could observe in the clinic. She told me to sit and wait. Ten minutes later a physician approached me with a silver tray of syringes and ampoules. He motioned to a crowd of twenty mothers and children standing against a wall and said, "You see those people over thah? Go and vaccinate them. One cc each. I will be on rounds until late-ah." That was it. No paper work. No licensing requirements. It was enough that I was a foreigner.

Now, at Mulago Hospital, on this sultry evening, I'm trying to find the Pediatric clinic and the two doctors, Liz and Don Hillman, the Canadian pediatricians running a program called the Child Health and Maternity Program—CHAMP. I knew the program was part of the adjoining university, Makerere, but I had no idea if they were even in the country. All I had done, with the help of my professors back home, was get a telex to them. We never heard back and, just before I left, the conflict in Uganda started escalating and we all put the idea of my going to Uganda aside. My professors were saying it was too bad. That it would have been a brilliant brushstroke on the canvas of my education and so interesting to have met them.

As I leave the building, two guards take up their night positions in the shadows of the main gate. I can't see their faces behind their hoods but think I'll approach them to ask about finding the Hillmans. I heard people call them "goon guards" because they were tall and unsmiling and cloaked in large winter coats, even though it was sweltering. But before I reach them, a man with a briefcase and short grey stubble on his head sees I am lost and walks me around to a desk in the administration office.

"Doctari," says the woman behind the desk. "Good to see you again."

"It can't be me. I've not been here before."

"Before with the engineers, yes?"

"What engineers?"

"Oh, oh. You are not with the Soviet?"

"No. I'm here to see the Hillmans."

"Not with the engineers, no? Some other engineer?"

"I don't know anything about that."

She looks at the letter of introduction I had. Then she puts her hand to her forehead and motions for me to sit. "You are just arriving here, sir?"

"Yes, from Jinja this morning."

"Any trouble?"

"Huh?"

"Any trouble coming here?"

Some others come in the room, introductions and handshakes all around, everyone wondering if I am the engineer. One of them is reading the letter and then he suddenly understands. I am not the engineer and I am in the wrong building. Lots of apologizing and back-slapping.

"Doctari. You come."

He holds my hand, and walks me past several dark brown wooden wards and up over a hill to a whitewashed building lit up against the night, with a sign that reads CHAMP.

A woman in a lab coat standing by the entrance introduces herself as the intern on duty. She tells me it is very difficult these days because most of the regular doctors are on strike. Nobody has been working regularly for half a year. The remaining interns are working double shifts to get by. Their chief resident on the ward has left to be with his sick mother in the village, so now the ward has only one intern for the last month and likely the next. She is paid ten dollars a month to be there.

Then other staff arrive and it is as if I am being welcomed as some kind of visiting dignitary or emeritus professor. Evidently the Ugandans are having a hard time estimating my age and standing in the medical community. I keep saying they were the ones who know far more than I do and that I am not even a doctor yet. But they thought I was being modest and making a simple joke. So they all start belly laughing, patting me on the back. They keep referring to me as doctari and professor and what a great honor it is for them to welcome such a highly respected international colleague.

One of them escorts me hand-in-hand up to the top of a lane to several modest one-story homes to find Don and Liz. Up there are guest bungalows kept by the university. The insects and frogs are screaming from the tree branches. The moon's making inky shadows of us as we walk past the white walled homes. We enter one of them and find Dr. Liz at the sink cleaning up.

"Oh, my, look at you," she says. "You must be him. Our visitor is here. We knew you would be here. Come give me a hug."

There are potato chips by the sink, a two-week-old copy of the *International Herald Tribune* on a table, and a bottle of Canadian Club whisky by the coffee pot. I have found a momentary home.

Liz asks me to join her on the wards for the evening rounds. I find her unassuming, like somebody's mom, as I hear her tell me all about living in a war and how to make a hospital function under the eye of a defunct government in a broken society. She said things in the country were indeed worsening, particularly in the countryside. They thought there would be a coup d'etat any day. She didn't know who—maybe Okello or the Tanzanians. And just in case, Liz and Don had made a few contingency plans, talking it up with the other expats who were hoarding a little gasoline and foreign currency, but mostly they were counting on the university being a free zone, off-limits to the soldiers and their guns. A rebel leader named Museveni could also take over, she said. It was just a question of time. But the two doctors hardly carried themselves like there was a war going on. They just got up every morning and went to work.

During our rounds, Liz wanted to hear all about Canada and the colleagues we had in common back home. She was so curious about my medical school, McMaster in Hamilton, and how we self-directed our education and learned in small groups. She was struck by the fact that the school allowed me to come to Africa so early on—amazed they approved my visiting a country at war. That's when I told her they didn't actually know I was here. That no one did. I told her I basically ran away from the hospital I was supposed to be working at in Kenya to witness what was happening here. I had to see the war. And this she understood.

I told her about Nairobi where I met with Dr. Roy Miller, the local medical legend who had been the personal physician of Jomo Kenyatta, the founding president of modern Kenya. She said she had heard about Miller. I said he shared amazing stories from the colonial days and I got a tour of where he worked, the pristine and private Nairobi Hospital. I told her all it took for patients to get admitted there was money. They would be well cared for, just as if they were patients in the premier hospitals in London or Boston. It was Roy Miller who helped modernize the health system. Not a small achievement. But Miller was prescient to know I wasn't in Africa to learn Western medicine, so he sent me to Kakamega, in the west of Kenya, to work in a rural hospital with a Dutch surgeon named Dr. Henk Verberg.

Liz didn't know of Verberg, so I explained the whole thing. I said he was stiff and proper and his hospital was on a dirt road outside town. He arranged lodgings for me—a very small room in a back alley just off the main road. It was a lime green, cement-walled room and there was a communal shower in the courtyard. I was handed coupons for meals at the tiny hospital kitchen and was even paid something like two dollars a day. The plan was for me to learn surgery working alongside Dr. Verberg as a kind of intern. So there I was, in Africa, committing to memory the names of muscles and bones, something I could have done back home. The days started early and the nurses and other staff often slept in the afternoons. So it was a kind of banal existence for a while, not what I crossed the ocean to experience.

But it was cool simply being in rural Africa, living with the local people in Kakamega, with ample time to just hang around. One balmy evening at a party for the doctors and business types, the party kind of disintegrated when someone's dad got potted on the gin and started smacking his ten-year-old on the face, scolding him in front of all the elites in town, saying, "You'll never be like them." There was some rotund banker type laughing along with the boy's father. No one said anything until Henk Verberg said, "He's only a boy," and I guess it stopped the assault, for a while anyway. Somebody brought the father's car around and he wobbled up to it, shouting nonsense to the crowd, his son in tow.

The most interesting things happened when we were on call. Often the worst cases were simply dropped at the front door of our clinic. We had a man with a tumor the size of a rugby ball in his abdomen. A nurse brought me to see him lying there, curled up in a ball. When we straightened him out, it looked like he was pregnant. Another man had been in a fight. He somehow drove a car to the front door and collapsed on his horn until we came. Apparently he had been delinquent in repaying a small loan and as a reminder, some thugs had beat him up rather thoroughly. He had what you call a flail chest, where several ribs in a row are cracked so badly the chest can't suck in air properly.

But the worst I saw was a young mother in labor. She was attractive, modest-looking but lovely and maybe twenty. She wore a plain light-brown dress and we were told she and her midwife had trekked from way out in the bush, more than a day's travel by ox-cart, and she had been bleeding the whole time. I don't know what tribal language she was vocalizing, but it was hysterical and her moaning filled the operating room. It was like she was calling out to spirits. The two physicians in attendance were working fast, telling her to keep quiet while they went inside trying to clamp anything that was bleeding. All of us were up to our elbows in blood and it took me a few tries to get a second IV into her arm.

A tall obstetrician arrived and took over. The doctor was joking with the staff, carrying on a monologue in Swahili. He wore a mask so I just saw his eyes and he leaned over the patient to show me how under her eyelids, where it should be pink, the tissue was white and where the skin on her neck was supposed to be warm, it was cold. He was wielding different clamps and silver scalpels and he kept up the funny monologue, telling the nurses he was late for supper and they better hurry up with the saline. Everyone was belly laughing along with him.

I didn't really know what he was saying but I couldn't help it, I laughed too. He was going on about how patients like this should come to the hospital sooner, how it was rude of them to galumph into the clinic so noisily. The patient and her midwife should have known better. I'm thinking, Do I ever have a lot to learn. I mean it looked to me like she was exsanguinating before us but the surgeon was laughing and I was thinking, good, the young mother was going to make it. But when they lifted her to the operating table, she started shaking with a seizure. Her plain brown dress was black with blood and it was spilling over the table, pooling on the floor. The obstetrician was working as fast as he could, and he kept up the monologue, still some laughing from his audience but not as much, and then the shaking stopped. He reached up and closed the IV drips, and then he stepped back. The young mother was dead.

I told Liz that two weeks into Kakamega, I took the surgeon's kids to a rainforest tree house hostel for a weekend to watch the birds and the monkeys. They were fine kids, totally at ease in Africa, and about halfway through I came down with brutal cramps, some kind of food poisoning, maybe shigellosis. Never had it that bad. Twelve hours writhing on the smooth wood floor beside the bed gritting my teeth every thirty seconds as the cramps hit. You could time the cramps. I truthfully thought my insides would split, that I might succumb up there in the jungle canopy with the kids and the monkeys. I had heard of this happening.

A day later at the surgeon's house, I fell unconscious in their spare room, dehydrated and limp. It had been forty-eight swirling hours in that jungle without sleep, and I could not move. The surgeon came and woke me to say there was nothing really the matter with me and that I'd have to move into the nearby hotel. That lime green room. So I didn't feel too welcome, and I didn't want to memorize anatomy but most of all, I wanted to see Uganda. I needed to see the war and what was happening over here.

I probably should have said goodbye to the surgeon and explained why I left Kakamega. His wife kept saying, "You should at least wait for him to come home on the weekend. Then you can explain it to him, in person." But really, I couldn't stand the guy and his way of being uptight. I was supposed to be with him in Kakamega for six weeks. I left for Uganda after two. The next morning I squeezed into the back of a Mutatu and headed west. And so here I am.

Later that first evening when Liz and I had finished our rounds, Liz's husband Don finally comes home. What kind people, working so late and welcoming me so generously. Before retiring, Liz and Don show me a narrow room at the back of the house where I am to sleep. It has a dark wooden table with an old Singer sewing machine inside a broken casing. There is a couch to sleep on with fresh sheets. Against a wall, floor to ceiling shelving houses two or three hundred books: classical literature from the Greeks to Francis Bacon, and modern stuff like Greene and Huxley. There are school books, atlases, volumes of Ugandan poetry, aging *National Geographics*, and picture books with plastic covers.

It reminds me of medical school. My professor Jim Anderson had a similar study back home. Same as Norman White. It seemed that all of the professors I had become close to had studies filled with literature and art, and a few tomes about medicine. And they all seemed to be psychiatrists too, all of them interested in how things went wrong with human thinking, how bad it could get, how mix-ups and horrors danced in people's thoughts.

I happily browsed through the many books. I pulled *Hamlet* off a shelf. What a perfect way to begin a work of fiction: "Who's there?" says the castle guard to the night. And there is a very old atlas. Some modern nations didn't exist and borders had shifted. Up in the Sahara there weren't even any countries. Chad and Mauritania were empty. The entire region was labelled simply Western Sahara. And I found an art book. Masterpieces from the Uffizi.

I listened to the shortwave as I leafed through the art books. The BBC was very clear. It was the "Africa Report," so the lead stories were about the wars in Africa. Uganda, they reported, was deteriorating. They said various factions had a strong hold on the regions outside the capital and there was speculation that Obote might eventually surrender or even leave for the Congo, but there was no mention of an impending coup d'etat. An official from the government laughed off the rumor, saying Obote would never leave his country, and that the capital was perfectly safe and stable. I put the book aside and drifted off to sleep.

In the morning, between slumber and consciousness, I have a waking dream about feeling hungry. And remembering about my hitchhiking days and how it was difficult to find food as a student traveler thumbing rides through Europe. None of us had enough money to eat at the nice restaurants in the capitals, the ones that catered to the well-paid foreigners and rich local elite. We always had to cross town on a hunch or inside tip that some restaurant on the outskirts was offering decent fare at a good price. It wasn't uncommon to wait an hour for a local bus that never showed and then walk five miles, soon past the point of simple hunger, only to find the restaurant was closed. We dreamed about food, mouth-watering dreams, and we went hypoglycaemic, blank from too little sugar in the veins.

But I awake in Uganda to real food. Liz and Don's cook, Jeremiah, has prepared toast with orange guava marmalade, thick salted pork slices and mangos from the market, drizzled over with lime juice, and a pot of steaming, sweet milky tea. Every morning before going off to the wards that week, we would eat outdoors on the terrace shrouded by banana trees and bougainvillea overlooking the Makerere Campus and the city below.

The wards at the CHAMP program are painted bright white; all the light bulbs shed light; there are neat sheaths of paper for all of the clipboard charts. In every bed are one or two little Ugandans, some managing smiles as they sit up beside their mothers. Many have IV solutions dripping into their arms or a leg pointing straight up to the sky so the thigh bone will set properly. But some of them are much worse off and don't even notice us pass by. Those ones are in a delirium, usually from having malaria in their brains, but not one of them would die the week I was there. I was thankful for that because I couldn't imagine anything as difficult to accept, to see one of them die. But equally, the opposite was true; maybe there was nothing more satisfying than seeing one of them turn the corner. Many times that week I saw this happen. Liz saying, "And how are we doing?" and the mother's enthusiastic response, "Much, much bett-ah." Liz smiling, "Ah, better is good. Better is very good."

At the end of the first day on the wards, Don hands me a report describing conditions in the north of the country. He is pleasant, just like Liz, with rounded features and wire-rimmed glasses and is wearing a tie even though it is a very warm country. He retires for the night. Liz is already asleep. I read the report in the screened-in terrace. The wars have destabilized everything up north. What I'm reading is a health report but there isn't much in it about medicine. It's all business and economics and those economic indicators had plummeted, and with it everybody's health. I am reading at a window looking out over Makerere University and Mulago Hospital, listening to the roar of the insects and frogs up in the trees and everywhere in the atmosphere. So loud you have to raise your voice to be heard. There are hundreds of insects stuck to the screen door and behind them millions in a chorus all over the campus. The sounds are layered together in intricate ways. It is impossible to decode and decipher the message, though it was indeed Mother Nature. Just a massive fuzz of noise.

Liz, Don, and I are finishing up dinner. On this night, a pediatrician colleague, Dr. Mushari Kenaji, and his wife Duella are visiting with us. Everyone takes turns telling stories and I am fascinated by their life here and how very normal they all seem to be even though the country has been upside down for so long. Dr. Kenaji wants to know what I think of Africa, but I decline to say much. I tell them I'd rather hear their stories but he presses me and says they are interested to know what others think of them. He says at the very least I should share with them my first impression.

My first impression was strange, I tell them, not very African. On my arrival in Nairobi, I was totally jet-lagged and went directly to the Y, the YMCA, where I knew I could get a cheap room. I was sitting by myself in the cafeteria when an older man showed up at the entrance to the restaurant, walked in like he owned the whole building and as he approached our table, he clapped his hands for service. He was maybe sixty while everyone else was in their twenties. He waved at one of the staff, demanded tea and then looking down, he noticed me and began a monologue:

"I haven't seen you before," he said, pulling at his white moustache, filling the room with his rich tenor, "You don't seem to know how it works here. I'll help you. Oh, and I better introduce myself before you think I'm mad. Kenneth Mason, actor."

Someone brought him tea.

"Are you expecting them to serve you here? No, no, that's not the way they do it. You must obtain a ticket, and then you help yourself over there behind the hallway. Here, have a ticket. I've extras for guests. This one's free. Go on. Now let me have my helper get the chicken. It's not terrible curry. You're not the first who has sat here waiting and then no one brings something for an hour. It's a ridiculous system and we've all complained but it never changes. Some of the members have their meals brought directly to their rooms. They've given up on this place, this cafeteria. They eat peacefully in their rooms now. They hate the system. But I think it's much too lonely."

He sipped his tea.

"The staff brings you drinks, you see, just not food. Well, not real drinks. For that there's any of a dozen places or, better still, have you had a proper sundowner yet? I'm trusting you have," he said. "What's a sundowner? Oh, dear? How long have you been here in Nairobi and you haven't been for a proper sundowner? We'll put an end to that tonight. Not just now, of course, I've got engagements. Acting. I'm something of an actor. Well, as much as you can be in this place. I suppose it's impressive enough for here. You'll see, the only serious actors are part of the expatriate guild. I'll have you over to a play. Have you acted? Everyone should act once in their lives. You've got to have a strong voice, a voice that projects and fills the back of the room. There's a trick to it. You speak to an imaginary person seated at the back row. Could you do that? Oh yes, Richard Burton could do it. But that was before he became wrapped up in Hollywood. That was the end of him."

Kenneth paused to assess the speech he had just delivered. Satisfied with it, he barked over to the staff. "Here. Yes, he'll have tea.

Anyway, are you free around five? Arriving at five is crucial for the full effect. I've a special place for sundowners. Best view of the city, and the other best part of tonight's sundowner is that it is free. I'm sure that's not a problem. You haven't bags of money or something do you? No, I didn't think so. I should have found you at the Safari Club if that were the case. What did you say your father does? Oh, aren't you lucky? Now have your chicken and rice and don't be late for tonight. It gets dark much faster here than in America. Where did you say you are from?"

He didn't invite any of the other guests at the table. I guess he had already had his turn with them. We walked out of the YMCA cafeteria around back where some bicycles lined the wall. There were half a dozen big black bikes, the kind you see against the cold stone walls of the Oxford colleges but also, there was one solitary child's bike, three quarters in size, done up colorfully with streamers and flags. Remarkably, he pulled *that* bike from the bunch, hopped on, tested the horn, and gave a smile and a "hurrah." He peddled away saying, "See you at five."

I had my first sundowner that evening, a rum concoction in a fancy glass. Kenneth Mason went on and on about a movie he was to play a bit part in as I gazed upon Nairobi and its hotels and boulevards and shantytowns.

5

The Hillmans' Home at Makerere University

Kampala, Uganda / June 1985

Liz and Don are away from the university at an NGO forum for the day and they said I'd worked enough on the wards during the week. They said I should take it easy, feel free to lounge around their house, maybe go see the city in the daytime. I overslept and am propped up in my skinny bed leafing through the books from the shelves. The cook, Jeremiah, traipses in carrying sheets and a towel.

"You're still here! I thought you went out with Dr. Liz. Not going over there to the meetings?"

"I think I'm just going to lounge around today. Don't feel like working. I think I'll sleep again."

"Yes, Doctari. You must rest. Tell me when you want some lunch. Dr. Liz gave these sheets and blanket for you."

He notices the book I have in my hand and says it is from his province. He starts flipping through the pages and shows me children posing in uniforms by a school and tells me there are Russians in his home town now. There is something unnatural about the photos in the book. The photographer must have told everyone to stand without smiling. The children are looking into the camera like it's taking something from them. There is a photograph of a man in uniform standing beside a passenger bus filled with children. He is holding his belt buckle and looking into the camera, appearing haunted, as if this was the end.

Jeremiah draws a bath for me and then sketches out a crude map of the streets to follow down to the city. An easy walk, he says. He explains he must go to the market. I have the house to myself.

Yesterday, Don came home in the evening after a long day of work—warm greetings all around. He adjourned to the porcelain tub where Liz lovingly brought him a neat rye whisky to enjoy. He soaked away a day of standing on his feet, all day, attending to patients on the wards. Such civility in the middle of civil war and insurrection.

So, seeing it's acceptable to drink in the bathtub, I send one of the local boys who was always hanging around the compound to the market with a couple of dollars. He comes back with four ice-cold Nile Brewery lager beers wrapped up in newspaper plus an exceptionally rare ten-day-old *International Herald Tribune*. He has a friend with him, tall and smiling, holding a chicken by the neck "buck, bucking" away.

"How much?" I ask.

"One dollar. We cook."

"What about my clothes. They need washing."

"Yes. We wash."

"How much?"

"You decide. You tip."

From behind the bungalow, two more friends show up, smiling, asking for the clothes. The tall man Isaiah is West African, a refugee from the Kingdom of Dahomey. He strings up a line on the terrace to hang up the washed clothing and one of the men dunks my pants and shirts in a bucket filled with soapy water and plunges a smooth, melon-sized stone in and out, going after the clothes. He puts his back into it. He keeps it up for an hour, washing each item alone, changing the water several times. I wonder how my clothing will survive. Then he delicately pins all of it up on the line.

Isaiah and his friends walk me down a lane, saying, "Don't worry, don't worry." One of them comes over with the chicken, holding a razor to its neck for me to cut. I say not today but they insist. Isaiah holds my hand in his as we let a ribbon of ruby-red blood darken the soil. No more "buck, bucking."

In a minute they have a tiny kindling fire going and twenty minutes later we are feasting. I pass out the beers and ask the boy to get more. One of Isaiah's friends starts smoking what he calls deng. Then Isaiah stretches out on the balcony steps, claps his hands and tells the West African story of Ogu, Agwe, and Legba from his animist faith, and how all the spirits of the dead are forever walking around us during the day and night.

I sleep much of the day away. As evening descends I am feeling recharged, ready to go. Liz and Don arrive back from their meetings and retire early. I have yet to explore the city of Kampala below—a capital in wartime—and my time in Uganda is about to end. I have Jeremiah's map in hand, so off I go.

Down the fascinating Livingstone and Pool Roads, I walk past the grand gates and homes and gardens where the university president used to stay, past the two goon guards with their clubs hidden under their winter coats. I tell them who I am—that I'll be back in an hour or two. They grunt and avoid eye contact; no way they understand me. I left my passport and money behind. I thought it would be safer like that. Without those things what would be the point in robbing me?

The city is still and black. Only through windows and cracks in doors can you see the light of cooking fires or weak light bulbs powered by car batteries. I assume all of the children and their families are asleep. A few men are still up playing Abyssinian dominoes or talking, sitting in chairs or on their haunches, a few of them maybe smoking cheap tobacco and drinking banana beer. Ten cents for a pack of local cigarettes, a penny for a mouthful of beer.

There are goon guards at the gates and walls of all the bigger homes outside the university. Walking down Buganda Road the bigger residences give way to smaller and smaller ones; then dull two- and three-story flats take over. No more goon guards. I make sure I know where the main boulevard is in relation to the smaller roads, because the street layout doesn't fit much of a city grid. Isaiah's map is off quite a bit. The lack of light makes it hard to get a proper bearing and those streets don't always turn at ninety degrees.

After a half hour I thought I found the Old Taxi Park but there weren't any mini buses, so it must have been City Square in front of me—why else would there be such an open place in the middle of the city? It has a gorgeous appearance at night, the outline of a fountain and an ornate plaque whose inscription I can't read in the dark. But I can smell some awful stench, and when I get to the center of the park there is just enough light to show that garbage is everywhere. The water pipes to the fountain are ripped out and the fountain's bowl is caked in bird droppings.

I don't know what happened to the light from the beacon at the top of the university hill. There are too many buildings in the way. If I go to the far end of the park maybe the beacon will reveal itself and I will have a chance to realign myself with Jeremiah's map and find my way back to the university. But I can't even see the lane I just came down.

Around a corner I see the silhouette of some men standing by a pile. It looks like they were tossing bricks and scraps into a pile and I wonder why were they working so late? But when I get within ten feet, I see it isn't bricks at all, it's simple garbage, and the silhouettes aren't men; they are giant Maribou storks standing hunched over, pecking at the garbage, each holding its place. Five-foot-tall white birds with long bills standing like old men around a fire.

Somebody shuffles along the ground to me. It is a man, whose legs are all crumpled up, sitting on a tiny skid with wheels. It is as if he is sitting on a skateboard. He has tucked his thin and useless legs under himself onto the dolly so he can push around with his hands. He paddles over to me.

"British. Come here."

"No, thanks. Everything okay."

"What are you doing here?"

"Walking."

"Walking where?"

"Where is the university?"

"Okay, I don't know."

"You don't know where the university is? Makerere? Mulago hospital?"

"Okay," he says.

"Hospital? Doctors?"

"Yes," he was smiling now. "This way."

He uses his hands to propel himself along the street. The poor man's legs are very thin and knotted up underneath him. Every once in a while he has to push his knees down onto the concrete and lift the skateboard up over a crack. The streets are confusing. After a while he has to rest to have a smoke. We try to get moving again but he soon stops again.

"Where's the hospital?" I ask.

"Okay. Hospital."

"Yes, where is it?"

"I will find it for you."

"Is the hospital this way?" I point down the street.

"Yes."

"Right. And is the hospital also this way?" I point the opposite way.

"Yes."

I show him the map. He assures me he knows Jeremiah personally and that Jeremiah is a great man. He tells me he's down to his last two cigarettes and would be grateful for ten cents to buy more. While smoking, he studies the map and looks down the alleys trying to figure out the puzzle in his hands. He is thinking. And after another smoke, my friend falls asleep on the skateboard. Everything is possible. The map is wrong or the map is right. Jeremiah will suddenly appear from an alley or I will be up all night waiting for daybreak.

Some men down the street point at me. They are walking fast and yell at me, telling me to wait, so I go around a corner and through a lane to where some boxes are stacked up at the rear entrance of a cinder block building and wait for them to pass. I think they are going to stop me and ask for an explanation of why I am in their neighborhood. When my explanation fails, they will ask for a better explanation. Then they will become tired of my explanations and tell me I have to pay some kind of neighborhood tax. Some trespassing fee.

But I hear the men go by. I sit in the alley, trying to pinpoint my whereabouts. I remember having no doubt that the Kampala Road crosses the Speke by "The Square" and that it goes all the way up the hill to the university. If that park where I saw the Maribou storks was indeed off Nile Avenue, then all I have to do is go west past the river. The problem is the two roads, Ternan and Nehru, look the same. The streets are not lighted and there are no signs. I thought I found a street name painted high up on the corner of a building but the paint was chipped and partly covered with war graffiti. No car headlights careen around the corner to illuminate where I am.

There is also no university beacon to see at that point, and now all the streets look the same. Empty. Just a few lights in cracks. Nobody around. The plan was that if I crisscrossed through these streets west or even south I would have to cross the Kampala Road and then it would be a matter of time, a matter of simply following it to the university beacon.

I could ask someone but, then again, what a giveaway. I might as well wear a sign saying "Rob me. Rough me up—give me flail chest like that patient in Kenya." And there's also the official curfew to worry about. What did the guy call it: "Right Time"? Right time for what? It would be pretty weird to find a "British" like me walking the streets of Kampala nearing midnight. I thought eventually some authority was going to stop me. Perhaps a gang of soldiers with their Russian automatics would start the questioning.

"British. Stop. What are you doing he-ah?"

"I'm just out for a walk."

"Why? Where are you walking? Passport!"

"Well, I don't seem to have it with me, etc., etc. I couldn't sleep. You see, I'm at the university staying with the Hillmans and I just wanted to see your city, you know, how it looks at night, etc., etc. The Hillmans? Oh, they're foreign doctors and I'm not causing any trouble, am I? A fine? Because of the curfew? You know, I don't even have any money with me. Isn't that funny? I didn't want to get robbed, you see, so I thought . . . no, no, let's not go to headquarters. Of course I'm not resisting, I will come along peacefully."

So I go darting down a dark alley, towards the park again, where I'm invisible in the shadows. My sense of direction has never been very keen and I must have guessed wrong. After a while I am back again in the thick part of the city where all the small wooden homes are pushed together, where the three-story cinder block structures look ugly even in darkness.

At a crossroads by a market I sit on a crate. I'm not particularly thirsty and I don't need to eat anything. I don't need to be anywhere really, and there's no one around, so I have a realization that I could just sit there, just be. Just being, being patient like Bob Lieske, a monk I knew in the Caribbean. He had Trappist monk patience. A core virtue. You'd say, "Hey, Bob, wait here a bit," and it was all the same to him whether you took five minutes or five hours. He would just sit there, his eyes closed, doing nothing for a time, perfectly content in a kind of suspended state.

Sitting on that crate it was good to see the moon coming out to rescue me. There it is, an equatorial three-quarter moon sitting on top of a row of wooden homes, the kind of big clear moon you witness in the tropics that makes you say "Is it real?" The moon climbs and the streets are lightening. The monotone black color of the walls softens to grey and then, when the moon is high enough, its light gives the buildings colour and texture. All of Kampala is revealing itself in the moonshine.

One spring in Paris I had to stay up all night because I had no money left for a hotel room. It was the last night of a six-week hitch-hiking tour of the continent and all I had was twenty francs for some espresso and a Metro ride to Roissy. At four-thirty a.m. Paris is a dark capital but, an hour later, at first light, you can walk around the white walls of the city and it is fully lit up. It's like walking around a massive movie set and you are completely alone.

But here in Kampala, I see a clock in an office. It isn't that late after all. I thought I was alone in those streets but in the door cracks and windows, there are women and older children still up. As I walk along it is clear they have all been looking at me, eyeing the "British," politely watching as I walk through their space. I suppose a hundred people had watched me mumble to myself on that crate, blinking at me with some kind of respect through cracks in their homes.

Up over an orange Fanta billboard, not too far away at all, I now see Kampala Road and up the avenue, past the park and river, there is the white light of the Makerere University beacon showing me a clear path back to my temporary home.

PART II

6

The Home of James E. Anderson

Hamilton, Canada / July 1985

It is after midnight in the old neighborhood, where many of the medical faculty live in stately brick and limestone homes. I tap on the study window of Professor Jim Anderson's house, trying to wake him without alerting the neighbors or his wife upstairs.

He is slumped in his black leather recliner and there is a book in his lap and a bottle of Teacher's Highland Cream Scotch Whisky on the floor. His glasses have slipped partway down his face and his belly is slowly moving up and down. All around him are shelves heavy with books that go floor to ceiling. And there are two other props: an art nouveau ashtray beside him, loaded with the stubbed-out white butts of his Player's Specials, and up above on the window, a stained-glass design of a man's bust that looks like the Pope. He said a former student made it for him. Going to Jim's was like going to church.

Jim is known to be Edison-like, cat-napping in his study. He has some kind of unusual energy and is one of those people who only needs four hours of sleep each night. He's always been like that and loves it when students drop in on him for advice and company any time of night or day. I keep tapping his window but he must have been in a deep, delta-level sleep, where distractions and disturbances like my window rattling didn't register. So after ten minutes I give up and walk along Herkimer Avenue to St. Joseph's Hospital and find a telephone. That always works. In every other way he can be asleep and closed to the world, but, perhaps from decades of being on call, he always leaves that one channel open, the telephone. It is some kind of mind trick.

The phone rings once and his radio-announcer baritone automatically answers.

"Hello."

"Are you up? It's me."

"Hang on." The receiver goes clunk on the table. He must have put it down beside his smokes because I hear him fumbling through papers until the Zippo clicks.

"What's wrong?"

"Nothing. I got the grant for the elective. I'm going to Grenada."

"Where?"

"I told you all about it. Are you up?"

"I must be. We're talking."

"I'm serious, I'm at St. Joe's. Can I come over? I kept banging on your window. You were dead asleep."

"No, I wasn't."

"Yes, you were. I was just there."

"I wasn't asleep."

"I was banging so loud I thought I'd break the glass or wake Helen. You were in your chair."

"Come over. Don't knock. The kitchen door is open."

But when I get there, the door isn't open. He is asleep again in his chair so this time I rap on the kitchen door, loudly enough to get him up, and a minute later, he looms in the door frame—tall, sporting a Harris tweed, glass of scotch in hand, smoking, shaking his head at me, pointing to the study, telling me to keep it quiet. We sit and he lights a cigarette and I start laughing.

"You've got one going already."

"No, I don't. Oh."

"You chain smoke those things every time I'm here. I've seen you do a whole pack."

"Oh, well. People like me better as a smoker. Here, want one? They're the ultra-lights. They can't hurt you as much. In fact, did you know it lowers the rate of Parkinson's Disease. Did you know that? A study showed it protects you from getting Parkinson's. It's true."

He swings the whisky bottle out from under his chair, pulls a glass from a shelf and tilts the bottle for me. I want to tell him about Grenada, get his take on it, but he starts a story.

"Did I ever tell you about Kyle? A sweet kid. He was sent to me from the justice system. His case worker marched him over here herself on a Sunday. You know what she said? 'I can't help him anymore. He's impossible.' She said it right in front of him. Really. The kid was seventeen."

"So what did you do?"

"I told her to leave him with me. To come back in a couple of hours. Kyle told me everything. How he was injecting heroin in the park across from the hospital. He said he was stealing television sets and shoplifting to pay for it. He stole from his parents too. Such a smart kid. His father is a businessman, and he was in the habit of hitting Kyle's mother and as soon as the boy was big enough, he started standing up for her, and now his dad had disowned him. So sad. His father even whipped him when he was younger. Kyle said that's why he kept injecting. He said that. So the police came by the next weekend, with his case worker. They took me to the park and we found him out of it and out of sight in the undergrowth of a hedge and he had a book under his arm. Do you know what the book was? It was *King Lear*."

"And what happened?"

"We got him into the detoxifying center. It took a month and then we brought him into the Cool School. He was such a bright kid. He was reading at the university level but he couldn't write. He had an expressive dyslexia. His penmanship was grade-eight level, so we worked out a new system of writing and taught him to type. The computers are going to be wonderful for him. We got special permission to let him take his exams using a typewriter. He got his high school diploma in four months and he's going to graduate next year from York. He's going to be a teacher."

Typically Jim would slump his shoulders after one of these stories. It was body language for "Where does such bad luck and wonder come from?"

We stumble on something that night. I tell Jim that the way he is finding these broken, brilliant kids on the streets and getting them back into society reminds me of my grandfather, Arthur Doyle, and what he accomplished as a psychiatrist. The coincidence was that Jim knew my grandfather. In fact, my grandfather had taught Jim at the University of Toronto back in the Fifties when Jim was in medical school. That floors us.

He knows all about Arthur and how he moved the forgotten patients languishing in the massive provincial asylums into the mainstream hospitals, where they were given medical diagnoses and helped back into society. No more "Keep them in the dungeon and throw away the key." It was a sea change in mental health care, and Jim said my grandfather was well known. Quite famous in certain circles and at the top of his field when he taught Jim. But that's all he knows about my grandfather. He doesn't know the path Arthur had actually taken to get to the top of his field. He's in the dark about what had happened during the war years.

"Did you know what he did in World War II? He was a lieutenant-colonel, in charge of an armed forces psychiatric unit in the Mediterranean. I guess that's a huge thing. But what he did for all of those soldiers who were shell shocked, instead of letting them get arrested or shot like they did in World War I, he made sure they were diagnosed properly. He turned shell shock into something legitimately medical so the soldiers were rehabbed and not executed as cowards— trauma diagnoses instead of traitor labels. He became a Member of the Order of the British Empire for that, from the King himself at Buckingham Palace. I don't really know what happened. But I've read his letters. He wrote the best ones from the Italian theater to his friend Rusty and every letter started off with, 'I'm here at the front enjoying this damn fine scotch . . .'

"He smoked Player's just like you, only his weren't ultra lights. His had the green package and he mostly drank Schenley Canadian Whisky, not scotch. Anyway, I was twelve when he died and he wasn't well for some years before that. I remember him mostly up at our cottage on Taylor Island in Muskoka. I don't think he got over what he saw in the war. What a combination, war and all of those insane asylums. That was the core of his professional life.

"When he was in Europe, he didn't see his family for a half decade. Imagine not seeing your wife for all that time. And he would have missed watching my mom grow from six to ten. I discovered a letter she wrote: from his little Jane to him over there. I remember finding the letter in an envelope taped to the back of a picture frame with all his medals. My hands trembled when I read it to my mom.

"It's crazy, I had so many relatives in the war. An Uncle Henry, he was in the Air Force in England and before that, I had an Uncle Will, a great uncle, also on my mom's side. He was in the First World War. Can't imagine I saw him more than ten times in my life and all of that was before I was eight. He had had his hand shot up in the trenches and he was mustard gassed. I was told he never really recovered but all I remember was a warm old man who always brought a book for me at Christmas. That Uncle Will, as kind a man as you'll ever find, and yet there he was with everybody else going up over the top trying to shoot and bayonet the enemy.

"He was trying to kill Germans and Austrians—that's my other family, on my dad's side. There was a whole set of great uncles, many of them just as active in the wars but they were on the other side. Uncle Karl was the only one I got to know. I remember arriving at the Hauptbahnhof train station in Styer in Oberösterreich, Austria, on a hitchhiking trip through Europe when I was nineteen. I was the first of our Canadian family to visit the Austrians in decades, had almost no German words at my disposal and only a hand-written set of addresses to find my family. I stepped off the milk-run train and plopped my blue backpack down and stared out at the anonymous crowd. Yet there they were, standing abreast on the platform, waiting for me, the four great uncles I had never met, each one of them clones of my grandfather Roman, and each one of them taking a turn to hug me and bless me.

"Karl was the youngest and in the war he was an officer assisting an attaché to the Nazi mayor in a town in Yugoslavia. I think he was second or third in command. Do you know what they did when the war ended? I don't know if it is true, but the story I was told was that my uncle was benevolent, helping people where he could, and somehow not caught up in the indoctrination so much, the hatred. Apparently when the town was liberated the people held an improvised show trial in the *hauptplatz*. The three ranking officers were put up on stage: the Nazi appointed mayor, the top SS officer and my Uncle Karl. It was a swift summary judgment and right there in front of the town's people, they shot the mayor, shot the colonel, and then slapped Karl's face and sent him back to Steyr. He lived out his life there raising his family and running a successful tailor shop called Heinzl Modesalon."

Jim slumps his shoulders at this. He says it's everywhere. You don't need to fly far away to see it. You don't need to go to Africa to understand it because it is right here, right across the way in the parks and homes. But he says I better go to Grenada all the same. He says my wanderlust problem means I wouldn't be happy staying home and he knows I'd go there without his blessing anyway. Shortly after that, Jim falls asleep, but I keep talking anyway.

"That was the thing," I say. "I had family on opposite sides of the war and they were trying to kill each other. As I grew up hearing these stories, it didn't make sense. War didn't make sense."

7

McMaster University Medical School

Hamilton, Canada, and Springs, Grenada / August 1985

During the first months of medical school, a small group of us didn't have apartments close to the university. Going home late at night was often inconvenient and always undesirable. Instead, we'd sleep on a classmate's couch or floor, staying up late with them, and getting out early in the morning, straight to the library. It was better than waiting in the cold and taking a plebeian bus home in the raw Canadian weather. The favorite place to crash was 43 Traymore because the medical school was only fifty feet across the street. The school's factory façade looms over the house. A bunch of us kept up this vagabond approach to accommodation until Christmas and I guess I kept it up the longest. Nobody seemed to mind.

Still, for me, Africa is out there, with its palm trees and infinite sky. The simple memories are the most powerful, like drinking sweet steaming tea under a corrugated tin roof in a rain storm. The tropics have a way of hooking you. It was three months after Uganda, when a bunch of us started scheming and figuring out a way to get back over there again. Anywhere poor and tropical. We wanted back under the corrugated tin so we can hear the pulse of the rain again.

We learn about a research program the university is running in the Caribbean. It's focused on rural healthcare with local nurses and traditional health workers. A psychiatrist named Norman White runs it with professors and students from the department of geography, and his son Sean is already down there helping the project along. White's home library holds twenty books of English literature for every one of science or medicine, and in his office at the medical school, on a lectern, he has the First Edition two-thousand-page *Compact Oxford English Dictionary*, the one that comes with a magnifying glass to verify the slightest nuances of the language.

We can't believe it when we get the go-ahead to work in the gorgeous Caribbean. The thing about Grenada at the time is that it had just been invaded by Ronald Reagan. We're excited about being somewhere with armed conflict. It's extra cool because it offers up a chance to see the extreme human condition. War amplifies everything and the pretext for the American presence in Grenada was a handful of Cubans on the island: they were building useful things like airports and clinics. Somehow this was supposed to lead to a toppling of the spice island, the other islands nearby and then Latin America. Eventually this was supposed to destabilize the United States. This was the Cold War. One morning there were a thousand US helicopters on Grand Anse beach. The locals told us all about it. New leaders were put in place and the foreign humanitarians on the island got to live through a coup d'état.

Soon after our arrival, the vice president of the United States landed for an inspection. Our group happened to be passing time up in the hillside communities with the nurses. Overnight people noticed graffiti spray painted around the island: "Grenada welcomes Bush" and "We love America." Our local friends had never seen graffiti and wondered why it was there. Someone said it was the CIA who did it. They had seen outsiders spray painting these slogans on the cinder block walls lining the streets. Some kind of phoney war was going on but the locals loved the fact that their tiny island was at the epicenter of world affairs for a brief time. How else would they make the cover of *Time*. In the coming weeks they would march around their streets in amazement with their fingers in the air chanting, "Grenada Number One." It was entertainment.

Our team is based in a nice house in the Bau trees up in the hills, in Springs where the terrace overlooks date palms and wild weeds that roll down to the Love Boat where everyone dances in a half-trance through the night. A few hundred people are packed so tight that when the rhythm goes good, the mass of people move up and down as one. Everyone jumps through the ceiling of burnt ganga, rum on everyone's breath. And there is that constant sweet smell of the tropics, a mix of rotting vegetation, something fermenting, the mildly acrid odor of human sweat. What is it?

On those twilight nights we'd head off to the Love Boat, an easy trip if you left before the light faded. The roads up in Springs all converged and led down to the ocean and the main road that rings the island shore. You couldn't miss it. But coming back, the roads diverged, there were choices to make in the night and it wasn't difficult to get it wrong. The locals had no problem walking the streets and trails in black night. They all had a second sense about navigation. But the clumsy foreigners did not possess this skill. If not for a last-second dodge, they could walk directly into the white eyes of someone standing noiselessly at a roadside. A bit disconcerting but nothing so dire as the dreaded spirits they called the "Jab Jab."

Not long after seven a.m., on a day that threatened rain again, the sun is already making ink black shadows of palm fronds against the white walled home we have on the Springs road. Everyone is tired from the late Carnival partying, so brewing up the Maxwell House and a modest breakfast is a local friend Bosch, tending to the kitchen quietly, trying not to wake us. He has also brought Sean and me a local tea, a very special tea from the mountains that he said would "wake the dead Grenadians and call the Jab Jab out."

Bosch wasn't his real name. Some Dutch tourist gave it to him and he had misinterpreted. It should have been Boss, but now it stuck. Bosch came from Sauteurs, up in the mountains where people just subsisted. We knew all over Grenada there were poor families living in shacks and bamboo homes and that ten US invasions could come and go and those people would still be the same. We knew they were up in the hills under Bau trees far from the beaches and the yachts and we wanted to see them, to get data for the research program, but mostly we just wanted to be up there and see the idyllic simple life on the top of their island.

"Come with me," says Bosch, smiling very wide. "We have to find the Jab Jab."

"Okay. But after, let's go up in the hills."

He says today is the island's Carnival and there is going to be a big parade and it is not a good day to go to the hills in the middle of the island. He wants me to see it tomorrow, on a Sunday, when, he says, all the families would be resting up there, leaving their plots to be tended another day. He says he'll show me some huts up by the old airport where we could find "six children in a bamboo and thatched hut living only from the land. Maybe ten!" He adds that sometimes you will find an old man in a different hut. He will be living alone and he is ninety-nine and has one hundred great-grandchildren. "We can see them lands. Show you them poorest people. See how those families live."

But first we have to see the ghosts of the island, the Jab Jab. So we walk down to the Love Boat where a crowd is gathering and where the parade will pass. Local boys, Henry, and his brother come running up behind us. The two have multicolored necklaces of ribbons and Christmas ornaments draped over their necks and they are giddy, elated with the holiday spirit.

"Much bigger than Christmas," says Henry. "Christmas is very small. Carnival is the biggest day of the year." He has his hands in the air and he is doing a stationary dance. His brother is bent over doing a funny walk in circles to get everyone laughing with him.

Jacana, the neighbor, is at the corner, swaying to calypso under some palms. She is covered in sparkles and trying to hug everyone who comes near. Halfway down to Belmont, the roads are filling up with people. Bosch says there are many tourists flying in for Carnival and that everyone from the countryside is coming down. Everybody is out. Some kids run by yelling they have seen the Jab Jab. Henry's eyes pop out at the news.

"There's Sean," says Bosch, pointing ahead, but we lose him around a corner. We run to catch up to him and see him again a hundred yards ahead for a few seconds, but then there are too many people in front and he disappears. Swallowed in the crowd. Bosch and I go down through someone's yard and step on a chicken coup which explodes with noise as it breaks apart. The birds are pecking at us, flapping their wings against our naked legs as we step over the crumpled poultry netting. We launch ourselves blindly over a fence to get away and land in a yard inches from a filthy dog showing its teeth. Bosch picks up a rock and hits it hard enough to make it yelp and run away. We squeeze past a shed out onto the street.

There are drums booming not far down the road now and we are squished five people deep against a wall, everybody's voices swirling and echoing off the wall. I feel Bosch grab me by the arm but I can't see him the crowd is so thick. He says he has seen Sean on the other side of the street, and then he says, "Here comes the parade."

Some elders and police march along first, giving stern looks to the crowd. They are pushing people out of the way, clearing the road so the parade can come through. Two police motorcycles are doing figure eights. They get too close and accidentally lock undercarriages. The one skids around and the officer falls. Everyone laughs but snap their mouths shut when the policeman shouts a warning. Someone starts yelling that it was the Jab Jab, that the Jab Jab had made the motorcycles crash.

A powder-blue convertible with classic 1950s-style tail fins inches along. The man in the backseat is wearing a fur coat and sunglasses.

"That's Jimmy McFarlane. He's very rich. Rich man. But look behind him. Look at the bus! There!"

"What is it?"

"That Magic Bus. All painted. Every year you see that."

"Where are the Jab Jab?"

"At the end. At the end."

A wall of women ahead of me have their toddlers on their shoulders so we can't see. Bosch spies his cousin across the street jumping up and down trying to get his head above the crowd. We are packed in tight, swaying. A very drunk man sags into us and then falls onto the road taking down a few people with him. He gets up, toasts the crowd, and everybody cheers. Now a curvy woman struts along with wings made of rainbow-colored feathers. All done up in glittering sparkles, her wings extend naturally from her voluptuous body. An old seafarer and colonial soldier circle her, shouting to the crowd. A man follows banging a drum. It is getting louder and people start pointing down the road, yelling, "Jab Jab" and "The Devil comes." People start hugging each other.

Down the road you can see them, about twenty men covered in thick black grease, wearing only loincloths, marching in a pack, so black all you see is white eyes and red mouths. Every few moments one of the Jab Jab lunge at the crowd and hug spectators, covering them with grease. Children dive through our legs to get away and one mother becomes so covered in grease she runs away from the parade in a trance, arms above her head, screaming about the devil.

"That is Margaret, my cousin's friend. Jab Jab got her. She okay."

Bosch is jumping up again, getting me to look out over the crowd at something in the parade. There is a man all covered in the black grease, far worse than the woman. It looks like he might have been a tourist in a Hawaiian shirt and Jesus sandals—someone who has made the ultimate wrong turn off a cruise ship. The man's shirt and jeans are all black, dripping with grease, and he is on his knees after being run over by the Jab Jab mob.

"Look," says Bosch. "It Sean! The Jab Jab got Sean."

It is our friend Sean all right, so dirty he is hard to recognize. He is sitting on the road, trying to light a cigarette, but his hands are too wet from the grease. Bosch tries to go over to him but an official gets in the way. Bosch is yelling, trying to get Sean's attention, calling, "Mr. Sean! Mr. Sean!"

But just as Bosch gets around the official, Sean summons some hidden energy, jumps up and runs up the road to get back in with the parade and the Jab Jab. Bosch puts his hands in the air to say, "No more Sean." We get one last look at him as he is sucked away down the street with the parade. It's like he is taken away in a river of people.

I watch the rest of the parade from a tree about twenty feet up in the air on a limb with a couple of kids. There were more fancy cars, a band or two, and some community groups. When the official parade finishes, the road is overrun by a dancing crowd and the party continues.

Somebody must have helped Sean back to the house. He is coated in grease, head to toe, and slumped on the only good couch in the house—and it is a white couch. When he rolls off there is a life-size image of him in black grease on the nice white fabric. He said he'd replace it, or get it reupholstered, which was impossible in Springs. The couch was a casualty of Carnival.

By late afternoon we had had enough. The island quieted and everyone retreated indoors. We tuned in a mediocre local radio station and listened to Seventies pop trash and just slept that afternoon and then through the night.

Perhaps the Jab Jab were affecting me. As I drifted off to sleep, for some reason, I had a clear image of a man I knew named Melville Watts. Melville was the uncle of my high school friend Jim Lane, and Melville lived in a four-hundred-year-old manor built for monks on a massive estate in Bream, near the Welsh border. The manor, named Prior's Lodge, would have been built at about the time Grenada was founded. It had its own lake and by virtue of his charity to the community, the Queen had made Melville Verderer of the Forest of Dean.

The rooms at Prior's Lodge were massive and beside the bedroom was a long double room on the second floor. You'd have to call it a museum, though it was cluttered more like an attic. Melville loved to walk through it and had a story for every item, and every story invariably ended with the question "What?"

"These suits of armor were bequeathed to father. Looks like a sculpture by Rodin. Know him? What? Look at these coats of arms. They go back to Wellington; that's a long time, wouldn't you say, two hundred years, what? We're not sure about these items. This one's unsigned but it could be by one of Turner's contemporaries. It's possibly worth a lot. I should have it appraised, huh, what?"

Melville moved a chair out of the way and lifted a stack of grey movie reel canisters. He said he had commissioned a movie crew to film the laborers at the Gloucestershire mines in the 1970s. He wanted to preserve their way of life before it was all gone. He started telling me about the ghost of Prior's Lodge. He had me going a bit, calling the ghost "Freddy" and creating an image in my head about the ghost's appearance in a war tunic and how people saw lighted flickerings in the corners of the Lodge, especially by the doors of the unused rooms. Or they simply said they "felt a presence."

Not very fair of Melville to put a seed in my brain about ghosts and then send me off to a massive room to sleep on my own at the end of the mansion's guest wing.

"Here, you'll have to use this torch, the wiring's not been working in your hallway, hmm. Sorry. You call it a flashlight, don't you, what?

And don't fret about Freddy. That's what we call him. Freddy the ghost. He won't hurt you, huh, what?"

And in that hallway, later, a presence of some type of wounded soldier standing there all night, just outside my door: sea blue trousers, brass buttons, red sash, white tunic.

The white sun poured through the living room window and by six a.m. Bosch was there, expertly tapping just loud enough to wake me and not the others. Time for our walk up into the hills. Up there, up in the cool highlands, the roads weren't paved and the bush wasn't as lush, but the wind came from behind and pushed us up. It made the walk effortless and the sun made it blissful, nirvana-like. After a while there were stretches with no homes, just fields. Then the roads thinned out to become foot paths, and a couple of hours later, the white sun forced us to walk without talking. But the air was fresh and as we got higher there was a constant wind making the trees bow. Now you could see the ocean from the east and the south and there were little dots of color down by the sea—wind kites flown by little boys in the fields a mile below.

Bosch points to a hill where he says we can see the ocean from all directions. The blue Caribbean Sea, aquamarine salt water surrounding the little spice island. It took us half an hour out of our way but when I was up on it I had my hands in the air, yelling, "Yay, yay!"

We come upon a little shack. Children spill out to stare at us. A young girl has a baby boy on her hip and a mother inside is nursing, surprised to see us through the window slats. Father is nowhere. Bosch points to a cluster of shacks up on a ridge. Smoke is exiting a pipe in someone's roof there. The steady wind takes the stream away at a right angle, sideways.

We see a simple graveyard with slanting crosses and stones marking maybe a dozen burial sites. I remember Jim Anderson talking about his archaeology expedition to Mexico. He had been walking in the hills above Mexico City just like this and came upon a woodworking factory. It was a busy place. In the back, stacked twenty high, was their handiwork: hundreds of miniature child-size coffins all set for those who wouldn't make it to their fifth birthdays in that poor land. And Jim remembers the workers giving a cheerful "hola" as he passed by.

As we traipse on that highland trail in Grenada, some goats make their sounds to give away our approach. A woman comes outside and steps up to Bosch all happy, calling him Traydon. He explains, "That my other name."

"Traydon, Traydon. You come all the way up to here?"

"This my friend." He pats my back. His large hand almost goes shoulder to shoulder.

"Okay," she sings out.

"This is my sister-in-law. Yeah. I know her since she was a little girl. Now look." More of the laughter. Bosch is pointing at her belly.

"Okay. Ting all right?"

"Fine. Okay. Jared, he here?"

She points to a shack.

"Come see."

After a minute, a tall man comes out from the other shack. The man has to duck under the cracked doorway frame. He has a baby with him, not much bigger than the man's knitted red, yellow, and black Rasta hat. He is smiling wide, very wide, shaking his head at us.

"What is dat?"

"Dis my baby." The man opens the cloth; the baby is maybe a couple of weeks old. Everyone stares at it and then the man hands the baby over to the mother, who sings to it. She sings "Gathering of the Spirits."

"Jared my little brother. But now he got four kids. I only have two. He winning."

"It came last week. It a girl."

"That baby is fine. Lucky. And everything is okay?"

"Yeah, she very, very fine. No problem."

"Where are the other kids?" I ask.

"They went to Black Bay to see the grandmother. They go there for Carnival."

There was a lot of laughter and back slapping between them. No matter what they said, it was cause for the laughing to start again. The baby woke and the mother took her inside the hut. Jared went on his haunches, turning his back to the wind so he could roll up herb in a long paper. He bounced up with it already burning. When he removed his wool cap to let loose his dreadlocks, it was as if he had sprung out of the ocean to shake out the salt water from his hair. They stood for a while liming, and then we found shade and made a cooking fire between some boulders. Lunch was rice and peas and we looked around a bit more but there wasn't much up there, just a simple life, shrubs, and a constant perfect breeze.

PART III

8

Amsterdam Airport

Schiphol, Netherlands / July 1991

The 747 rolls down the runway and as it gains altitude, all three hundred of us are pinned to our seats as we skyrocket up and turn east for the eight-hour flight from Amsterdam to Karachi, then to Hong Kong, and finally Phnom Penh, Cambodia, where my year with MSF awaits. For some reason I start to think about Jim Anderson, remarking how he's getting older and more forgetful, with his walk becoming worryingly unsteady. He had taught me so much, offered guidance on what direction to take in my career—had given me more advice than any other professor, and he did it usually through his stories and parables about people who were up against challenges. As I watch the lights of Amsterdam disappear, I wonder if I will see him again.

I had been visiting him less and less, maybe only a half dozen times after graduating from medical school in 1987. That spring, when our class was making arrangements for the graduation ceremony, Jim came out to our student house in the countryside in his '85 Camaro to get ideas for the commencement speech he was going to make. He was going on about how he had been doubly lucky, first to study medicine at the University of Toronto when it was at its peak in the late Fifties, and now in the Eighties, as a professor at McMaster just as it was reaching the zenith of its imaginative power. McMaster was a singular school. Everyone was learning by the Socratic way, mostly in self-teaching tutorial groups with no exams and no lectures. The school was a kind of social experiment, something like Christiania, the fabled communal enclave in Denmark.

As soon as I graduated, I went straight to Jamaica and lived in a cave-like room right on the sea in Negril. At high tide the ocean spray wetted the bed sheets. After that I jetted to Peru and hiked the Inca Trail. About 16 kilometers out, along the viejo rastro, there is one of the world's rarest camps, beside a waterfall in a valley of boulders. It was something like the sculptures in the Henry Moore Room at the AGO in Toronto. Human-like boulders shrouded in a constant mist from the falls. Wherever you pitched your tent in the mini valley, the waterfall gave off a steady drone. Loud enough that you couldn't hear the words from someone a foot away. You had to lip read. It cast a perfect spell for sleep.

But sleep was in short supply during those days of medical training. I was advancing MSF, trying to get a movement going, talking about my experience in Uganda with anyone who'd listen and connecting with international humanitarian workers where I could. And then I was sucked into the vortex of my internship at Women's College Hospital in Toronto. All I remember was staying up all night two or three times a week for the year, learning how to run an ICU. I've still got those beeping noises in my head. I crashed my Toyota Tercel three times from exhaustion, twice on the same corner on the way home. It was the exact same corner and the guardrail dents are still there, side by side.

My problem was they didn't have a specialty called international health. The closest was public health, and it wasn't exactly prestigious. People actually looked at the ground in disappointment when I told them what direction I was taking. They said, "Not going to be an exalted surgeon or cardiologist, eh?" And my choice apparently got even more aberrant when I picked psychiatry as my clinical year after internship. But why not? It was an absorbing discipline and I was genetically loaded for it: both parents psychologists, and a psychiatrist for a grandfather. I was moonlighting up at a mental health facility in Penetanguishene, a place locals used to call the insane asylum, or what the guards call the Bug House, where they say the boogie men lived. I was working up there on weekends, living in a cottage by the lake, paying off debt for the first time, plotting to go abroad.

Then luck came my way. I knew a lawyer named Peter Dalglish who founded a charity called Street Kids International. Dalglish, totally energetic and visionary, was friends with Jacques de Milliano, the president of MSF Holland. When Jacques came to Toronto in the fall of '88, that was it. We hit it off and talked right away about bringing MSF to Canada.

Over the ensuing couple of years, we had quite a few late-night discussions in his home in Hemestede—smoking Indonesian cigars and drinking brandy by his fireplace, scheming and making plans. Jacques said MSF was unique in the world. He thought of it in corporate terms, like it was a franchise, and "an organization in a state of chaos." Jacques had done a brief stint in Chad with MSF Belgium, and afterwards the Belgian president, Reginald Moreels, helped him found MSF in Holland. And now Jacques was continuing the cycle, handing MSF to me, helping it come to Canada.

He said if you put MSF out there, people will come, and they will risk so much for the movement because they see the gap between rich and poor and how it's mind-boggling and absurd. Beyond that I don't know how it all happened so fast. It caught us off-guard but the movement had begun over here.

I had inveigled two others to get going on it with me: Jim Lane, my best friend from high school, who was now a lawyer, and Marilyn McHarg, a nurse I had worked with during the summers at St. Joseph's Hospital in Hamilton. The three of us formed the early triumvirate to build MSF in Canada. When we sent out our first press release one morning and didn't hear back from anyone all day, we went home dejected, doubting we could get the organization to germinate. That evening a television news crew showed up, unannounced, at Jim Lane's door. There we were on TV, and by the end of the week we had been covered by national newspapers and radio. Lots of volunteers joining us, a trickle of funds, people flying in from Europe—all of us congregating at the meeting room for humanitarian causes at the local Quaker House. We knew we had something. It all snowballed.

One spring day in '89 I flew to Paris to firm up support for MSF in Canada with the French. I met with one of their leaders, Francis Charron, who sported thick white hair on a large head, and after a few minutes of him majestically puffing on a Cuban cigar in front of me, he just said "Non," there wasn't going to be a chapter in Canada after all.

He said there was a moratorium: no new sections and especially none outside of Europe. He ended the meeting abruptly, saying he had other things to attend to, and wished me bonne chance anyhow.

I sat alone at Café Lipp staring at the white walls for a couple of hours fighting the jet lag with my espressos, trying to figure out the next move. Then I took a KLM commuter from Roissy straight up to Schiphol near Amsterdam to meet with Jacques de Milliano and the other co-president of MSF Holland, Roelf Padt. Downing a few blonde *presions* later at the Schiller House to satisfy our thirst, we firmed up the connection between Canada and Holland. The Dutch were keen to back us, obviously delighted to have a Canadian source of field volunteers and donations, and we simply needed the support. There was no other way. Jacques said he'd figure out something with the French—the alternative was being sued by them or blackballed in the movement. But the Dutch told us to move forward very quietly and to slow down. Stern warnings about all of that. Such politics in this apolitical organization. They wanted us to pause until things warmed up a bit in unreceptive Europe.

The slowdown with MSF meant I could pursue plan B, studying international health. I had a spot reserved in the masters program at Harvard. It was an opportunity I thirsted after. Talented, left-leaning people, and every night you could listen to the poets and other writers and the musicians, politicians, and scientists. That was the coolest part of Harvard—all the big names came through to speak and make appearances. They all wanted that experience for their careers and on their bios, so we got to hear them in privileged small groups and then, not uncommonly, accompany them to the cafés or pubs. It wasn't rare to dine with a vice president of a foreign country, and I once stood at a urinal beside Seamus Heaney and Ted Hughes before they spoke at Lehman Hall.

To push MSF along, every other Friday I skipped my classes in Boston and took the Green Line from Brigham Circle to Logan for the hour-long flight to Toronto, where MSF had a fledgling presence in Peter Dalglish's Street Kids International office. On those trips home I got to see my girlfriend, Carrie, and earn some money at Penetanguishene, the hospital. I attended meetings in Holland a few times. Jacques de Milliano flew to Canada, and over to Harvard once as well. We hatched an idea to send me on a month-long mission to Mozambique and Malawi. It was a Dutch national working with MSF in Maputo named Jos Nolle who set up the brilliant trip. I took a month off from Harvard to go, in April, a month before final exams. It was essential to get more experience with MSF in the field and good to be among the palm trees again. I toured village hospitals and refugee camps teeming with children. There was a place over there called Vilanculos. The local MSF teams called it Club Médecins Sans Frontières because it was a small project in a quiet town on the ocean. All of the expats got their own thatched homes right on the beach and for a hundred miles north and south it was virginal sand and occasional palm trees.

Halfway through 1990 there was a kind of thawing with the French and we got a call from Jacques saying now is the time to push. Marilyn McHarg was already traveling through Africa, visiting MSF programs, amassing experience. I finished up at Harvard, and when I came back to Toronto, our MSF group dropped everything and waited to go abroad.

In January 1991, I was sent to Cambodia, the first from our Canadian group to go on an official mission. Jim Lane took my place as leader and Jos was in from Holland as general manager. It was to be a year-long placement for me. Jacques kept saying how important it was to spend a full year abroad. Everybody loved the plan, though it was tough on me and Carrie. I was supposed to be going to a flagship project in a place called Sisophon in the battered north-west province of Banteay Meanchey, but the war was unstable and it escalated the week I arrived. So I waited it out in Phnom Penh, the capital. It was like being unemployed, hanging around a tropical capital for a time looking for work. After a while I was dispatched to Pursat, in the middle of the country, to relieve a burned-out French physician. It was a temporary placement—not the nicest living arrangement and impermanent, so there was no rooting, no deep new friendships. The priority was getting to Sisophon, but the war was too close and we had to wait.

I lived in Pursat with Caroline and Gerald, an administrator-logistician couple from Strasbourg. Caroline insisted I enunciate her name fully as Car-o-line, and after I had been sick for a week, she looked me up and down and said, "Alors, mon ami, you used to be fine; now you are all awful and skinny." I let it go as being motherly. And Gerald, harmless enough but what a mess. When he started rambling, he spoke French so fast in his Marseillaise inflection, it was hard even for franco-phones to make out what he was saying. And if you asked him to repeat it, he'd frown and remind you MSF was a French organization and Cambodia was part of the Francophonie. So my inability to understand his mumbling became a "problème grave" for the mission. He would lit-erally sit down at breakfast, not make eye contact for twenty minutes, not say a word, and then he'd be gone all day out to the countryside where he built latrines and managed the water supply. At times the ga-lactic station in his brain took over, and he'd start rambling on and on. These tirades were about society in the emerging European Union or about his football team and their fans. I nodded along "Ah huh, ah huh, oui." His favorite expression was "supercool" and when I first heard it I thought how refreshing to hear a spunky word like that in the French language. But he overused it and after a while it wasn't cool at all.

But my brief time in Pursat coincided with the exact moment the Kurdish refugee crisis exploded in northern Iraq. The world was focused on it. I sent a message off to Jacques de Milliano and the others in Amsterdam telling them I was stagnating, languishing in Cambo-dia. I told them I'd come back to Cambodia and get up to Sisophon as soon as the fighting waned, but asked that they get me to Kurdistan where I could be useful and the next evening I got a telex with flight de-tails to the Middle East. One day I was in the middle of the sweltering jungle in Cambodia and the next I was up on a chilled mountaintop in Eastern Turkey on the Iraq border surrounded by a hundred thousand refugees.

There were other Canadians up there too, including a tree-planter-administrator-logistician named Ian Small. He said he wanted to commit his entire life to the organization; he was young and we all loved his enthusiasm and his mop of hair. Lots of long conversations, scheming about humanitarianism and working overseas and about building MSF in Canada. Throughout that mission we got the same comments from the French and Belgians and all the other sections about MSF Canada: ça existe déja? It exists already?

A few weeks later I was back in Amsterdam to get briefed before moving on to Cambodia, to Sisophon where our program was finally opening up. It was drizzling at five a.m. and there was litter everywhere on the Damstraat, the pungent stench of stale beer mixed with fresh-cut flowers. Outside the MSF Holland office men in blue smocks were sweeping the litter into trash bins while they smoked. I had a couple of hours to myself before the office opened so I walked around the canals and through the crowds. It was all like Pieter Bruegel the Elder, canvases with canals, bridges, and brick facades.

There was a backpacker sleeping on the steps of the Centraal Station. He must have spilled out of one of the overnight trains and he was bobbing in and out of consciousness, fighting Morpheus, the god of sleep. Dangling around his neck for all to see was his cloth passport pouch. He couldn't wake himself even though he was about to be plundered. An unshaven, wiry man was hunched over the backpacker, trying to look casual, like he was his friend. Twenty Guilders says the plunderer was in need of his daily dose of crystal meth or heroin and today's financing plan involved the sleeping student's traveller's checks and Eurail pass. The thief timed his cuts, waiting for the backpacker's head to fall forward into deeper sleep before dragging the blade further along the thin cloth of his passport pouch. There were hundreds of people walking past the thief and his victim. Every minute or two, a responsible Dutch citizen would stop and scold the man. The man would stop and pretend to walk away. But a minute after that, the thief was back, extending the cut a little further.

All of this occurred in front of a plethora of early morning commuters walking and cycling by. Those cyclists. What code were they observing? I watched hundreds of them crisscross the canal bridges and streets with no near misses. They all could do it. Punked-out teenagers with safety-pinned cheeks and young lawyers in Italian suits. Mothers with younger children in tow or teenage girls—one doing all the pushing and the other sideways on the pannier, nattering. Some instinctive Dutch navigation system preventing miscues and violent crashes.

And even though there was cloud cover dimming everything that morning, every few minutes a radiant Dutch woman would appear in the crowd, classic and elegant like someone from a magazine cover. But it was so common I don't think they even knew how attractive they were. Ian Small called them Dutch masterpieces.

At the MSF Holland office, I was to meet Lex Winkler, the operations director. He was older than most at HQ, a bit rotund and balding, and he wore wire-rimmed glasses. He came into the room saying he didn't have much time, something about a crisis in Chad, but maybe he could steal a few minutes to give me my briefing on Sisophon, Cambodia. Every time he started there was an interruption. He kept coming in and out of the room and other people came in to speak to him in Dutch, that flowery, guttural Dutch language, simultaneously soft and hard. Finally he asked me if we could do the briefing in the morning but I offered my regrets to that. I was to fly to Hong Kong in the evening. So he frowned, told a few people not to disturb him and shut the door.

Cambodia is a totally confusing place, he said, a mess, and everyone there is still stunned. He said they didn't really know if Sisophon would stay open. A rebel faction had already been bombing the little town again in the past week, but the violence in the northwest was supposed to slow down. Something about a French-backed peace accord. He said it was important to get in there, strategic because none of the other aid organizations had managed to operate there and this would be good for MSF Holland. An achievement—good for our image. And he said I was going to open up the project with a very experienced Dutch physician named Rob Overtoom. The team was going to be Rob and me.

Lex started giving me a lecture about the history of Cambodia, how it was an ancient Buddhist nation and a former French colony. He said Cambodia avoided most of the Viet Nam war until the very end in 1975 when the pro-Western government started to crack and Lon Nol was ousted. That's when the communists and Maoists stepped in. He said most of the population was out in the countryside simply subsisting, not that interested in politics at all. But the B-52 runs turned opinion against anything Western and capitalistic. It opened the door for the Maoist Khmer Rouge. He said in '76 and '77 the killings were heavy. Thousands of people disappearing. Villages liquidated. They even drove dump trucks around the capital filled with people's heads. That's when they emptied Phnom Penh, making it a ghost city in what they called Year Zero. But it wasn't until '78 when things became unimaginably worse, brainsick and mad—over a million people were killed and starved. In '79, the Vietnamese moved in and for a decade they occupied most of the country. The Khmer Rouge hid out in the north and west, and there was another faction, the Monarchists who wanted King Sihanouk back in his Silver Palace. The armies were hiding out on the Thai border about fifty kilometers from Sisophon, living off the proceeds from the gem mines in the west. Not an ideal place to go to. Very, very poor.

But Lex said Cambodia was opening up, Western capitalism was infusing some color, at least in the capital—the grey-brown wood and mud roads were being replaced by fresh whitewash and neon signs. But the Khmer people were still in shock, millions of broken families, fractured cities, people with missing limbs living on a quarter a day in a dissociated state. It was beyond-belief stuff and Lex said it would be an ideal education for me. He predicted that I'd find it fascinating. And so did Jacques de Milliano. He said that my year abroad was important for MSF, essential for the movement in Canada. He was counting on me, told me to do a good job and he said that I had to enjoy it over there. I *had* to like it.

9

MSF Holland / Belgium Compound at Siem Reap

Cambodia / July 1991

There is sweat soaking through my clothes as I lie on the smooth mahogany floor of the MSF headquarters in Siem Reap waiting for Rob Overtoom. The ceiling fan is seized up, so behind my neck and all down my back and legs little pools of perspiration have formed—there is a sweaty imprint of my body on the floor. I couldn't get up. After fifty hours in and out of jets across three continents and two oceans, any major muscle command was impossible. The office staff just stepped over me.

I ask them if they know when Rob will be arriving. They all put their hands in the air—no idea. "Ott deng" is how you say it in Khmer. They tell me that it is permissible to sleep on the floor, that I am not bothering anyone.

I did sleep for a while, dreaming about something that happened earlier in the year during the Chaul Chnam New Year festival in Pursat, where I was temporarily running the medical ward. I was seated in the Salle Réunion of our hospital. Chairs had been set up so that the entire hospital staff was in their white uniforms, seated tidily in rows, with the medical doctors in front. There were two special seats, one for the medical director, a Cambodian named Dr. Monkgol, and one for the visiting German surgeon, Gunter Haus, mid-fifties, bald, and thick-boned.

Everyone referred to it as Haus's hospital. He had been there a long time. Such vast experience. People kept telling me they were so lucky to have him there. They all uttered the same phrase: "Médecin extraordinaire." Especially Monkgol, who between his many cigarettes, had a way of shaking his head in disbelief at how magnificent the doctor was.

As usual that morning, Haus waited outside by the Banyan trees with two or three senior colleagues until everyone else was seated and silence had fallen in the Salle Reunion. Then he paraded in last, alone, at a good clip, took his seat and said only, "Le mis a jours, s'il vous plait." We're seated in strict order: I'm up front in my chair beside the hospital director, who in turn is seated beside the great visiting surgeon. The other doctors follow some kind of seniority order, timidly speaking up one at a time to offer their overnight reports from the wards. It was always the same: three patients died, all expected; four new admissions. One was a blessure from a mine, one was a suspected case of typhoid, two were malarial, and two were proposed for surgical intervention.

At that final mention, Dr. Haus spoke up. "Why? What are these cases that require my surgical intervention?"

The nervous Cambodian doctor explained in front of the audience why he thought a fractured femur needed an external fixation in the salle d'opération and why the patient may benefit from one of Haus's revolutionary fixation devices that utilized a local iron wood. Another anxious physician suggested that a distended abdomen was possibly a ruptured intestine full of pus. The patient needed an "intervention rapide."

Haus remained silent, staring out the window long past the conclusion of the doctors' reports. The Salle Réunion somehow fell silent even more, dotted with nervous coughing.

"Expliquez-moi," Haus began. "Why not use Ivermectin tablets for the abdomen, and what's wrong with a simple plaster of Paris casting?" The doctors did not answer.

Haus asked, "What was the condition of the man who died on the medical ward? Someone?"

A junior doctor answered in bad French. "Paludisme cérébral."

Haus asked, "What did he say?"

A colleague answered in better French. "Cerebral malaria."

Haus retorted with, "Oui, and what was he administered for the cerebral malaria?"

"Intraveineux avec de la quinine."

"I see, and what kind of intravenous?"

The junior doctor put his head down. He knew there had been a mistake.

"What kind of intravenous perfusion?"

"Saline."

Haus's timber raised a notch. "You gave him saline?"

Rising, Monkgol proceeded to go into a tantrum: "Why are you giving saline to a man with cerebral malaria? Why not dextrose? Pourqoi? Why?"

Haus summarized: "You knew he had cerebral malaria, yet you declined to give him the dextrose. Interesting. The brain requires dextrose sugar in these situations yet you decided to give him saline. Is this correct?"

Still, the man kept his head down. He didn't know what to do because this situation involved honor—maintaining face.

In front of the doctors and nurses, Dr. Monkgol practically screamed. "Who told you to give the wrong medicine?"

No answer.

The director asked again. "Dites-moi, qui a prescrit ce médicament?" But now he was so mad he reverted to Cambodian and his neck veins were distended. Who had told him to give the wrong liquid solution to the patient?

From among the dozens of people in the room, the junior doctor lifted his head, and then raised his clasped hands, extended a finger and pointed at me.

Fifty people twisted their necks to look at me. No one knew what to do. No one was speaking. Then Monkgol broke the silence like a gunshot. "If he told you to do it, you do it. Don't be an idiot. It's completely simple, isn't it? Don't be so stupid. If the bar rang (foreign or white) doctor wants something done, you do it immediately. I cannot believe we are still having these problems."

Monkgol caught up with me and was so upset he couldn't even light his cigarette. "That doctor is so stupid. Completely stupid. I'm sorry. This is what we have here in Cambodia. Problems." He said it wasn't my fault. Then Dr. Lean Kong said the same, not my fault at all.

For a moment, I had no idea what had happened. I didn't tell anyone about any malaria case. That wasn't even my ward, so I didn't know why this exchange would be directed to me. We had all treated hundreds of malaria cases, all with dextrose. No one knowingly would have given saline. Nobody should have. The directives are on posters in bright red ink.

The junior doctor pointing at me didn't look familiar and I couldn't place him on my wards. After a minute he began to look more familiar to me. Then I remembered. Just as Haus and Monkgol dismissed everyone in the Salle Reunion, it all made sense.

Only yesterday, in the afternoon, after it had rained and the grounds were almost dry again, I was walking with Dr. Lean, a talented pediatrician from Phnom Penh, and some nurses. Everyone was smoking and talking, meeting for coffee before going home for the day.

A junior doctor came running across the grass to us with two intravenous solutions in his hands. The whole exchange took sixty seconds. He wanted to know which one to give the patient. We all told him to discuss it with the senior doctor on the ward. But the junior doctor thought he had better run it by me, the foreign doctor.

I said, "Ott deng," which is "I don't know." I couldn't fully understand his French, so we were speaking a mixture of French and Khmer, neither of us truly comprehending. I did tell him I wasn't working on his ward and that I don't make decisions about the surgical patients.

But the junior doctor was persistent. I told him again to ask his senior, Dr. Buen Low, for help, but he wanted some prescient teaching from the expat doctor, so I said, "What's wrong with the patient?"

He mumbled something in French. All I could make out was, "I give this, oui?" He showed me the saline solution. I know this doctor is from the surgical side, so giving saline is reasonable sometimes.

"Is he dehydrated?" I asked.

He said yes, so I replied, "Well, if he's dehydrated and he's low on fluids, he might need saline, but it could be anything. I haven't seen the patient." I spoke to him as professor to student. But I was distinctly keeping the conversation theoretical.

The others in the group had walked ahead now and I wanted to catch up to them. I wanted a piping hot chai tea and sweet tolcut chma biscuit. So I ask him quickly about the patient's diagnosis, but he can't make himself understood.

He pushes the two IV bags out for me to pick. One bag means life.

Now he is annoying me, so I tell him he needs to go back to the ward and talk to Buen Low, but he asks me to choose. My group is now across the compound, and they're yelling for me to come on. So I give him one last bit of medical teaching. "If it's dehydration, typically, you give this one."

"This one?"

"Oui, but what's the diagnosis or is it just post-surgical dehydration? I don't know the case."

He thinks for a second and then says, "Oui," but I remember now it sounded more like "okay."

"Well, if it's simple dehydration you can give saline in these cases." I touch the saline bag.

The junior doctor seemed relieved at that and, right away, I thought to myself, Hang on, I'm not instructing you to give that one. You need to check it out with Buen Low. But the junior doctor darted away, so I shouted after him, "C'est votre decision. It's your decision. You understand. That's not my patient." I even yelled it over at him again, "C'est votre decision."

And there was no mistake in understanding my French this time, he was all smiles now. "Oui, oui," and, "Bat hoy!" he assured me. I didn't think about the incident again because, in the end, I hadn't told him to do anything. It was just a casual discussion about saline and dextrose. I told him it was his decision and didn't even bother to look back to watch as he went back to the ward, ready to give a man I had never even seen the saline that would eventually kill him sometime during the night.

I wake up to an empty room, still lying on the MSF compound floor in Siem Reap waiting for Rob Overtoom. I start to hear thick raindrops plopping on the tin roof. They land one at a time, and then come in twos and threes. In a minute the rain escalates and sounds like a machine shredding the tin roof. It's mesmerizing, and it traps me in a half-sleep, a kind of waking dream.

Peering out a window, I see two Cambodian men in front of a banana tree handing food to a Bonze monk who is draped in traditional orange robes. The sacred robes look neon orange against the gravel. Those monks, it was almost as if they were toying with everyone. They float into your present space with no eye contact and no words. People bring them warm food and money. Then they float away. Not even a thank you.

A tall Belgian translator named Gerome, from a local water and sanitation NGO, marches with perfect posture into the room with a Cambodian woman on his arm. Both are drenched. She is wearing a long purple dress and makeup, which isn't typical for Cambodian women. Gerome sees me on the floor, and all I get is a nod as he walks through the room. I thought, "What a nice couple," but I was told by the giggling cook that the woman was a meretrix and there was an arrangement. Gerome would help her financially to some extent and she, in return, would be faithful to her only client.

The Belgians I happened to have met had no shame about having meretrixes. They didn't try to hide it and didn't understand why the practice might be questionable. I remember watching some journalists from Brussels arguing about it. "But I made them rich," was one defence. Some of the French were right there with the Belgians on a financial exchange for personal favors, but most of the Dutch and Brits and North Americans were mortified by it. In one town in Cambodia, a group of European nurses tried to outlaw the use of these convenient local girlfriends. They said it was bad for public relations, but I don't think the Cambodians even cared. Having a mistress was a sign of social standing to many of them.

One hot night a few months earlier, we had been at a provincial state function in Pursat. These were always such gaudy affairs. An outdoor garden beside the government building, raked clean, with tables set out under Viet Namese patio lanterns to make way for a four-piece band, tables, and chairs. To bring it to life, a portable generator was fired up so the instruments and microphones could be amplified. What unsavory music. So odd to a Western sensibility, and ear-splitting at that. The generator and band fought it out into the night.

The few expats from the international aid agencies in town were routinely invited and always sat at the head table where everyone had to look attentive during the propaganda speeches. On my right were Caroline and Gerald, the MSF volunteers from France, and on my left, Manuel Chaves, a Swiss prosthetics fitter working with landmine victims. We were expected to knock back the brandy and cream soda. Such an awful drink, but it was their beverage of choice, and I sure didn't feel like any of it.

These events always ended with everyone drunk, arm in arm, saying how great everyone was and how wonderful the government was. They all yell, "Kampuchea la or! Cambodia the good," and then cheers of, "Cent pour cent," meaning you had to drain your glass a hundred percent. In the shadows the soldiers stood by their aging jeeps, mounted machine guns and grenades ready in case there was an assassination attempt on one of the town officials.

The guest of honor that night was the non-military governor of Pursat. I could never pronounce his name but I can see him clearly: almost sixty, straight black hair, thick purple lips, even thicker glasses, and bad teeth. His eyes were tiny and when they caught you, they were cold.

He smoked throughout the ceremonies and speeches, kept silent and never showed emotion until after dinner, when he had had many brandies and cream soda. That's when he started leaning into people, mouth agape so you could see his foul teeth, laughing louder than everyone at the party. His aides hooted it up along with him to smooth out his artless manner.

Despite all this, he certainly had a pretty woman on his arm. I was told these girls accompanying the officials were all "orphelins"— orphans from the Seventies whose parents had disappeared a decade earlier under Pol Pot. The government in its kindness had gathered them up when they were five or so and kept them safe in a résidence officielle where they learned many traditional arts such as Bopha Lokey dancing. But the nurses told us they were being taught other skills as well—ones to please the governor.

The girls put on the traditional Wishing Dance, and I'm enchanted by the governor's companion. Her arms and hands flow like a harpist's. Manuel Chaves and I flirted with them, enjoying the way they move under those lanterns in their clingy dresses.

The governor's girl was avoiding me, so I asked the other girls to bring her over, to come sit and have some of the brandy and cream soda. They shouted, "No, it's not allowed." They cupped their hands over their mouths in modesty, looking past me to see if the governor noticed. They're not encouraged to speak with the foreigners.

When the governor's back was turned, Manuel and I ambled over to her anyway and offered the formal greeting, "Choum reap sour."

She bowed with her palms pressed together in prayer and offered the same measured welcome. She could not help giggling and had to hide her mouth with her hand. She couldn't understand what I was saying but speaking with a bar rang seemed to humor her.

This orphelin, she was rather angelic, maybe eighteen, and I was guessing she'd never spoken to a bar rang before, let alone danced with one. Her eyes were screwed up tight, almost closed and she was giggling. Manuel was saying she's the prettiest one out there tonight. He was ranking them top to bottom, toasting them one by one across the crowd. Down went the brandy.

The band was playing and the other orphelins came over to dance with us. Manuel was bopping around. Even Gerald and Caroline. They're doing a variation on their square dance. Everyone was laughing. I don't think this happened often, having the foreigners dance. The orphelins were bent over in laughter, covering their mouths.

"Yeah," Manuel said, "the governor's is fine, very fine, better body but none of them would do anything. Nothing! I'm telling you." He explained it in French, making a face like he was disgusted. "On doit se marrier premièrement," he said. "You have to get mar-ried first. Married. Nothing till you get mar-ried."

They have a chaperone with them. An older woman, all business, barked at the girls, telling them to keep their distance from the bar rangs. I'm pretty sure the governor has noticed us now. I got one strange look from him anyway and for sure one of his aides de camp was subtly trying to dissuade me from talking to his girl, tapping my shoulder as we danced, saying, "Yes, docteur, oui, oui, bien sûr, but why don't I introduce you to M. Riapeth. He is the manager of goods procurement for the entire western provinces."

Sure enough, now the governor noticed us. He was pointing at me through the crowd and asking his people questions.

Here comes the governor, stumbling right up, shaking my hand, and he wasn't letting go. He smells of brandy and cigarettes and his face floats in and out as he mumbles indecipherable Khmer.

"Yeng som orkun som rap karngea nao knong brotes Kampuchea. Karsvakom pi rothapibal knong Phnom Penh!"

The translator said: "The governor is very grateful for your presence in Kampuchea and for the wonderful work that is being done at the hospital. He brings greetings from the government in Phnom Penh."

The governor's face was an inch from mine. He yelled across the lawn for drinks. Two or three others started echoing his request. He wanted the drinks right away. Someone came running over, head bowed, and poured brandy and cream soda. The server then stood at attention with a brandy bottle in one hand and the cream soda in the other.

"Tekkork! Tekkork!" yelled the governor. He wanted ice for the drinks. Now everyone was yelling for ice and several people were bowed low, apologizing to him for the delay. He waved them away as a bucket arrived and the ice plopped into our drinks.

He wanted to make a sincere toast and was waiting for everyone's silence. His people yelled at the band to stop playing. He was holding the drink out at the end of his straight arm as everyone at the party came in close.

"Khnom orkun lork vech doctor," he said.

It was a solemn expression of thanks for the foreigners but, just as he continued, the governor slipped into the server and had to be steadied. A little too much brandy, it seemed. Two of his men were holding him up. Everyone laughed it off. It's nothing. The governor very much wanted to continue his speech but his aides advised against it. He was in no state to speak in public, so the aides got their arms around his waist and walked him back to his seat.

For a moment the party was uncomfortably quiet. Manuel Chaves rolled his eyes at me. Then somebody started clapping and then everyone joined in on the applause. What a great speech by the governor. Shouts of praise for the governor. Then they yelled, "Kampuchea la or! Kampuchea la or!" He was slumped in his chair, waving at the crowd.

A minute later the soldiers came in from the shadows, put a flak jacket on the governor and eased him into the Jeep beside an anti-aircraft gun. They handed him a cigarette but he dropped it. I was looking around for the orphelin and, sure enough, there she was being ushered through the crowd into his Jeep.

I'm stretched out on the floor again when I hear Rob's staccato laugh flowing in through the window. It makes me smile. I think, with a laugh like that he can't be all bad. Then I see him walk in to an enthusiastic welcome. He's tall like many Dutch, dark haired and tanned, older than me by a decade, and he has a burlap pack over his shoulder. He looks like a Beatle in the Seventies, or maybe like one of the less-flashy Rolling Stones, maybe Ron Wood. There are some lines of experience around his eyes. Everyone is speaking Dutch and there is a lot of hand-shaking and hugging plus the obligatory kissing on each cheek. I make a move to push myself up to greet him but he can see I am drained, paralyzed with fatigue, so he motions for me to remain on the floor. He lets sleep overcome me.

10

Angkor Wat

Siem Reap, Cambodia / July 1991

An hour or two later, Rob and I are pouring beer over ice cubes that melt as fast as we talk and drink. He tells me all about Sisophon, saying it's a Wild West town, and I fill him in on Holland where I had been the week before. He misses Holland. I tell him how goddess-like the women are in Amsterdam. He knows, he knows and he misses the not so glamorous things too, like his canned herring most of all. He was glad to receive my peace offering—a smoked sausage from Schiphol. He holds the meat up like a sacrament and says something in Dutch I don't understand. We trade travel stories, and I tell him I've seen over fifty countries already; but Rob no longer knows how many he's been to—maybe a hundred—and he starts to count them, offering a story for each, telling me about all the time he spent in the field, especially the work he did with the Cambodian refugees. Years at the refugee camps like Site II and Khao I Dang on the Thai border. Work with this organization and that. The list kept growing.

Rob sure liked to laugh and seemed laid-back and tolerant, not the kind to make problems out of nothing. For the coming year the two of us would be two astronauts rocketed into a new colony. We were going to eat every meal together, rebuild a provincial health system as a team, and live in a house under night-time curfew. But first there is something we both must see, so Rob and I tell our driver to take a detour leaving Siem Reap on that initial day together. How could we miss a chance to look in on the majestic ruins of Angkor Wat, the ones built during the reign of Suryavarman II? We go north up Sivatha Boulevard over to Pokambor and speed along for a few kilometers until we park the Land Cruiser beside a Ta Prohm Kapok tree opposite the temple. It is well into the rainy season, so the rice fields are green lakes. That's all you see. Green lakes divided by long brown walkways creating massive squares. It's an ocean of green patchwork that goes in all directions from the road to the horizon.

Those rice fields and the Angkor temple in front of us have been there a thousand years. The temple looks like an enormous black cloud rising out of the fields. There are five distinct peaks surrounded by a moat big enough for skiffs. As we walk up to it, you can see the black structure is covered in carved faces—round faces with thick lips and dreaming eyes. There are very few people at Angkor Wat this day, maybe a dozen. The country is at war so there are few foreign airplanes coming in and virtually no tourists. Getting all the way up to Siem Reap, even if you were granted a visa, was rare. That is one of the principal benefits of working in these war zones: walking through astonishing, famous places all alone.

They say the Angkor Wat temples in front of us were hidden by forests for most of the last millennium, and were only rumored to exist. The tropical forests swallowed everything, strangling it. So dark and tangled it would take an hour to move through fifty feet of it. Chuon, our driver, is walking with us, smiling every time I look at him. The sun glints off his gold-capped teeth. But as we get to the temple gates, he stops smiling and hesitates going forward. He taps on his chest, something about his soul. He wants to stay by the truck.

"Come on, Chuon. Come see the temples of Angkor. You can explain to us what it all means."

But Chuon doesn't speak English and barely any French. So we have to motion to him, saying please many times until he comes, shaking his head.

Leading up to the temples, there is a three-hundred-meter-long walkway. Suryavarman II had his workers lay massive black square stones about the size of church doors. The black stones roast in the equatorial sun and burn our feet. For the most part, the stones are neatly aligned in a grid, but here and there, over the centuries, some of the bigger ones had sunk into the earth at odd angles. It disoriented us.

At the entrance, the first rooms are illuminated by narrow shafts of light, giving them an ambient glow that flickers on and off as passing clouds block the sun. The spaces inside are cooler, small and catacomb-like, sized to fit the diminutive people of the twelfth century. You can look from the entrance way of one room all the way through ten more identical rooms and doorways until your line of sight escapes outside. We ascend stairs into an antechamber Chuon calls the Room of a Thousand Buddhas. He doesn't want to go in but we drag him up. It's darker in there but has nothing creepy like bats or rodents and there aren't any secret doors opening up or anything unearthly. Still, Chuon is so hesitant I have to drag him along, holding the toughened hide of his hand. We were admiring a nine-hundred-year-old frieze when he throws my hand away, yells, "Khmon neng tao krao!" and runs back down the steps.

Rob shouts for him to come back. "Chuon! Mowk nee!"

But Chuon runs away through the catacombs, shouting, "Khmoch! Khmoch!" which means "ghost." We lose his voice in the maze of stone rooms and find him an hour later, bug-eyed, standing by our truck, having smoked half a pack of 555 cigarettes in succession. The orange butts are stuck in the mud around his toes.

Cambodians believe ghosts are everywhere. They feel the presence of all of their ancestors walking around the villages and forests. They see life here on earth as just one step in a beautiful never-ending cycle of birth and death and rebirth. Little boys growing up to grow the rice and herd the animals and little girls growing up to get married and raise their children in the thousands of peaceful villages in the serene countryside—unchanged for a millenium. It's fitting that one of their most important national holidays is the Pchum Ben Festival, during which everyone offers gifts of food to their deceased ancestors and feasts with the spirits by their side. Angkor Wat is at the center of these beliefs. So when we find Chuon by the truck smoking, he is shaking his head at the temple, still saying, "No good, no good." But he is allowing a slight smile now. There in front of him in the hundred-degree heat is a ten-year-old boy sent by Chuon to the market. There are cans of Viet Namese Heinekens wrapped in newspaper and the boy is busting up a ten-cent chunk of ice, putting the pieces into cups for Rob and me.

"Well done, Chuon," says Rob with a staccato laugh.

Imported Heinekens on ice. It is soul-reviving and with that burning sun way up there, Rob admits they are almost as good as the presions at the Schiller House in Amsterdam. We are not going to say no to these ice cold mid-afternoon libations. Not on this day.

Later we stop at the west end of Siem Reap and eat rice, sugared pork, and Chinese bunching greens. It wasn't that bad—maybe too much fish oil—still, we ate it gratefully in silence, waving away the flies. But when it was done, we started complaining and wondered why we couldn't have Thai food. It's only a hundred miles to the border and their exquisite cuisine. We had been hearing stories about how savory the food is and how the Belgian mission on the other side of the border ate it every night and it was only a dollar or two. No matter, really. The food sustains us as we venture west, towards the front to see our home in Sisophon. Rob gives me the front seat for the five-hour ride. I have the view. He wants to stretch out in the back and sleep. The Land Cruiser has a factory-upgraded stereo, and three of the four speakers still function. What great fun zooming along with the music blaring. But it's too bad about the air conditioning. No one can fix it in the north of the country. No parts.

On both sides of the raised road, bamboo thatched huts on stilts are surrounded by an ocean of green rice field squares linking one horizon to the other. Some miles straight ahead there is a black rain cloud that forms a curtain across the road. It is more like a wall moving away from us, but we are traveling fast and Rob says we'll eventually hit it. There's no avoiding the midday shower in the rainy season. The roads are pretty bad, with pot holes six feet deep every fifty meters, and because they are surrounded by deep watery rice fields it's impossible to drive off-road; we have to go through them. Down into the hole and up into the light. Tossing you up, slamming you down. It is possible at some stretches to get the truck up to fifty miles an hour but only for a few seconds, until another pot hole makes us slide to a stop. The stopping and starting throws us forward into the dash and then backwards into our seats.

On our side of the rain cloud wall everything is well-lit—calm watery rice fields, not even a ripple, and white ibises standing unnaturally still. On the other side it is wild and dark. Sure enough, somewhere around the edge of Sisophon we penetrate the wall. We drive into a curtain of dark rain. The rain hits the windshield so hard the high-speed swish of the blades can't clear the water. Banana trees bend over to the ground, giving up pieces of their massive fronds to the wind, and the car-sized pot holes fill with water. All the people we had seen along the roads by the huts are gone. We just inch along.

It is getting dark when we make our entrance into Sisophon at around five-thirty. Thankfully Rob has instructed Chuon to take the High Road, for the rain has turned the Low Road into deep black soupy mud. It is a drab street scene, and with the fading sun and light rain, everything looks fuzzy and misted out, like a Georges Seurat pointillism. There are boarded-up two-story homes, some of them on stilts, and occasionally there is something more modern—a galvanized tin roof, or even a slab of pavement for a car port, but we see no vehicles in this town of thirty thousand. Actually we did see one car—broken down, abandoned to the earth. Other than that it is pretty much a characterless town in the grey rain. People in conical woven straw hats have their sandals in hand so they can move barefoot through the mud. I see a boy carrying his bicycle overhead and watch a group of men help a driver pull his horse-drawn cart out of a pot hole. This is the code of remoteness. Some communal way.

After passing over a plank bridge repaired with bamboo, we see our neighborhood for the first time. People watch us from under dripping palms and from the glassless windows of their simple homes. Chuon brings the Land Cruiser up to a two-story wooden house painted blue. It has a wooden gate, a tin roof, and a cinderblock perimeter wall. Not a thing of beauty. He gets out and swings the gates open while Rob drives the truck in very carefully, because there are only inches of clearance on either side. This is the MSF Blue House.

11

The MSF Blue House

Sisophon, Cambodia / July 1991

I am waiting for someone to turn on the house lights. I want to see what is to be my home for the next year. "Ott mean," says Chuon. There are no lights. No electricity since the bombing started again that week. No plumbing either. Nothing is working. No batteries, no demijohns of water and straight up, you could tell that the roof was leaking in many places.

"Don't you worry," says Rob.

I fumble in the glove compartment of the Land Cruiser for a flashlight. No flashlight. Chuon comes out balancing three kerosene lamps, all of them lit. He is smiling at his balancing act and I thought, Don't drop those, this is a wooden house. The lamplight reveals a cinderblock garage, two spare tires and a tire iron as well as other tools. Over our heads are blue-painted rafters, and along a wall a staircase leads upstairs to our living quarters. In the corner there is a generator, along with several large wooden crates bearing the MSF logo. It looks like enough medical supplies to seed a tiny hospital. Rob wants to show me around our home: the kitchen is a worn cement table with a conical indentation for the cooking fire. The bathroom is a closet-sized room with a hole in the ground. Chuon chases away something from the cooking table. We both come over to look. Something had gotten into the tin food box and helped itself to some of our precious nourishment. What is left of the turnips and carrots can't be used and sugar is scattered everywhere, so long lines of red ants track up from the floor. Rob reaches carefully into the mess, pinches a chewed box of white soy nuts between his thumb and forefinger, and pulls it out. He utters a Dutch profanity and then lets his staccato laugh fly because, small triumph, he finds an unscathed can of butter with the words *beurre français* written across the red label in yellow letters.

"Don't you worry," he says again, a little more confidently.

Rob tries his best Khmer on Chuon. He repeats several times what we need in the way of food and then carefully hands over two 100 hundred Riel notes. Chuon seems to understand. We need him to succeed because it has been many hours now since we ate the Chinese bunching greens at the roadside back in Siem Reap and we are weakening, feeling edgy. Chuon repeats the Khmer equivalent of "No problem" and ventures out into the dark town to find food. As he leaves I think, That's probably more money than he sees in a week, maybe a month.

A minute later we hear raised voices. Chuon is in some kind of trouble. A robbery? I can see him down the street walking directly back to our house. There is a shadow beside him and as they come closer I see it is a soldier. The man has a gun, is asking for a cigarette, and has a few questions. Chuon is saying, "Ott laor, ott laor,"—no good, no good. The soldier wants to know why he was in the Blue House. The Blue House is off limits. He doesn't believe his story about foreign doctors and a new hospital in town. Rob heads toward the stairs wanting to know what was going on. I call him back, telling him to stay quiet and not to move.

In comes the soldier with his Kalashnikov, and Chuon is bent over in respect as they walk, marching right into our house and up the stairs. You can hear Chuon doing his best to explain but the soldier is clearly ignoring him, pushing him aside to get a careful look around. It is dark and the rain on the roof is loud. The soldier walks up the stairs and doesn't see Rob until he steps right into him. There is a foot difference in height between Rob and the soldier, so the soldier cranes his neck to look way up at Rob, who says something in Dutch. The soldier freezes. Then he notices me, grips the banana clip, and moves the weapon off his shoulder. He is stunned and for another five seconds he stares at me and nobody speaks. With that gun between us, I was thinking somebody should speak very softly right about now. Someone please calm down the man with the gun.

Chuon spits out some words. He must be saying something like, "These are the bar rang doctors I told you about and there is no problem here." When he says it, he is smiling and throws in a laugh to smooth things over; the soldier picks up on it. Everybody exhales, and our shoulders relax in unison. The spell is broken and the soldier starts laughing, then so does Chuon, then Rob, and then me. That was the order of the laughing.

"Bat, bat, bar rang," the soldier says. He understands it now— these are the foreigners he was talking about.

And Chuon adds, "Yes, and they are doctors."

"Bahn, lok doctor," the soldier is nodding.

But Chuon isn't done. He sees his efforts are of great benefit to the situation, so he adds, "Okay, these two bar rangs are working in the hospital. That's their truck. This one is Dr. Rob from Holland and he worked for years at the refugee camps like Khao I Dang and Site II in Thailand."

That is a little too much information. The soldier now has his hand back on the banana clip. He is thinking fast. Why was the foreigner in those refugee camps? There are KPLNF cadres in those camps. They are his enemy and they have been trying to kill his comrades for years. What is someone from Thailand doing on this side? Chuon notices and starts laughing again, this time louder than before. He is laughing but his face is taut with concern.

"No, no, there isn't any problem. Doctors. They are just doctors working in the hospital." The soldier joins in again, laughing, but it's a bit halting. He is far more interested in the house now and is looking right past Rob and me, checking the house for anything untoward such as guns and crates of ammunition, or maybe a military radio. Chuon points to the MSF logo on the wall. The soldier looks at it like it is a puzzle.

It's Rob's turn to smooth out the situation. He says in Khmer, "Let's have a beer." Good idea. That seems to work right away. Rob explains everything again. Shows him the crates of medicine. The soldier becomes very happy and even puts his gun down. We are down by the Land Cruiser as Rob hands out the last beers we have. No ice. No cups. It doesn't matter and everyone drinks them fast. Everyone is having a laugh and Chuon is filling in any conversational gaps with Rob cautioning him about saying too much. I am wearing the soldier's green cap and Rob has draped his stethoscope over the soldier's shoulders. The man shows us a picture of his wife and child and also how the gun's safety and sight works. He puts the butt of the gun between his feet, two latches go click, and he hands me the heavy banana clip. Rob is now holding the machine gun. The soldier is about thirty. He is not much more than five feet tall and has several gold-capped teeth, just like Chuon. He is from Battambang and earns about ten dollars a month but hasn't been paid in half a year. We all finish our beers and the soldier appears genuinely thankful for the encounter. He and Chuon get ready to go together, the soldier off to patrol the streets of Sisophon and our driver out to find food.

Chuon looks a little taller this time as he ambles down the Low Road with 200 Riels in his pocket. He shows it to us to prove that he is trustworthy. No tricks tonight. He is on a straightforward mission to find us some decent food. I still haven't been to the upper level of the MSF Blue House, so Rob escorts me up. It is much better up there. The air is cleaner and with the rain abating, there is a bit of moon so you can see the old colonial outline of the town. Our house has a balcony of worn mahogany wrapped three quarters of the way around the second floor. It flows to where Rob has his bed off the main room. "This is where the office will be once we have a few supplies," he explains. I get a self-contained, tiny room at the back. Fair enough. Rob gets a bigger room but has to share his space. I have a room on my own, though it is notably small. In fact, the room is so small we start calling it the coffin room. It's six-and-a-half feet long and four feet wide. There is mosquito net rigging covering the ceiling rafters. You can just barely stand beside the bed without banging your head on the low ceiling. It has one window the size of a magazine and offers a view of a government loud speaker on a pole across the street. It is pointed right at my little room.

We take a moment to sit on the wooden balcony in the dark overlooking the streets. I rest my aluminum suitcase on the floor, get a mosquito coil going, and pull out my Sony SW1000. Rob starts fiddling with my preset buttons. First channel: BBC Asia, a retrospective on Lucien Freud and his stark realist paintings. Next was Radio Moscow, something about farm equipment, the people this, the comrades that. The Cold War is still on. And on Radio France International, someone from South East Australia is speaking flawless French, going on about wine and food. Rob spins the dial. It sounds vaguely like a roulette wheel going slower and slower until it sticks on a channel that is playing a waltz. He has found Radio Polskie and stands up, pretending to conduct an orchestra. He was overdoing the dramatics with his playful hand movements, calling for more from the woodwinds and brass. That's when we heard children's laughter down on the street and looked down to see them; we can just make out their shadows in the bushes. The kids are nearly invisible but we can hear them. "Bar rang," they sing. But just as Chuon arrives, the children run away.

Chuon comes up the stairs with some items wrapped in newspaper which I immediately start unraveling.

"Mean tekkork," he says. Good, good, we have ice.

"Mean, tek." All right, fine, we have water.

And then, he pauses for some drama. "Mean bières."

Rob is cheering. Very good, Chuon, we have beer and ice. Well done. But where's the food? Where's our splendid bounty? Rob takes a turn unwrapping the newspapers but it is like peeling onion skins away until there is only air.

"Ott mean," says Chuon. There is no food hiding in the newspapers.

Rob asks Chuon whether he went here, and didn't he go there? Yes, Chuon says, he's been here and there and everywhere, which is not true because he was only gone ten minutes.

"Impossible," says Rob, but Chuon is sticking to it. He says no one's able to get food at night. Rob doesn't believe it and wants his change back. He counts it out right in front of Chuon and wants to know how much everything cost. Item by item. I am thinking we might starve. Chuon has his palms upturned to the moon, plus he is shaking his head. It's the universal "What can I do?" gesture and he can't believe this is causing such a problem.

There is something else. Chuon has a touch of alcohol on his breath. Maybe banana beer, or possibly the vapors of Cambodian moonshine. He also has a new pack of American cigarettes in his shirt pocket. I notice the package because the rain has made his white shirt transparent. He didn't have those before.

We are hungry and feeling a bit miserable, but Rob says we'd be well fed soon enough. He started to say, "Don't you worry" again but I cut him off. He started laughing and hinted at how the locals would celebrate my arrival; that they would honor me with dried pork fat, warmed on the hood of a car. Maybe I'd even get some of that soup made from the leftover bits of a goat. He said that's what happened to him. Then he started listing his top ten favorite meals. Number one was canned herring washed down with a liter of Dutch pilsner at his neighborhood pub. I said something about steak tartar and a pinot noir at the old first-class waiting room in the Centraal Station in Amsterdam. It was not the last of our conversations about food.

That first night in our new home was July 14, 1991—Bastille Day—and dinner at the MSF Blue House, Low Road, Sisophon was white soy nuts, a red can of beurre français, and beer over ice. Nothing as appealing as the French cuisine we knew our colleagues were enjoying in the capital, Phnom Penh, or, more vexing, what the Belgians were no doubt feasting on at one of the numerous cafés and restaurants along the Sukhumvit Road in Bangkok. They told us all about it. Local seafood shops, the day's catch on ice. You just pointed to whatever you liked. One restaurant slogan said, "If it swims, we have it."

12

The Hospital

Sisophon, Cambodia / July 1991

At five a.m. the loud speaker across the street from the MSF Blue House wails with traditional Cambodian music. The free-reed mouth organ and gourd wind chest song has a tasteful hauntedness to it, but the shrill singing that follows is crude, unbearable. It blasts into my room as if the walls were made of paper. Rob is fine with the noise, used to the cacophony after years in Southeast Asia. Deep asleep in his hammock and shrouded in a mosquito net strung up corner to corner in his room, he couldn't be more content.

The night before, in the grey drizzle, the town was drab and dull but the new day is already bright, illuminated by an infinitely pale blue sky. I walk out to the balcony to see my new town in a dazzling morning light. It has gone from a dreary Turner landscape to a tropical and vibrant Gauguin Marquesas scene. Color everywhere.

Rob joins me on the balcony, and we watch the people below drifting happily by on foot, on bicycles, or crouched on springy horse-drawn flatbeds going clop, clop, clop. Here and there ancient motorcycles and newer scooters dodge puddles, and we see a tall truck loaded so high it almost topples over as it corners. All of the townspeople point up at us as they pass below our balcony, calling, "Bar rang!"

Across the street is a family with seven or eight children hiding behind a durian tree. It might be the little ones from the night before. Rob hoots at them and they all run away laughing. All but one. A ten-year-old girl beams up at me and she can't stop smiling. She has her baby brother on her hip, her hand covering her smile. An insuppressible, radiant smile. It is very hard for her to pry her eyes away. We decide to call her "Smiles."

A barefoot man in a straw hat with a burlap bag over his shoulder stuffed with baguettes and other fresh baking makes his way up the street. He is calling out, "Nom pang! Nom pang!" and banging two sticks together to get everyone's attention. When Rob hears the man he comes running out of his room saying we need some of those. He lets a 50-Riel note float to the street below, and motions for the man to throw some of the baked goods up to us on the balcony. The man looks at the 50-Riel note like there is a mistake, so I add a couple of fifties. He then throws up his entire bag. Inside are about four dozen little sugar donuts in the shape of X's like chromosomes and a handful of petit pain baguette loaves—and they are still warm. We are soon flicking ants off the pastries and digging in while Chuon is down in the kitchen boiling water for coffee.

He had been trying for a half hour to get the cooking fire hot enough, bent over, blowing at the embers. I tell him to forget it. We are going to the hospital and have to get ready. Chuon points to the "ung" pot. It is a four-foot-high pot filled with water for washing and cooking. There is a tiny, silver fish in the pot swimming in nervous circles near the surface. The fish eats the algae so the water stays clean. Chuon pretends to scoop water out of it and dumps it over his head. He scrubs his hair and body under an imaginary shower. Rob and I take turns under the ung pot showering. That water is cold first thing in the morning—the only cold thing in the country. Rob and I put on fresh shirts and start marching down the low road to the town center and the provincial hospital. First day on the job.

People stop walking in their tracts and stare at us as we pass them. They get off their bicycles and come out of their homes to gape at us foreigners. Children are cheering, "Bar rang! Bar rang!" and some of the older ones try to touch us as we move along the mud road. When we get to the hospital the director, Monsieur Mogiath, and two of his assistants come out briskly. Mogiath has his hand straight out to greet Rob, calling him the grand doctor, saying what an honor it is and what a tremendous opportunity it is for the Sisophon Hospital in the new province of Bantaey Meanchey. He refers formally to the hospital in

French—l'Hôpital Sisophon dans la nouvelle province de Banteay Meanchey. Mogiath holds my hand while he finishes up his perfunctory morning salutation to Rob, and then he turns his substantial chin my way and basically gives a welcoming speech as if he is addressing a crowd of fifty people.

"My friend, docteur, you are, pardon me, please accept our humility, it is a tremendous privilege and honor for the government of Cambodia to welcome you to our province, Banteay Meanchey, and this grand assistance will aid many here in Sisophon and in all of Banteay Meanchey, the new province in Kampuchea. Oui, oui, especially the children, the poor children of Cambodia. For us, this is an unprecedented, oui, unprecedented. . . ." He was trying to come up with a word, and one of his assistants suggested "event," but he waved the word away and came up with "milestone." He says "étape importante!"

During his delivery, Rob was trying to catch my eye to get me to laugh. It was exactly the same speech he had received a week earlier. Mogiath finishes with, "You are most welcome. C'est un grand plaisir. This is now your hospital. Your new home." He makes a sweeping gesture with his hand, displaying the bedraggled hospital grounds, and then they all clap—including Rob, who is cheering and patting me on the back.

Monsieur Mogiath didn't really have a huge chin but it was bigger than most, and he used it to emphasize the points he was making. I would have put him in his late thirties but later found out he was already fifty. What a well-preserved man. He had identical twin daughters, age ten. Very privileged and beautiful kids, just like Mrs. Mogiath. We walk to the near side of the hospital compound to a café, which is most welcome because I am hungry for something more substantial than pastries, and I am still hoping for a coffee. I need to tighten up my thinking and be present, awake. I envision an extra large coffee with milk. Maybe two, just like back home. The caffeine is going to help. So is the sun. How could I feel sleepy with a white-hot sun like that?

We are served coffee in green-tinged glasses. But no milk. None for the year. Not much dairy in Cambodia. And on the tray are the exact same X-shaped sugar donuts. The server asks if I want an egg.

"Sure, I'll have an egg. Can I have a couple?"

The server looks at Monsieur Mogiath for approval and Mogiath waves the man away. Of course I could have two.

The hospital grounds are surrounded by a faded yellow masonry wall. There are maybe ten buildings inside the grounds making up the hospital and they are all single-story, dark brown wooden edifices with thatched roofs. We are sitting in the café next to the main arch of the hospital entrance way. Painted onto the faded yellow arch are red Khmer letters, and beside the letters there are numbers that seem to be monetary amounts. In front of each number there is a large R for Riel, the Cambodian currency. Mogiath gets up from his seat and touches the numbers on the wall. "These are the great donations from the hospital patrons." Everyone at our table starts nodding. He begins naming names and the amounts the benefactors have given. "Meng Chhay, ten thousand. Monsieur Chea Phirun, five thousand. Monsieur Vy Kong Kea, seven thousand five hundred. He was a businessman." At the top of the arch is someone who had given one hundred thousand. The next closest is ten thousand, and there is a handful at five thousand. That seems to be the lowest. The official conversion rate is 100 Riels to the US dollar, but we had been getting closer to 500 on the black market. So the grand total of the hospital's endowment is, at best, less than 300 US dollars.

My eggs arrive unopened in a cup. They are large for chicken eggs. Are they chicken eggs? I am assured they are indeed eggs, but their ancestry is a mystery. Rob is trying to figure out the Khmer word for egg. I make a sound like a chicken and everyone thinks it's very funny. I point to the eggs and make the sound again. More laughter. We are getting along fine but what kind of eggs are these? Even Rob isn't sure. He, too, is suspicious of their size.

Mogiath describes how delicious they are and I am given a special spoon with which to eat them—a long-handled metal implement with a spiral stem. It looks like a surgical instrument. I break the top off and can see a mixture of runny egg white and blood inside. I feel the spoon crunch on something as it goes down through the contents of the egg. Mogiath's assistant holds his egg high up in the sun and keeps it there while he scoops it out into his appreciative mouth. He just feasts on it.

Then they all watch me eat. I do, haltingly. My toes are curled up as I try to think about anything but tiny chicks pecking at the inside of the eggshell.

Lumbering trucks roar around the corner kicking up dust. Mogiath reflexively covers his plate and continues on with his description of the hospital, chin up and out, hands gesturing to this building and that. Every time Mogiath hints at a plan that might require financial assistance Rob says, "Just you wait." A pig comes from around back of the hospital kitchen. Nobody shoos it away. No one notices it at all. I had counted a pig, two goats, one cow, and several dogs inside the hospital compound. Bitches with twenty nipples hanging from their undersides.

Mogiath holds my hand, nodding at things as we tour the compound. Rob and the others follow. We walk up to the maternity building. There are eight bamboo beds, several smiling expectant mothers and two newborns wrapped up tight in silk cloths. We had been told by the World Health Organization that this has been the most successful ward in the hospital and that the success was due to Madame Boran, a French-speaking, Thai-educated midwife. How she lived through the genocidal horrors of Cambodia was a mystery. Anybody else with her Western skills had vanished. Yet there she is in the delivery suite with her back to us. She and two nurses are leaning over a woman groaning in childbirth. Blood and fluids are everywhere and the woman is hysterical. Madame Boran has her hands on the baby's crown, scolding the mother to slow down. Without taking her hands away from the baby, she casually twists her head around and cordially smiles, offering a measured greeting in faultless French. Perfect control.

Like a Soutine painting, the mother is lying on her back in the blood and mess on a stainless-steel table that has a drain for easy cleanup. Soutine, because that Impressionist had a way of painting from the inside out, first bones, then flesh, then skin. Madame Boran has plastic overalls covering her simple hospital whites and she is standing there in yellow rain boots. Those boots were as high-tech as it got at l'Hôpital Sisophon dans la nouvelle province de Banteay Meanchey.

"Time to visit the medical ward," says Mogiath.

The entourage follows to a slightly longer building with the same thatched roof and weathered wooden walls. It has maybe twenty beds inside, but fewer patients.

"Where is everyone?"

"Der leng"—they are all out walking, promenading. Out with their families getting food, clean blankets, water, all the things the hospital didn't provide.

Underneath each bed there is a clutch of loose crumpled papers with details about the patient's case. Mogiath begins to tell me about the kinds of problems on the ward. This one is malaria, that one is typhoid. Intestinal parasites here, abscess there. He waves his hands around, pointing out this and that, and his chin helps him point out things as well. But it seems as though the diagnoses he is throwing around are simply words he has overheard his doctors using.

"What's wrong with this one?"

"Ott deng—I don't know," says a nurse.

"What about this case here?"

"Ott deng," she says again.

"Where are the doctors?"

Someone points out it is Tuesday. Rob and I say, "So, it's Tuesday." Is the hospital closed on Tuesdays? Where are they? But no one has an answer. No one thinks there needs to be an answer.

I read through a chart. The man has a fever and without any tests they had given him tablets and injections for half a dozen major illnesses—anything that causes fever. The chart said the man had typhoid, shigella, dengue, cerebral malaria, and tuberculosis, as well as fever of unknown origin. What an unlucky man.

"It's amazing," Rob laughs. "They give medicines for all illnesses, all at once, as long as the patient can afford the pills."

We go over to the minor surgical ward. Docteur Sann is waiting there in a perfect white uniform with his neat black hair parted to the right. We are told this was his ward and that the hospital has a special arrangement with him for his services. Rob wants to hear more about this arrangement but Mogiath and the others laugh it off saying there is no problem. Sann has been saving a case for our arrival. It is a man in his thirties with an apple-sized swollen mass at each groin.

"Maladie vénérienne," we are told—venereal disease. "Too many visits to the meretrixes," giggles Sann, and all the staff laugh with him. They stand around the patient in a semi-circle laughing. But the man doesn't hear them. He has his eyes riveted to the silver surgical tray with all the scalpels and syringes and clamps. The doctor puts on his surgical gloves. He uses a clamp to dab a square piece of gauze into a silver dish containing a generous puddle of brown iodine and then proceeds to paint the man's groin with it. People are nodding at the doctor's quick work. Where the iodine drips onto the white cloth, the brown color expands in all directions. He then pulls a sterile scalpel from the autoclave—a number three quick bevel. He points it like a matador in for the final kill and stabs at the man's groin before Rob can intervene.

Rob cries, "Oy yoy yoy! There are arteries there."

Sann isn't deterred. He strikes again and is squeezing at the mass and it comes out like milk from a garden hose.

"You see," he says as he lances the other groin with equal speed, "maladie venériénne." Everyone is groaning at what is coming out, pinching their noses as Rob says, "Oy yoy yoy," again.

But now there's a problem. Where he made the first cut there is ruby red arterial blood coming out, and not that slowly either. Rob asks for a number seven-and-a-half-glove and gets his hand on it to stop the hemorrhage. After a few minutes he takes his hand away very gingerly and for a moment everyone is relieved that there is no more hemorrhaging, but then the blood comes again, worse than before. Rob has to spend the next hour with his thumb pushed into the wound, leaning into it to improvise a groin clamp before the bleeding is under control and the man is safe to be left.

This is Sann's ward.

Later that afternoon, Sann came skipping over to me. He wants a word and he has my shirt sleeve in his hand. His French is pretty good and he starts explaining that there may be a "gros problème" developing at the hospital. Something grave, and he doesn't want me mixed up with it. He says he is concerned for me, and I notice he's still clutching my shirt. He's worried about what he calls "interference" and wants to know what Dr. Rob has been saying about him. Wants to know if he has said anything to Mogiath, the director, and could I help him because we are such good friends. He ends by saying MSF is a great organization and that I am a great physician and that Rob is a great physician too, but he prefers me and hopes Rob can be reasonable. He requests that I smooth things out so Rob doesn't cause a "grave problem" by saying something to Mogiath. He wants me to promise before letting go of my shirt.

13

The Public Market

Sisophon, Cambodia / August 1991

We heard about a restaurant just this side of Mongkol Borei, a neighboring town about half an hour away, where rumor hinted at the chance to find something sapid and savory. It's a sunny late morning and beyond finding food, the point of the mini excursion is to find Rhee, an eighteen-year-old friend of Chuon's. He tells us she is keen to work in our home as a cook and maid and has experience. What's more, she speaks fluent French, a huge advantage for us. Rob begins calling her our saviour and we fantasize about all the great baking and grilling we will soon be eating daily.

Rhee apparently lives in a wooden house with a large arch somewhere between Sisophon and Mongkol Borei. That wouldn't narrow down our search very much, so after lunch we drive a lot slower, keeping an eye out for anything that might resemble the large arch. By all reports, it was always safe on that road. Lots of military checkpoints to keep out the bad guys and there hadn't been any reports of roadside landmines in a month. No sightings of the KPLNF.

Then we round a corner where four people at the roadside wave us over. Standing by a modest home in a sarong and sandals is Rhee, her hands clasped, patiently waiting for us to pick her up.

She seems very young and after pressing her hands together in the customary offering of "Choum-reap-sour" she just helps herself to the front seat where Rob had been sitting. Rob looks over and says, "Did you see that?"

Rob and I try to speak French to Rhee, but she doesn't seem to understand what we're saying. Same with English. Chuon hadn't been ambivalent: he said she spoke French and that he knew her well and could vouch for her "sans réservation." I was present when he said it. When Rob questioned him that day, Chuon pretended it was all a mix-up. He said someone at the market recommended her, that he'd never actually met the girl. Our Khmer was only just hitting some kind of conversational stride, so to have a cook with whom we couldn't communicate was trouble. We needed to be able to tell her what to buy in the market and when to fill up the great ung pot with fresh water. We needed the help now, not later when we had the luxury of improving our Khmer. It wouldn't be the best use of our time to have two physicians haggling about turnips and laundry when we were facing long days at the hospital.

We try our best in the truck, fumbling along in Khmer. It is a junior-kindergarten kind of give and take. And after a while, the conversation goes dead. When it gets to the point of uncomfortable silence, Rob just laughs. Rob laughs when things are funny and when things are stupid. Cambodians laugh when things are funny and when things are unbearably sad. Rob and I have maybe a couple hundred words in Khmer each, and Rhee doesn't understand a third of them. Some kind of dialect problem. So Rob and I carry on the conversation in English, making plans for the hospital. Rob thinks we should paint all the buildings white. Rhee stares out the window and giggles whenever we try to engage her.

Khmer is an easy language to speak badly but nearly impossible to speak well. We had all been taking informal lessons in the coffee shops during the mornings. Fifty cents for an hour-long customized lesson from a former teacher who had laid low during the purges or escaped to Thailand. Generally, if you had been a teacher or a midwife in Cambodia, like Madame Boran, you didn't survive. Rob had been learning the language very well, better than me. He had a head start from all his work on the Thai border camps but also, prior to becoming a physician, he had studied speech therapy. So he was more easily able to replicate a diphthong and glide. Anyway that was his theory. Before long he was speaking Khmer better than Maurits van Pelt, our head of mission in Phnom Penh, a man who had lived in Cambodia for several years.

We creep into the Sisophon market. Everyone is checking out the Land Cruiser, calling us bar rangs. Rob has an idea. He wants to test Rhee, so he identifies a modest list of foods we need. Where he doesn't have the correct word in Khmer, he draws a picture. Rob is not a great artist, but how do you draw a tangerine versus an orange anyway? He hands over 1000 Riels and sends her on her way. Rhee's eyes light up. A whole thousand Riels. The market looks like a country fairground after significant rain. Many were barefoot moving through a foot of dark chocolaty mud. Some of the stalls have glass cases with gold jewelry and thick stacks of worn Khmer banknotes. Evidently the black market was quite open here in little Sisophon.

"How many Riels for a US twenty?" asks Rob.

A Chinese man behind a glass case holds a calculator out for us to see what a US dollar will buy. There were rates for the Cambodian Riel, Thai Bhat, Pound Sterling, and US dollar. Hmmm, thinks Rob. We go to the next stall. This man can do a little better but Rob is not impressed and waves him away. They are all signaling each other, telegraphing exchange rates. They don't know how to deal with Rob, the bar rang. At the third stall, we get a good rate. Six hundred and twenty Riels for a dollar. Last week it was five hundred. Since the fighting began again in the northwest, the Riel had been plunging. Too bad for the Cambodians.

We weren't supposed to be trading on the black market. Well, it wasn't clear what the exact MSF policy was on that. Some said we could, some said we couldn't. It was always like that. No clear policy. We still had US $10,000 I had brought from the Amsterdam office. At the official exchange rate set by the government of 140 Riels to the US dollar, it meant our money wouldn't go a quarter as far. A friend in the capital said trading our funds at the government rate would be like killing people.

Rob goes off to buy batteries and Chinese neon lights. I start strolling through the market and everyone is calling me "bar rang." They want to know if I want to buy an eggplant or if I need a gasoline container. I'm holding back. A vendor comes out from behind a stall and holds a Vietnamese T-shirt up against my body. "Oh, saart nas," they say, "it's beautiful." But I'm thinking a gold-colored T-shirt is not in vogue and just doesn't suit me. Perhaps I'll get one for Rob.

"How much is the nice shirt?"

You wait, I am told. Someone comes running back with a calculator to show me that today's price is 1000 Riels. A dollar and a half. As the shopkeeper is showing me the price on the calculator, a few of the other vendors in attendance are giving each other looks.

"Way too much," I tell them and begin to walk away. The shopkeeper is frozen. He stands there in the mud working his calculator. He's got a new price, runs up and taps me on the back.

"Two hundred."

I show him a 100-Riel note. He doesn't need the calculator this time. One hundred is too low. There's no sale. But he gets the message, it isn't so easy to fool the bar rang.

The market is crowded with goods and wares, but there isn't much that I need personally. One after the other, the stalls look the same. I am walking past a shop that sells cooking supplies and oils and little ovens to cook in. I'm thinking, Why buy an oven in this heat? Just leave the food under the sun and it will bake to a crisp. There's a pharmacy with many French pharmaceuticals and some naturopathic items from China. Pills for cancer. Pills to treat skin rash. Powder to ensure you get a baby boy. Injectable morphine and intravenous steroids. No prescription required. They have several boxes of IV fluids as well. What was it about getting intravenous fluids from the doctor? We heard that wealthy men visit the clinics to get pumped up on steroids and saline for an evening with the meretrixes. Friday evening was the busiest time at the doctor's offices.

There were all kinds of rumors about this. That the IV made you virile and it purified your blood. More than once we were told that high-ranking officers got perfusions before battle. The fiercest officers sometimes took the fluid directly from a coconut. Clear, sweet, sterile, isotonic coconut water has the same solute content as ocean water, to match the body's blood. An aide would hold the coconut up in the air above a general as he reviewed battle plans and barked orders. We heard Dr. Sann was offering this kind of service on our ward and at his home clinic. He would typically have three or four men lying in beds, IV lines run up their arms with saline and whatever else drip dripping away. For a special price, he would don his sunglasses, drive out to find you on his motorcycle, and make a special house call, IV bags in hand.

Cambodians use the word "Mean" for everything. It means "Have," and "Ott mean" means "Don't have."

"Have you got any beets?"

"Mean!" they say, laughing at our accents.

"How about potatoes? Pomme de terre? You know, apples of the earth?"

"Mean!"

"Well, what about chocolate?"

"Ott mean." There isn't any chocolate on that day at the market. We would have to come back. There are a lot of things missing. Almost everywhere you go in the Third World you can find a Mercedes Benz, Marlboro cigarettes and Coca-Cola. But not here. Not yet.

I notice a stall to buy stationery where gaudy Chinese calendars and Buddhist posters of Indian children are displayed, and I swear some drawings show children involved in sex acts. There are school notebooks, envelopes, accounting ledgers, and ink stamps. Even knock-off Bic pens. I say knock-off because whichever company in China made them spelled Bic like Bick. Here at the stationery shop, we can't find anything un-Chinese. Everything, including all the merchants, seems to be ethnic Chinese. I go through the shop's inventory searching for a journal to lodge my notes and sketches. But there are no Grumbacher 7194-2 sketch books. Nothing close. I will have to wait a few weeks until the IndoSwiss Courier Company delivers them to me from home via Phnom Penh. But they have accounting ledgers. We did need those accounting ledgers. Rob was already complaining about losing bits of papers with the project costs on them.

"How much?"

She hesitates. I know she's trying to come up with a higher price. Something to her advantage. Staring right at me, she is calculating something extortionate. This is so insulting. She's seeing how much she can get out of the foreigner.

But I want the real price, and it's hot, so I rush her. "How much, how much, tell me?"

"Forty Riels," she blurts out. It's almost nothing. The price is very low, so low I buy four of them. I pick out some blank pads too, some poster paper for the hospital, and ten of the Bicks. It was still under a dollar. How does anyone get by? I tip her but know this will make Rob mad. Every tip fuels inflation in the bar rang economy.

Some farmers are selling their produce from the countryside. In one stall they have big burlap bags full of turnips, other ones full of corn and rice, and what's this? Right in the middle was one full of cannabis. It was sitting out there in the open, maybe fifty pounds of it.

"Is that . . . ?" I didn't know the word for it.

"Konch chhar," they say, matter-of-factly.

I hold some of it in my hand. The dark sticky buds are still on their stalks and they've tied ten or so stalks together to make a bundle the size of a small loaf of bread. I'm very curious about this. I didn't think you could get it so openly anywhere. There it was in a bag just like the rice and corn. You didn't really see it or smell it around the cities but I was told the teenagers smoked it at parties and that some older people thought it helped them get closer to Buddha, although it was a soldier who told me that. He said smoking konch chhar here made him afraid. Something about all the murders and ghosts. And there was that gardener I knew in Pursat. He kept a glowing konch chhar cigarette dangling from his lips while he did the raking. I pick up one of the bundles—fairly good weight to it. I look up and down the rows of stalls expecting the locals to notice the bar rang checking out konch chhar, but no one cares.

"How much?" I ask the farmer, but she is speaking fast with a dialect and I can't understand the numbers. I thought I heard the price but it seemed inconceivably low. Someone comes over with a calculator to help out. I keep saying I don't want to buy, I just want to know the price. I also want to know if the police have any problems with this. I must have confused the issue, because two or three of the farmers start a diatribe about the police, but I have no idea what they are talking about. Every so often, one farmer in particular points to the konch chhar in the burlap bag and waves his hands around his head.

The price they mention couldn't have been right, not for so much of the God-touching vegetable. I try to explain I am only curious and just want to know the price but I'm not making much sense with my Khmer. The farmer assumes I am doubting how potent his product is, so he calls over to some older man who takes me aside, holds my hand in a solemn way, and utters some lengthy testimonial. Neither of us have any clue what the other is saying.

I hold out one of the bundles in my one hand and a 100-Riel note in the other. This is about a dollar. I motion like I want to make an exchange. How much of the loaf-sized bundle would I get for the dollar? The woman seems to get it. She takes both from my hands, disappears behind the burlap bags and comes back with the entire bundle wrapped up in a plastic bag and some money in her palm. It was my change. I counted out 93 Riels. That was approximately one Troy ounce of fresh, local konch chhar and it cost seven cents.

I find Rob down one of the market lanes at a stall trying to buy some car batteries. "These are the ones," he is saying. "This will give us electric light all night and some hours of music as well."

Rob wants six of them. He says we need that many to adhere to the strict security policy. We do need to ensure we'll always have enough juice on hand to power the military band on the radio, but it was really for our music. In another of Rob's previous lives, in the Seventies, he had been a photojournalist covering all the big rock bands in New York and other venues. Rob loved his music, especially the British bands like the Stones and Elvis Costello; he loved the idea of rock and roll. He had photographed the big stars and sometimes cajoled security to let him shoot the musicians offstage, where they were smoking and drinking in the catacombs of places like Madison Square Garden.

People can play all their lives at things they love. That is Rob. Or enter into drudgery.

Rob is walking a little faster in the afternoon heat. He's after his music again. He shows me a booth offering bootleg cassettes and movie videos. This is an astounding discovery. The shop has many boom boxes and even one television for sale. The good equipment is from Singapore, the bad stuff comes from China. Rob says, "How much?" but was ready to laugh no matter what the price was. We start going over the cassettes. Wouldn't it be nice to have a few dozen albums to enjoy up there on our balcony, up where the sugar palms shaded us from the moon and sun? But the titles were all Thai and Chinese. There wasn't a single Western recording artist amongst them. "It's all garbage." Rob makes a face like something was off. He says we'll have to wait and pick up some music in

Bangkok in a few months when we are on leave. There were thousands of cassettes just over the border and not even one worth listening to here. Thailand was a land of plenty. Here we were in the anti-Shangri-La. "Don't you worry," says Rob.

Rhee manages to find us at the market's restaurant. We were making our way through a kind of sweet and sour pork dish served on rice. I think the cook snuck some fish sauce into it. You had to watch out for the pork dishes. There was pork done the way Western-ers prefer. And there was traditional Cambodian pork. This was to be avoided. On just our second day in Sisiphon, Monsieur Mogiath and another government official put on a meal for us by the roadside. We were being feted with an honorific delicacy. It was dried pork fat. I couldn't possibly lie about this. During that exceptionally hot day, our hosts had dried some of the fat on the hood of a government car for us. A chef of some notoriety had cleaned off a portion of the Peugeot 404's hood and had laid out the strips side by side to warm them. I kept waiting for the next course of the meal to arrive and our hosts kept waiting for me to try it. They wanted me to tell them how good it was. In the end I snuck it off my plate and into the mud beneath the table when everyone was laughing about something. Thank god for the Mekong brandy. They didn't see me do it but some dogs across the road zeroed in on the pork's scent. They tried approaching and Mogiath's assistant had to throw a rock to keep them away from under the table.

Thankfully, Rhee didn't have any of the dried pork fat with her as she joined us after her shopping spree on that first day in the market. In fact, she had nothing with her. What had she been doing?

"Where is the food we asked you to buy?" asks Rob.

"Ott mean—don't have," she replies.

"Yes, we can see that. Why didn't you buy anything?"

"Too expensive," she says.

"Oy yoy yoy."

"We are starving," I say.

"Too expensive," she says again.

Rob wants the money back. Rhee is surprised.

"Okay," she says, "I will buy."

Rhee ventures off into the market for round two. She has been told exactly where the MSF Blue House is. She is asked to meet us there in one hour.

"Well," Rob says "we should have an extra beer each because it is so hot here in the market."

"I believe we should. We don't want to become dehydrated."

The heat and the beer and the food make us sleepy. So we ease the Land Cruiser down the Low Road. Everyone is yelling "bar rang." We are small-town celebrities. Small-town oddities.

We arrive at the hospital. It's one or two in the afternoon by now. The wards are empty. Some of the nurses in their white uniforms are sleeping on chairs or in hammocks by the staff building. A horse-drawn cart comes in clop, clopping. Rob and I stop the driver. It's not a good sight. There's a body in the back. Rob checks the eyes, then for a pulse, then frowns. He extends the man's arm to show the rigor mortis is already setting in.

"Slap hoy," says the driver. "The man is already dead."

"Was it a mine?"

"Oui, une détonation de mine," agrees the man. He points up to the northwest where everyone knows there are many hundreds of thousands of mines.

We'd hear the low distant boom of an antitank mine every other day. It was usually a cow taking one. What an unlucky final step. That's how the Cambodians clear the mine fields. They would let their herds graze them. The grasses were thicker in those fields because no one dared walk there for so long. So it was cheap fodder, though risky for a farmer who had maybe only three or four Bali cattle.

There is a small commotion by the administration building. It's Sao Sim, the top government official in Sisophon. He has a bunch of administrators bowing around his short, substantial frame. They are all bent over meekly, showing great respect. He carries himself around town in such a conceited way, chain smoking 555s. He brings his grumbling laugh over and one of the bent-over administrators introduces us. We are all standing around the man on the cart. Sao Sim seems to be personally offended by this problem. He raises his voice above our own and says the government has told everyone where the mines are and that the man should have been more careful. He curses and spits little bits of his mashed up toothpick on the ground as he chews it. Then his rumbling laugh takes over.

He extends his hand to shake mine. As he does, his little finger wiggles in my palm. At first I think this is a fumbled handshake, but the finger keeps on wiggling in my palm and he keeps on belly laughing. The finger was saying, this is the secret handshake of the elites in town. As we talk, there are no extended platitudes about how great it is to have the foreigners in town, nothing to suggest he's wanting to be deferential, as Mogiath had done. The way he holds himself, it's as if he is saying while we could bring our money and know-how to Sisophon, he wants us to know that we should not ignore his presence. He wants us to be aware. It's not that he's distempered or humorless, in fact, I can't seem to conjure him up without seeing his smile and hearing his laugh. But on the other hand, he is all politics and business.

We get back to the MSF Blue House. Everything seems to be in order. Chuon is standing beside a bucket of soapy water washing the truck. Rhee is up on the balcony pinning up some white bed sheets to dry. The hot air will super-dry the wet sheets. Time for a libation on ice, a chance to watch the town go by from our box seats up there on the balcony. Time to enjoy the lighter side of humanitarianism. Rhee begins making dinner. Whatever she is cooking wafts up to the balcony where Rob and I are resting, he in the hammock, me on the mahogany floor getting some oblique five o'clock sun. Down on the Low Road are the kids playing games, dogs, carts, fruit vendors, old people sitting on their haunches, others talking and smoking. Rhee comes to be with us. She sits on the floor beside me in the shade. Rob doesn't look very comfortable with this. Doesn't she have work to do?

The sun is setting so fast I have to relocate frequently to catch the last oblique rays of the sun. Every time I get up to reposition myself, Rhee groans. It's like "Humph, did you really do that again?" It takes Rob a few more groans to understand what is going on. As I lay out my towel, I naturally had to step over the stuff that had accumulated on the balcony floor: cans of juice, the cooler, the Czech shortwave, plus some cassettes, my books, and Rhee. What this meant was I was lifting my feet up and over Rhee. I was lifting the soles of my feet above her.

In the Khmer tradition, where people often walk in bare feet, walking through the mud shared with animals, this was the rudest thing anyone could do. It was saying "I stepped in the dirt and manure and now I am holding my dirty feet above you." And Rhee wasn't going to move. No, no, she had found a nice spot on the balcony floor and was not going to get up. So when we moved around, we dragged our feet along the floor so as not to offend our cook and maid.

Not unexpectedly Rob and I were unable to eat the meal Rhee prepared. She had cooked up the traditional Cambodian pork dish with extra fish sauce, precisely what she was told not to do. Rob and I shared a can of nuts and took turns dipping into the last can of beurre francais. I told him about a Belgian national who worked in Chad. He was a fruitarian, strict about eating only fruits and nuts, things very, very difficult to find in the Sahara. He got thinner and thinner, and they eventually sent him home in just under a month.

We had heard rumors about how the other missions in Cambodia had it easier than what was in store for us—how others in the field had decent restaurants in town and excellent cooks and maids. In Kampot, the MSF workers even had a gardener. All the other missions were three or four hours from the capital so they could go there on weekends and watch movies and play tennis. They had swimming pools, and even phones to call home. Rob and I were two full days' travel from Phnom Penh and all those luxuries, close enough to the front to feel the bombing and watch stuff fall off our shelves from the percussion.

When it was time to figure out who was going to drive Rhee home that night, we flipped a coin and Rob lost. When he returned, it was another meal-less bedtime.

14

S'isophon

Cambodia / September 1991

The government loudspeaker—the "haut-parleur"—goes off at five a.m. again. The same penetrating song to start the day with. What a fancy name, "haut-parleur," but there are so many grand sounding names like that in French. Words like pâté, which really just means paste. And what is worse, lately, there has been a pig coming around the Blue House. It's a big sow and for twenty minutes before the haute-parleur starts its morning cacophony, this pig would rub its sides up and down against the rickety tin shed under my window. It sounded like someone raking. And when you made it past the full half hour of propaganda from the haute-parleur, the next set of noises emanated from the neighbor who ran a Chinese school in her house. Twenty ethnic Chinese children singing Maoist slogans, squawking away.

At that hour Sisophon is still dark but in minutes it started brightening. The day illuminates faster here on the equator, and it keeps intensifying, past normal brightness until the town is lit up like a movie set. There are some kids outside our fence whispering "bar rang" to us and "om" for uncle, seeing if we'd come over and talk to them through the fence, maybe give them a pastry or a balloon. The one we had started calling Smiles motions for me to come around to the front where the trucks are parked. Some problem perhaps, but no, it's just the ice man, the one who sells chunks of ice from an insulated box on the back of his bicycle. Smiles says she'll handle the purchase for me and adopts a tough-customer air with the man. She is ten and he is thirty. She peers into the ice box, starts fishing out chunks and passes me her baby brother. We are always holding the yearlings.

I buy two brick-size pieces of ice wrapped in newspaper. Five cents each. That's how they do it. No one has freezers—there isn't enough available electricity for that. Power is turned on once daily, in the evenings, and is never reliable, so no one can keep ice. Instead they get ice from a forty-year-old ice factory, a dark industrial building ribbed with scaffolding and corrugated tin. You'd expect an ice factory to leave you with an impression of silvery-white or windows of clear see-through ice. This one was a study in contrast.

There are two parts to the factory. A rickety conveyor belt system pulls blocks of ice from icy pools, pools that look like something from an underground cave, and each successive pool is colder and colder until ice forms in the last one. At the other end of the factory there is a diesel-powered turbine the size of a locomotive engine. Horse-drawn carts and men on bicycles arrived during the day to take out chunks of ice, some as big as a treasure chest and others the size of grapefruit, all wrapped in newspaper, placed deep into tin boxes lined with Styrofoam so it won't melt. Arctic nuggets for sale.

We have a "Deluxe Supérieure" cooler box now but it still contains no food. Rob wants to see how well the ice will last, so in goes the ice, each brick on either side of a six-pack of Vietnamese Heineken. If the cooler is of good quality, Rob said, we'll have ice-cold beer tonight. And then maybe we'll be able to find a way to store Vache Qui Rit cheese and keep it from spoiling.

Rob plans to hang around the Blue House and tally up some expenses; anyway, he tells me, it's my turn to go to the wards. Actually, the way we divided up the work for the first month was that I would directly attend to all the patients on the wards. My French was better than Rob's and that helped because French was the operational language at the hospital. Rob's Khmer was better and he knew how to maneuver around the government and the market and the shops. The supply situation was meager and we needed Rob to get out there and find stuff.

So off I walk along the Low Road to the hospital. By six-thirty the sun is drying everything, such a bright equatorial sun and the temperature is perfect, maybe eighty, and the sky is clear of clouds. I walk by a woman in a traditional sarong. She has a basket of heavy plantains on her head, an infant strapped to her chest and a two-year-old by the hand, walking at her side. Actually the child is probably four. The children are always older than you first think, and when the boy looked up at me he stared right into my eyes and said, "Bar rang."

Every day feels a little more like home at the hospital. I know everyone's name and there is a polite greeting or handshake in return. Some joking-around too, like the past week when we raced each other up the sugar palm in the courtyard. There we were climbing the trunks in our lab coats. They all taught me so much and I didn't make the mistake of pretending I was all-knowing or some kind of great Westerner. I was learning more than teaching.

Madame Boran waves from the maternity suite. She is busy with another delivery again. She might have been up most of the night, but there she is, her smile undiminished.

I say, "Call me when the baby's coming. I want to deliver this one with you."

"Oui, monsieur, but this one isn't coming quick. Pas très vites."

The ward nurse, Monsieur Sok Samuth, is there. He's got jet-black hair, a round, kind face, and is wearing a clean white lab coat. I don't know what time he showed up but he had done a quick run-through with all the patients, plus he had had his breakfast already. Sok Samuth is very competent but guarded. When you get too close, he laughs to keep you away. It is his favorite tactic: a shrill, high-pitched giggle. He holds my hand and brings me to the medical ward where we have most of the sick kids staying. He's smiling about something.

"Where's the little boy?"

"Der leng," says the boy's mother. He's out walking so Sok Samuth shouts over to a nurse to fetch the boy and a minute later he shows up. The little boy is beaming, standing up straight, looking a bit thin but healthy and not coughing at all.

"Well, well. Somebody's all better," I say. "The other day, we thought you might not make it. He's still taking the erythromycin?"

"Oui, oui."

"And we're doing the TB testing again?"

"C'était negatif."

"It's negative for sure? I don't know—that's probably worth doing again. But, obviously, keep on the antibiotics, and uhm, get a weight on him, we should do those every day. I think all the pediatric cases should be weighed daily and we've got to figure out how to keep track of the food and fluids better. Any ideas? I'll get graph paper. Even a rough estimate on the urine. It'd be the only way to gauge things. I can't understand this chart. Is that Khmer?"

"Francais."

"Really?"

"Oui, oui." Sok Samuth is showing me how to read the notes and how the temperature graph already has the fluids in and out written underneath.

"The boy has something for you."

He reaches under his bed and drags out a reed bag. The boy's color is good but his back is bony and his arms too thin.

Sok Samuth says, "Skorm," the Khmer word for skinny. The word sounded wicked. Skorm.

"Have we got a weight on him today? I know he's skinny but he should be gaining weight. At least by the end of the week. Doesn't he look better than before—I mean heavier?"

"Oui, oui, he's eighteen kilos now. Only sixteen last week."

"Okay. That's very good. That's what we wanted. Is it enough?"

The nurses in the room are waving off the idea that the boy is too thin. They are all saying he is doing much better, no coughing and that he is eating well and has had no fever for a few days, so I think we saved one here. They know best. The nurses have a sense for these things. The boy reaches into his reed bag and uses two hands to pull out a green coconut. The kid is all smiles, saying, "Orkun," or thank you. I say to Sok Samuth that I can't accept it but he's saying I have to, and then I'm saying can I at least share it with everyone. No problem. He says we'll send it to the kitchen and cut it up for everyone. We can have it after rounds, and invite the boy and his mom to join us.

Now we have four nurses with us, all in white uniforms and white habits. Dr. Bun Thoeun arrives as well. He was just out of medical school, the accelerated program in Phnom Penh that produced physicians in four years after high school, and he was good—very skilled, always in a perfect white smock, hair parted neatly and always smiling. He had started teaching me about the ways the diseases present and how to interpret the symptoms and comments from the patients. He says there were no new cases the night before, and all the existing cases are stable or improving. The farmer with the snake bite, his leg wasn't so swollen now and he says the strength was coming back. Amazing, given that it was black and taut like a sausage two weeks before. There are a couple of typhoid cases and some other respiratory infections. The teenager who was hit by a motorcycle seems in good spirits, no fever and no pus, but the twice-daily dressing changes and the doubled-up antibiotics have to continue. Bun Thoeun uses a towel clamp to peel back the dressing and then he leans over to smell the wound. He doesn't think there is any infection. Then he squeezes the surrounding muscles to express the pus but only clean, transparent serous liquid comes out. Good. Nobody would win an award for the suturing job, but the kid should have full movement eventually. We didn't think the tendons got severed. He'll have quite a scar.

There is a man coughing in the corner. Why is he there? If he's got a cough like that he shouldn't be here and at the very least he should be wearing a mask.

"Ott mean," they all say. There are no masks. And there is, of course, no isolation room. Or a negative pressure room. That's a good one. There wasn't one in the whole country. No place to put him until we figure out what is making him cough and we can't send him to the TB ward yet, we hadn't confirmed anything. TB was just a suspicion. We weren't sure what to do. Maybe keep cases like his in a tent. Better ask Rob for a plan. Maybe a new room or building on the compound?

The next five cases are summarized by Mademoiselle Ly Leap and they are all the same: cerebral malaria.

"This one here is malaria—paludisme cérébral, oui, oui. We are giving the dextrose and the quinine. Yes, this one's conscious, he's just sleeping, see. And there is no fever. Pas de fièvre."

We double-check the chart and the medicines and solution—everything we are giving him and how we were tracking him. I think I checked everything a third time.

"This one is also paludisme cérébral . He's doing well. Oui, oui, ça va, ça va bien. Also this one is paludisme, also well. Ça va. And the same thing here, malaria, well. These two are better. They have malaria but they are all better and want to go home."

The two men are standing beside their beds, not sitting, and they have their personal effects all packed up. They say they need to go back to the countryside where their families have animals and gardens to tend to. They each have a bag of pills in hand with Khmer instructions written on the bags.

"Can they read?"

Sok Samuth and Mlle Ly Leap start laughing. Bun Thoeun just shakes his head. So one of the nurses goes to the men and starts explaining how they are to take the tablets and what to watch for and how they are to come back here for a checkup later. That's when one of the nurses from the maternity suite shouts at me to go to Madame Boran.

Madame Boran, perfectly collected as always, has my glove size ready and she is telling me to put my hand on the crown and to push a little but not too much. The mother is twisting on the metal table but she's not speaking, just heavy breaths and grunts, and Madame is reminding me to push because the baby's coming very quickly now and we don't want to have a tear but in another thirty seconds, pushing against the forces, out comes the baby, a little boy, and he was wailing away with his eyes shut tight.

"Was that the one you were watching all night?"

"No, Docteur, she was only here a few minutes. Eight children already for this mother. They come fast."

"Eight! Eight kids. Man." And there were the attendants tightly wrapping the little "koun" in a red checkered silk, handing him over to his mother.

Bun Thoeun and I zigzag to the tuberculosis ward to stay under the shade of the sugar palms. When we hear a solitary boom in the distance, he says it's a mine, one of the antitank ones. They can all tell the types of mines by ear.

"Do you think that person survived?"

"Peut-être, maybe. But probably it was just a steer or a goat."

Bun Thoeun points to the fence that lines the Low Road. Some local children are spying on us. One of them is Smiles with her little brother on her hip and her sister Genius. Bright, happy kids. Funny they aren't in school again. Many of the other children wear the blue and white uniforms and go to school every weekday morning, but not these children.

As we approach the TB house, with its flared arches and carved roof edges, you can see the towering thunderclouds are darkening. Strung up between the TB house and a sugar palm are about thirty surgical gloves, disinfected in peroxide, hanging out to dry. Three patients come out of the house with handkerchiefs pressed to their faces and, as we got closer, Bun Thoeun and I put masks on and have a listen. TB sounds the same all over the world. They are called crepitations, crackling noises especially high up in the apices. I couldn't get over how isolating it was for those patients. Most of them are from the countryside and their families don't come. It is hard for them to mix with anyone else because they are infectious still and shunned by the locals. They lie on their beds all day, sleeping or talking sparingly and then sleeping all night. If not TB, the boredom might kill them.

Bun Thoeun and I saunter over to the Salle D'Administration, retracing our route under the palms, when we hear another boom in the distance.

"Ah huh," I say. "That's a big one. An antitank mine for sure."

Bun Thoen says, "Non."

"No? You sure? Then it was an antipersonnel mine. A smaller one, but nearer."

"Non."

"Then what?"

"Dynamite. It's the fishermen on the Stung-River. They use dynamite to fish."

There wasn't much else to do that afternoon. We had rounded on all the patients, all forty of them, and it seemed everyone was stable. There were no new cases, but we were told some would be admitted later in the day. Not much point doing anything after eleven. Everybody sleeps then, or they go out for walks, even the patients.

So I retire to the little dark grey wooden building the hospital had given Rob and me as an office. It is a low edifice, with a simple table, one bench, a mud floor and a cooking fire. By the time I arrive there that morning someone has already fired up the coals for me and the water is hot for tea. I check a couple of facts in my worn green Guide Clinicale, have a cup of tea with extra sugar, and then stretch out on the bench.

When the rain starts, the first drops are so heavy they explode hitting the tin roof. Then the torrent comes and it's a buzzing noise like a reciprocating saw cutting into the roof. Twenty minutes later, the buzz ceases and it's funny, but when the storm is ending, you can sometimes notice the last solitary drop. Then it's over and the little rivers surrounding the office carry away the rain. Before long, the sun burns through.

There's a knock on the door. Good news back at the hospital entrance. Our first shipment of medicines has arrived. Mogiath and Sao Sim are at the truck. And another man is there, somebody wearing sunglasses, smoking.

"Who's he, the driver?"

"No, no. Pas le chauffeur," says Sao Sim, shaking my hand and laughing.

"Why's he in our truck?"

"He's from the government, working with me. You can trust him."

"Huh? These medicines are from *our* stores in Phnom Penh. They're not government."

"No, there's no problem. Pas de problème. Pas de tous—not at all."

And Mogiath adds, "Oui, oui, there's no problem."

So we have a look. There are boxes of chloramphenicol for typhoid, quinine for the malaria, erythromycin for the pneumonias, many boxes of surgical gloves and masks, and paper for the charts. We have more than a hundred treatments for TB, all in WHO boxes, and smear stain for the TB slides, plus—small fortune—a new microscope. We are going to be popular with our friends in the lab. There are about fifty boxes of drugs and equipment—more than what is in the little hospital at present. So I tell one of the attendants to go to the Blue House to get Rob. Rob needs to be here and he has the master list of what we were expecting. The entire contents were radioed to us two days before and Rob had already been going on about how everything better match up.

As we wait for Rob, I'm looking through everything for the non-medical boxes, the personal stuff Rob and I had been waiting to have shipped to us. The stuff that would make our lives more comfortable. But I go through everything twice and there are no boxes marked with our names—only pills and hospital supplies.

Rob comes in fairly fast in the Land Cruiser. A bit too fast, actually, because he forgets to put down the parking brake and after he jumps out the truck creeps along a few more feet on its own, and eases up against a barbed-wire fence and stops.

"Why's the truck open? Were they going through it?"

"Don't know. I just got here."

"Where's the lock? The back was supposed to be padlocked."

Sao Sim is laughing and Rob shakes his hand but there's not much eye contact between them, and Mogiath and Sao Sim are both saying there's no problem, not at all—that nothing's missing. Mogiath starts going on about the great partnership between MSF and l'Hôpital Sisophon dans la nouvelle province de Banteay Meanchey, but Rob is busy going through all the stuff. He's got his list in one hand and he's counting up all the boxes. He is in the back of the truck for about ten minutes.

"Well?" I ask.

"Maybe it's all there. Some of the boxes are open; I can't tell. We're never letting this come to the hospital again. Everything gets delivered to our house. Kijk! I have no way to tell if anything's missing."

Rob asks the driver about the trip. He uses Mogiath as a translator and gets the story of how it took two full days of driving, with an overnight in Pursat. The roads were very bad. There was a big detour after Pursat. They had to go overland west where there were mines and the KPLNF, but eventually they made it here. Then Rob goes back in looking for our personal delivery. We were expecting food mostly, some canned hams, pasta, tins of stew, all the things we couldn't get up here. And, as he was looking, I said for sure they said my cigars from Hajenius were included, plus the CDs from Toronto and my books from home. Rob comes out of the truck shaking his head, speaking in Dutch.

"There's no personal stuff."

"I couldn't find it either."

"Kijk! No fan. No music."

"No cigars either."

So we interrogate the driver a bit more. He doesn't know anything. He is swearing everything he was asked to deliver is still in the truck. That he slept in the truck overnight in Pursat. Nothing went missing but he does have an envelope for us. It is an oversized manila envelope with a note from the office and a list of all the supplies. It seems to match Rob's and there are also some private letters inside. At least we got our mail. It had been a month and we had no idea what was going on outside of Sisophon or back home. Wonderful letters. Contact with the outside world. It deserves a celebration.

We have dinner at the Lotus. The restaurant floor is covered in green cracked porcelain tiles. They extend all the way to the road and some kids sat at the roadside and watch us eat. We sit at flimsy white plastic tables, under fans that are still and as soon as we sit down, the owner puts on lousy Asian pop music. We are greeted by the same Mwan Rotee dish as always, but they have Beck's beer this time, real beer made in Germany. We ask Dee Ling where she got it, but she wouldn't say: Beck's are scarce and she wants to keep them to herself so she can over-charge the bar rangs. She has a way of shrieking when she talks, almost berating you. She is ethnic Chinese and doesn't sound like the other Cambodians. She doesn't have that strange "blub mnup pup bah" sound some of them make as if they are speaking underwater. All throughout dinner Rob is adding up the boxes and pills and comparing them to the official list, and while there is no box missing, he couldn't be sure the boxes hadn't been opened and pilfered. That will have to wait until we make radio contact in the morning.

We finish dinner and return home to the balcony of the Blue House where we watch the town people shuffle past below. The sun sets fast and within minutes the brilliant sky is ink black and dripping with stars. The Big Dipper is upside down and the nearly full moon gives a snow-dust quality to the zinc roofs along the street. It's an Edward Hopper street scene. Wooden homes on stilts looking like a ghost town at night. We douse ourselves with insect repellant and get a mosquito coil going.

I open my letters and read them slowly. Ian Small got rave reviews for his work in Iraq—that would be good for Canada—and now he's waiting in Amsterdam for his next mission. He doesn't know how but swears he'll somehow find a way to come to Cambodia. Next letters: family okay, Carrie okay, some clippings from local newspapers and even some from the hockey season. There is Mario Lemieux holding the Stanley Cup and a cassette from my brother John, no doubt full of wit, something to save for Sunday. And my other brother Mark didn't write me a letter—he drew me a comic strip instead. But there is one letter from Jim Lane. Lots of concern from Jim. Three more volunteers sent overseas. That was excellent; MSF Canada was growing nicely. Fundraising is steady, way more than we anticipated. We got a call from Robert McLure, a sage-like medical legend in Canada who had worked as a physician in China way back in the forties. He called our organization to wish us well.

But Jim was going on about how impossible it was becoming. How the office politics were souring. Badly. He was saying the Dutch were interfering with everything. They were screwing up all of our good work. They'd say do this and do that and then when we did it, someone else in Amsterdam would ask us why on earth we did it. They'd asked us to find a doctor with all the right experience and, after weeks of searching, we'd call them up and say here's your doctor, ready to go. Then they'd send a blunt message: the doctor wasn't needed anymore. They found someone themselves. And when Jim called Amsterdam to complain, they said, "Why are you bothering us? Don't you even care about all the poor people stuck in war?" It was their stock reply when they wanted to get their way. All this news was a month old and I was ten thousand miles away.

I scrunch up the letter into a ball and toss it from the balcony, among angry dogs down there on the Low Road. Snarling, filthy dogs, one trying to mount the other. Then they start fighting. They are a tangled ball, dust flying around them.

"Maybe they're rabid."

"It's possible," says Rob. "It's common here in Southeast Asia."

"Ever see it in a man?"

Rob nods, as smoke from the mosquito coil twists around our balcony. He tells me about a video he had seen of a man who had rabies in the camps. He was past treatment so nothing could be done. Rob's eyes open wide as he describes the condemned man who had to endure about twenty-four hours of a strange neurological breakdown before he could rest. La rage in French, the rage.

He says the video was handheld and shaky, but it showed the man looking spooked with the attendants around him. The man's gaze was bug-eyed and he was making some spastic movements with his limbs. Somebody thought it would be appropriate to film the man's descent. Rob says there's a moment in the video where someone pushes a bowl of water towards the man and he starts grimacing. Rob shows me how the man's neck and facial muscles were tightening in spasm as the water was brought up to him. Involuntary seizure-like spasms fearing the water. Hydrophobia.

The dogs are quiet now, apart on opposite sides of the road, but it doesn't stop a teenage boy from chasing them away with a stick and then flinging a baseball-sized rock at them.

The only other time I saw Rob get so creeped-out about a story was when he discussed Cambodian history and the architects of what happened here in the '70s, especially in the year it all went psychotic. There was one name, Khieu Samphan. Rob said that that man was worse than Saloth Sar and Ieng Sary. He took up the cruelty of the Pol-Potists with a kind of creative harshness. Hard to imagine the man had been an academic, held a doctorate from a university in France, and there he was ensuring that tens of thousands of people met an early grave. When Rob said Khieu Samphan's name he pointed to his arm to show how the name alone made the hair on his arms stand up. And the man was still out there in the countryside somewhere, a free man after what he had done. He couldn't have been more than a hundred or two hundred miles from us, living with an army faction somewhere in the jungle pushed up against the Thai or Laos border.

After a cool dousing from the giant ung pot, I lay in my tiny bedroom within the mosquito net, listening to the unusually clear reception of the SW1000 that night. It sometimes happened like that. The voices seemed like they were coming from the other room. There was a piece on China Radio International about ancient zithers. The announcer was mentioning how the instrument had a cherished place among the literati in Chinese culture and that when first invented it had only five strings. Five strings, each with a meaning or feeling. The legend was that an emperor added a sixth string which meant sorrow and a seventh which meant enlightenment. They were playing sound bites of zither music that evening. Strange bending notes with an echo, like it was a stream of water going over pebbles in a cave.

15

The Lotus Restaurant

We painted the walls and wood frames of the hospital beds white. Mogiath wanted this done. Rob and I contracted a group of carpenters to patch up the roofs, mortar the foundations, and wall off the latrines out back. This was on a Saturday—a special manual labor day. The animals were kept away from the wards. Madame Boran's clinic got new equipment for the deliveries, a new incubator, more boots, gloves, and needles—a new suite really. "Merci bien," she says and goes to work. The medical ward could wait; same with Dr. Sann's ward. Big problems ahead with him. Sann hasn't been showing up that often.

For a day we moved everyone out of the children's ward and doubled everyone up in the medical building so we could lay down a new concrete floor for the kids. That's where we did most of our teaching, on the medical and children's wards. We listened very carefully to our staff. They wanted to make their hospital beautiful and grand. We weren't the International Committee of the Red Cross, we said. We didn't have their bags of money and we kept saying money wasn't going to solve all the problems here. We asked that the tuberculosis medicines be delivered directly to our pharmacy. Pills were getting lost via the government stores. "Of course," they said, "we'll redirect them; give us a week." In a month, still no pills. We heard all the excuses: wrong paperwork, packaging not allowed, needs to be a different administrator. Who's profiteering, Rob wants to know. Was it Sann? It couldn't have been Sann, why would he bother with pills? We were watching him too closely. It was too risky.

127

We spent long days walking around the wards, everybody learning together, me learning so much from the nurses, all of us trying to make the fragile system work. Now that some time had passed, when a hysterical mother brought a limp infant in, we just followed the straight-forward protocols—a little rehydration salt, a touch of antibiotics, close watch and presto, the kid wakes up in a day and goes home the next. Might have been dead otherwise.

Once every day, the clouds gather and the hospital darkens. Up above us, the lightning is a skeleton hand cupping the sky. It storms for an hour and everyone hides. The roads go from dust to mud and back to dust every day. This is the rainy season, so it also rains at night. The rain and wind rip through the town, hurling pieces of corrugated tin and palm fronds. Sometimes when it gusts, a soldier fires tracer bullets up into the night as a kind of offering. The shots are so loud, it's as if the soldier is firing next door to the MSF Blue House, but we never see him. We see the soldiers during the day, sleeping in the shade of a truck canopy or off in some corner smoking. But at night, they are invisible. They must have safe homes, dark backyards next to ours where they station themselves overnight to make their presence known, attendants keeping the city safe.

The front is only fifty kilometers away, sometimes as close as thirty. We'd hear the solitary boom of a T-55 tank firing its 200 MM and the sickening screech of the Katyusha rockets. Nice World War II technology, those rockets—what a joke. When they hit, it knocked our stuff off our walls and shelves. And then in the morning they'd bring the injured civilians to us in carts clop, clopping along. If the patient's condition is dire, he might get a speedy motorcycle ride. The injured soldiers are taken to the military hospital nearer the front. We rarely see them coming and going from town and we only ever saw their hospital from the road. Bar rangs not allowed.

It was beyond comprehension the way the locals laughed all of this off. Their conversations are infused with laughter, the great leveler. They laugh when something breaks. They laugh when someone dies. They can't tell you about Saloth Sar and all the killings without smiling and laughing. Yes, I lost my brother and my two sisters and my aunt and my three cousins. Then, ha ha ha. It was terrible, oui, oui. And when they tell these stories, they cover their mouths because it isn't polite to show their open mouths. Many of them are broken and their emotions are disconnected. It is rare to see them cry.

On the inside wall of the hospital reception building, a two-room edifice touched up with uneven cracking plaster, is a fresco-like mural depicting what had happened in town in the late Seventies. It is a barbaric scene, something like Rubens's "Massacre of the Innocents," but the figures are drawn in a primitive, juvenile way. More like Marc Chagall and his childlike representations of dreams. It shows a group of soldiers attacking a pregnant woman as the townspeople watch. The first time I saw it, I thought, Can a society go mad? The next scene has the woman dead on the ground and the cut-out fetus thrown by bayonet up onto the roof of a hut. In the final scene, the fetus has withered and an image of Buddha is praying beside it. I thought it was all some kind of fantasy, the artist's depiction of hell. But the staff brought in a man from the post office who explained each frame of the mural and said the scenes were true. He said the fetuses were called "smoke children," some kind of magic talismans. He told me these very scenes had happened right outside the building. He pointed to a Bau tree and said he saw it happen there. He told me the government officials would never allow the mural to be painted over. Cultural bureaucrats in Phnom Penh said so. It was a way to remember the dead and not let all those souls slip away forever without proper deference. All the people carry those memories, their ghosts. They have some way of living with them that I can't fathom.

❧

One day we heard thunderclaps on all sides but we couldn't see any clouds. In fact, we couldn't tell if they were thunderclaps or landmines; there was just a fuzzy horizon three hundred and sixty degrees around us and the noise seemed to be coming from everywhere. I tell Chuon to keep a lookout for rainbows and I am trying to explain how you get rainbows when the sun and rain are out together. He finally gets it.

That afternoon a KPLNF commander arrived in town. He and his aides-de-camp are meeting with counterparts from the Hun Sen

Army, the government's army. We'd never seen this before. It is some kind of a ceasefire and the two sides are meeting only a few doors from the MSF Blue House at the Lotus, the town's only restaurant. I am at a table when they arrive, off in the corner minding my own business reading Celine's *Journey to the End of the Night*. I was at the point where Alasander had lost his job as a médecin and was now wandering aimlessly around the United States. Usually the military people make eye contact and say something cordial. Other times they ask insipid questions and you can't get them to leave you alone. "Are you truly a bar rang?" they ask. "Is that really a book you are reading?" But not today. There is military business at hand and I am not part of the equation.

There are half a dozen vehicles outside the restaurant and many soldiers. The Hun Sen commander comes out from the dark inside of an armored troop carrier squinting at the day. He is wearing impeccable army greens and has a briefcase. His aide carries a mobile radio on his back and occasionally answers messages, consulting his superior and making demands of the soldiers at the front.

The KPLNF soldier is a colonel. He wears a dirty uniform and has only a stump for a right arm. He is using the stump to great effect, waving it around to make his point. He has a Bowie knife in a sheath at his side, and a black-brown pistol, probably a Chinese Hanyang. Scary, brainwashed soldier from the front. The colonel has been out in the forests so long he has gone mad. Here he is deep inside his enemy's territory, drinking in a restaurant with a commander he has been trying to kill. He makes a speech holding the brandy and cream soda glass straight out while his right stump makes circles in the air like a mad conductor. Down goes the brandy.

Now it's the Hun Sen Army commander's turn. More nice words. He holds the drink with two hands in the subservient way, looking up at the colonel, bent over like he is sacrificing himself. They are all having dinner together and the brandy and cream soda is flowing. The matron of the Lotus, tiny Dee Ling with the squawking voice, is running in and out of the kitchen hoping she gets it all right. There are twenty soldiers from the two sides drinking and smoking and it is getting macho in there. I watch one of them kick a dog that gets too close. It goes halfway across the road. Everyone laughs at that and they have a special toast for the soldier who kicked the dog so well. Some of the opposing soldiers have their arms around each other now.

What do people like that say to each other?

At this point all of the townspeople stop walking by on the Low Road. The military is diverting them to the High Road. No one has seen that before. No one actually asks me to leave the restaurant but you can see in their eyes they want me to be on my way. Prudent to move along when the soldiers start drinking like that. But I know I can watch the rest of the meeting from the balcony of our MSF Blue House. The balcony is like having box seats for the main event. The soldiers keep drinking and eating Num Pachok Kari Saich Moan. Someone gets that awful Khmer music going. It is way too loud. I actually see enemy soldiers exchange guns. It is like, "I'll show you mine if you show me yours." I'm sure someone is going to fire one off just for the manliness of it all. Anything is possible way out here in the wild northwest. Let's all prove to each other how fearless we are.

"Watch while I shoot this dog. Bang! That'll teach the dog not come close to the table."

"Bahn high! You're not the only one who can shoot a dog." Pow and yelp, yelp, yelp.

"It's not even dead. Can't you kill a dog with one clean shot?"

"I can kill whatever I want without even looking. Want to see?"

"Dogs aren't worth the bullet. Why not challenge something more honorable?"

"Shall I kill a pig then? There seem to be lots of pigs here."

"Which one of us is a pig, then?"

"It's easy. Have a look around. You can tell by the uniform."

"I see clearly. Here, have some more cream soda. Or do you want some slop instead? Pigs like slop. Shall I ask my colonel to find some slop to lay you down in?"

"I don't want any cream soda. I want to go pig hunting."

But at that moment, the one-armed colonel gets up and waves at the crowd of soldiers. Time for one last drink, a mention of peace and the eternal greatness of the Khmer people, and then an orderly exit with the KPLNF going out first in their convoy, warm smiles and waves to their

Hun Sen enemies. They leave fast. All of their vehicles do three-pointers and vanish.

I go over to Dee Ling, but she isn't saying anything. She is shaking her head at the mess of plates and scraps on the floor. This time she doesn't mind the dogs in her restaurant helping with the cleanup. She begins to squawk away, cursing both cadres of soldiers. They hadn't paid enough.

16

Svay Chek

Cambodia / October 1991

Svay means mango and *Chek* is banana. Mango Banana could have been the name of a beach resort on the South China Sea but bad luck had put the town very close to the front lines. A little too close to the sun. Svay Chek had been overrun, they said—many, many times. And now the population was effectively zero.

We had been invited by the government to tour the city, or more accurately, former city. We were promised a chance to see the aftermath of the fighting between the Viet Namese army and Hun Sen and the various factions—crumpled corrugated tin and burned-away wooden row houses. Svay Chek used to be the size of Sisophon and now there wasn't much left of it.

We were there with a delegation of prominent European Union representatives and some Cambodian dignitaries. Everyone was eager to sort out the reconstruction of Cambodia. Someday in the future when the fighting officially stops, the mines get cleared, and the *deplacées* come back inside, people were going to be ready with their bags of money to rebuild Cambodia. Svay Chek had been designated as a "reconstruction city" by UNESCO, and the French construction companies were seeing ways to bring their "mutually beneficial" business plans back into Cambodia.

We also had our first visitors from MSF: the Asian medical director Eric Goemaere, Lex Winkler from Amsterdam, and our country director, Maurits van Pelt from Phnom Penh. They had come to Sisophon to check on us and see what support we might need. It was supposed to be great fun having them up there with us, but in between drinks and niceties it was pretty easy to tell there was a sliver of something intruding. It wasn't like being in the capital when we just laughed and enjoyed each other's company. This time there was something wrong, a problem in the way. Lex wasn't even making eye contact. When I confronted him, he just waved me away.

Here we all are in crumpled Svay Chek. The colonial architecture has been flattened to rubble and anything of any value left in the wreckage was mined by scavengers years ago. It is as if the place is still smouldering. Such a quaint, storybook name, Mango Banana. On the ground we look at the outline of what used to be a home and in the back is a four-by-eight foot section of blackened tin.

"What's this?" we all want to know.

"No. Don't touch anything," yells one of the delegation.

"No problem, ça va, ça va, it's okay," says the mayor. "The army has been through here. There are no more mines."

The mayor heaves open the metal and reveals a six-foot-deep hole lined with grass, broken pots, and plastic sheeting. Rob and I both think it is some kind of a grave.

"It's a bomb shelter. The families who stayed on used them during the raids."

I'm kind of hanging back from the delegation. Eric and I mope around the broken foundations. I don't need to go any further to find a place poorer than this. But it doesn't register fully because there are no people around to tell us their stories. Only ghosts if you ask the mayor. I am trying to make what I'm witnessing real by picturing what my home town would look like carpet bombed and razed until there was nothing standing higher than your waist. I keep remembering what the London *Times* reporter said when he entered the camps in 1945: "It is my duty," he wrote, "to describe something beyond the imagination of mankind." Same kind of thing all over Cambodia.

My dad, Rudy, did this trip when he was eighteen, with a friend, Hugh Little, a doctor. They went over to Europe a few years after the end of the war and just toured around. Nobody did that back then. He would have seen the Austrian side of our family, all the clones of my grandfather, and he would have seen the famous capitals and majestic Europe smashed into rubble piles.

In the middle of all this Eric is laughing with me, asking about me about staying on long-term. He and I are walking through the destruction and he is pointing out all the benefits of working with MSF, for example the nice view, how quiet the neighborhood is. This was a city the size of Sisophon and he and I are stepping over the rubble. It is the saddest thing and we are busting our guts laughing. He's saying if I could just convince my girlfriend to come live over here we'd have such a pleasant time. He makes a sweeping gesture with his hand, saying, "How could she resist this?"

But even Eric wasn't being himself. He was serious about my staying on. He thought I should get a few more years' experience in the field before trying to run things back home. It wasn't exactly a pleasant feeling having the three MSF bosses up there with us in Sisophon, giving me the cold shoulder with no explanation. I had been expecting something more like, Hey, good job, or, Keep up the great work. We had hit it off so well in the capital and I respected them. I was thinking maybe they didn't like what they saw in the hospital. But Rob said everything was fine. They thought the hospital and the outpost work was progressing well and he didn't sense anything. What was it I was sensing?

That night I was on the wards late. When I came back, they had all started dinner without me and then went to bed pretty quick. Lex hardly says anything as he went off. Eric is off in a corner writing some report. Rob's helping himself to some aged Gouda Lex brought from Amsterdam. Maurits is smoking, taking long drags, holding his breath then talking. He hands me a big envelope from home. Good, but I can tell it's been opened. He says it wasn't him. They don't open personal mail; that's their policy. I'm going through the envelopes and for sure someone's opened a few of my letters. I ask Maurits what's wrong with Lex and Eric and he says nothing, nothing at all. He has a way of smiling—a big, handsome smile—and he sometimes uses it to push you away. It wasn't like he was afraid of conflict, he was simply weary of the hassles. His way of dealing with it is to ignore it. Sometimes he'd rather smile and be superficial than engage in meaningless gossip. He had enough real responsibility:

a multimillion-dollar budget to look after and several dozen expats under his care living in a war.

So you had to press Maurits to find out things. Finally he tells me: they're upset because of MSF Canada. Not everybody wants MSF in Canada just yet; some of them in Amsterdam think I am trying to run it from over here.

Rob and I give each other a "what?" look.

"Don't worry about it," says Maurits. "It's just politics."

"How could I run anything from here? I haven't made a phone call in two months. Last letter I sent was over a month ago."

"Don't worry about it. That's my advice. Just focus on your work here, not on the international politics."

Rob let out his staccato laugh, saying, "It's amazing," and leaves to replenish his beer with ice chunks from the downstairs cooler.

"Focus on my work?"

"Don't worry about anything. It's just small things. I'll speak to Lex. I think they were upset because you went to meet Rony Brauman when he was in Phnom Penh. Why did you need to meet the president of MSF France?"

"That was two months ago. Why do the Dutch care?"

"It's very sensitive. It's not the right time for you to be meeting the French leadership. It's too sensitive. Trust me. The French don't really support MSF in Canada and America yet."

"What is it? Another one of these freezes on? No new MSF development outside of Europe kind of thing?"

"Don't worry. I think you're doing wonderful work. No, I *know* you're doing wonderful work. So does Rob. I'll speak to Lex about it. Just focus on your work here. And don't use the military radio for media."

"Huh?"

"You used it to get a message through to a newspaper in Canada."

"That was a month ago. It had nothing to do with anything. It was just a clarification about where I was in Iraq for a story. Big deal."

"Still, it's off limits."

Rob comes back with beer and ice for all of us. He and Maurits launch into a conversation in Dutch. I go back to my little bedroom and sort through my mail. For sure a bunch of envelopes had been opened. There is a letter from one of the Dutch managers. It says that I should "focus on my work in the field." It is the same phrase Maurits had used. It's like a memo had been sent around. The letter went on to say they had a perfectly capable team in place in Toronto and that I was to focus all of my energy on the extremely serious situation in Sisophon.

The next letter is from Jim Lane. Big problems unfolding. He says the situation has become unbearable, that the Dutch are interfering in everything, controlling the whole thing like they own MSF Canada. They kept telling Jim not to worry about Canada having their own independent and operational MSF chapter. That there is going to be a new kind of partnership, a new arrangement, and to stop asking about it because "didn't he care about the populations they were trying to help?" Jim says it was like the Europeans were colonial masters carving up the new world, and they were going about it silently, not bothering to fully inform us. He says he would have left but there was no alternative. He cared about what we had built and would wait until I got home as a favor to me.

In the morning I sent one of the kids to tell everyone at the hospital that I'd be late. I'd maybe not make it in at all. I remember what my mom kept telling me—that I should start a medical practice back home, perfectly safe, lucrative. But she didn't really mean it. Nothing was ever lost on her. She said it to ground me. She knew my wanderlust was in the way and that I had to follow some other walk of life.

She also said when it gets tough over here, that I should keep moving, get busy. So I take the Land Cruiser out on the Mongkol Borei Road. I get the truck going as fast as I possibly can. The road craters are so bad I figure an axle might break but there is a way of getting two tires up on the edge of the road where it's flat so the truck can skip over the pot holes and there is one stretch where you can get it up over eighty, but then you have to slam on the brakes and skid to avoid diving down into a crater. Quite a few stunned looks from the bicycle riders and farmers as they scatter into the ditches.

I take my lunch alone at the south end of the city, near the ICRC hospital. The restaurant owner brings me tea, asking me how I am. I look directly at his eyes and speak English. I say I am making fifty bucks a month, the armies are laying landmines outside of our town and occasionally bombing it. My girlfriend is ten thousand miles away, I have a painful, grinding stomach this morning, weight is down ten kilos since I arrived, and it looks like the organization I started back home has been hijacked. He doesn't understand a word and laughs it off, then so do I.

In the middle of my roadside solo lunch I think, why not take some of the Sisophon kids for a ride? Most of them had never been in a truck or a car. It would be like an amusement ride. I find them hanging around the Low Road, by the fat Chinese man selling fruit chunks, and they pile in my Land Cruiser. Smiles, of course, in the front seat right beside me, with her sister Genius and the baby brother, and Monster-man, Monster-boy, and Barbie in the back. Everybody close now. All those lovely kids and their pet names. We parade up and down the High Road and Low Road waving, picking up kids as we go. All the locals are cheering. At one point I have about fifteen of them in the truck with me. I buy them all fruit from the Chinese man and go to the end of town, out past the ice factory where the canals and farms start. We inch up to the water's edge. All of us climb up the side of the truck to sun ourselves and lay together on the roof of the Land Cruiser. We nibble our fruit, gazing upon the massive green squares of the infinite rice fields.

Rob and I kept visiting places like Svay Chek, each time pushing a little farther north and west to places where outsiders hadn't been in decades. One day Rob and I are going up the Thamar Puok road to see the nurse stationed on the road near Svay Chek. Nothing unusual about the trip until we pass the last temple. For the first time we turn the Land Cruiser north.

Right away, it looks different. We are pretty sure no one from the West has been here since the mid-Seventies. Later we confirmed this. Rob starts telling stories about what life would have been like up here in the remote countryside during the era of the Khmer Rouge. He knew the history well and his best stories were always about Phnom Penh and the early days when the Khmer Rouge moved in and emptied the million-plus city in a bid to create a Maoist agrarian utopia—what an American journalist called a Maoist agrarian utopia on very, very bad acid. Hard to imagine a bustling city with all the noises of traffic, children, and street vendors suddenly still and soundless. They said when the city was freed they found mountains of fridges, electric ovens, hair dryers, and fans. Anything modern or mechanized had been confiscated. It was a crime to own them. They were piled fifty feet high, left to rust in the middle of the formerly busy streets. Between us, Rob and I had read thirty or forty books on the political history of Cambodia, but you can read all the books you want about Cambodia or live there for a couple of years and you'll still never understand what happened. How could it ever have happened, a national suicide like that?

So up towards Samrong, where Westerners hadn't been since the Seventies, we didn't want to draw any more attention than we were already getting. We coast in. People stare at us in a way I've never seen. They drop whatever they are carrying and freeze. A few of them point and say "bar rang" or "blanc" but most of them just look at us in disbelief. They have never seen Westerners.

The thing is, we are inside the Khmer Rouge, and we are walking around their little village. Women are carrying their young on hip and balancing water pots over their heads. A man is tying off one of the bamboo hut walls with reed and coming from somewhere behind a thicket of bougainvillea, someone is singing. There are no telephone lines or cars. Nothing manufactured. I come up silently behind a mother and her child at a cooking fire. The child is in her mother's lap looking up at her, listening to her mother sing. I had heard the same song, an anthem in Phnom Penh, at an outdoor cultural event on the Mekong. The lyrics go:

Temples are asleep in the forest,
Remembering the splendor of Moha Nokor.
Like a rock, the Khamer race is eternal.
Let us trust in the fate of Campuchea,
The empire which challenges the ages.

PART IV

17

The Ministry of Forestry and Fisheries

Sisophon, Cambodia / October 1991

Some weeks went by. You could say we were making it okay, some progress, but no great sense of accomplishment. No streamlined hospital just yet, but the supplies were arriving regularly and the night shifts were smoother. The outpost in Preah Neet Preah had the basic medicines now and there was money to bring in the very sick from the countryside by cart. Still, it was impossible to get used to the heat, and the food was poor. Rhee wasn't learning to cook. It wasn't making our lives any easier.

It seemed you could spend many days trying to bring in a new process, a new way of doing things in the hospital, yet nothing would ever change. Inertia kept things the way they were. The Cambodians had reasons for doing it their way, ways we couldn't understand. And if you took a step back and looked at us, it was ridiculous really. Two foreign doctors move into a pulverized city hidden away from the world for a couple of decades and we try to suddenly change everything. We weren't ever going to be one of them and they still called us bar rang right to our faces. It was like we weren't real to many. But I was getting used to it. Less of a reaction as that ugly word "bar rang" hit my nerves.

One day Dr. Sann stops Rob and me as we cross the hospital grounds. There is an attractive nurse with him and she's not wearing the usual white uniform. She is new, a kind of personal assistant. Sann has been avoiding us for weeks but this time he has his sunglasses off and he is being as direct as a surgeon. He wants to know why we have been giving him a hard time and asks if we thought he had been stealing. That was the rumor. We tell him no. Rob says we know he had nothing to do with the tuberculosis medicines disappearing. And Rob says Sann is a fine physician, easily the most experienced here, but that the problem is his work on the side, in the private clinics, and how he is seeing private patients for a fee right here in the hospital. Rob tells him he is profiting and everyone else can't. It's a free hospital. It can't work if some patients pay and others can't. Mogiath and Sao Sim agree; even the governor is saying it can't go on like this. Sann doesn't say anything to that. There is no counter argument. He just walks away with his nurse a step behind. Sunglasses on, he heads straight for his scooter.

On a Saturday, the day of manual labor when only half the staff shows up, there is a five-day-old baby on the ward. It's having trouble breathing. Rob examines the infant. Lungs are clear, heart seems strong. Still, this little thing isn't really in a fighting mood. It wants to quit and go into the forever sleep. As we watch, the breathing gets slower, more shallow, and then stops. Then the mother shakes it a bit, and the breathing starts again just fine.

It is one of those immature lung situations. Back home the kid would get oxygen and a little artificial help with breathing, and most importantly observation. Some nurse or resident dressed in greens would doze in a chair next to it, ready to stir the child when an alarm bell went off. Just a little extra help to get it through the troubled day or two until the lungs awoke and the signals to the brain improved. Routine newborn care. But here in Sisophon the mom is alone, exhausted after watching her baby so closely for so many days and hours since the birth. She never did get a rest and wasn't able to leave the baby. So we draw up a schedule for the nurses and the doctor on call to watch her through the day and night.

The whole team has been doing well lately. The protocols are working. There is a lot more confidence in the nurses and doctors now. But it is Dr. Nhean's turn to be on call that night and Rob doesn't like it. "Couldn't we get Bun Thoeun to watch the kid tonight?"

"He's gone for the day already."

"Well, I'll watch the kid myself," says Rob.

There goes the baby again. It had been breathing fine for the last half hour, but then it started slowing to one gasping breath every twenty seconds. Not enough to keep its color and make it see another day. Rob gently rubs the sternum and voilà, the rate picks right up. Samphy and Bunroeun, the nurses, come over. Rob shows them how to record the breathing on a chart. He likes to teach the nurses and the doctors, and for the most part they like learning from him. But some of them prefer their own way.

The hospital maintenance man comes over with a helper, all smiles. They've got the brown cylinder of oxygen from the supply depot across the road. Mogiath says we can dip into the special hospital fund to pay the dollar for it. A family owns the cylinder; it's their business. They fill the tank when needed and rent it out at a profit. I never saw the family do anything other than sleep around the tank all day.

Rob shows the nurses how to adjust the valve and how to strap the tube in place with tape and put the tubing at the baby's tiny nose. Such high-tech medicine. Dr. Nhean shows up on his old motorcycle. He is one of the very few with a vehicle. Everyone else walks. He takes his helmet off but keeps his silver motorcycle sunglasses on. You can't see his eyes. You can see everyone's big dreaming Cambodian eyes but not Nhean's. All you see is the reflection of Rob and the nurses.

On the same day we were helping that baby breathe, there was a big upset in the out-patient clinic. Someone had collapsed and everyone was shouting for help. It was a nineteen-year-old girl and with her were four or five other teenagers, all hysterical. They said she had taken something from a bottle. There had been a fight with her boyfriend and accusations about fidelity. We sent a nurse to find the poison and ten minutes later we had it in hand. It was a Chinese pesticide and there was a skull and crossbones on the bottle.

The girl was really out, just flaccid, not able to breathe, everyone taking turns doing the resuscitation and her heart was failing. Rob figured it out, called for the atropine and an IV and had her stable in minutes. It was an instantaneous rebound with the atropine cancelling out the poison. And the instant she woke, she heaved it all out but it was still going to take hours before the poison cleared.

Suicides are quite common here, especially for kids in their late teens and early twenties. They were the ones who were between five and ten in the late Seventies. Their first conscious memories would have been of the Khmer Rouge and the atrocities. Not the most nurturing environment. These kids survived, but without food and clean water, their younger brothers and sisters did not. Those ones were known as the "Missing Generation."

We had a suicide case back in Pursat, a young dentist. He had just graduated and was setting up his practice. I saw him as he was coming in and out of a Valium stupor, although because he was from a wealthy family everyone pretended he had had a "vascular collapse." He had taken thirty little yellow pills, just enough to hand himself a three-day sleep. He was angry at his parents, he told me. They had surprised him by arranging a marriage. Something wonderful to complement his graduation. His wife-to-be kept asking me to explain what a "vascular collapse" was.

So now we had the two acute cases side by side, the infant with the troubled breathing and the poisoned teenager. We didn't stray. Rob keeps giving atropine and I keep giving oxygen. An hour later they are better and an hour after that the patients are stable. We stay an extra couple of hours and spend time with the nurses to ensure they know what to look for and when to act.

Dr. Nhean is ready for the coming night shift. Rob does not want any mix-ups tonight. He wants the infant and the teenager to live. So he has his arm around the young doctor and starts the conversation with, "Listen very, very carefully to my instructions," and ends it with, "Are you one hundred percent sure, I mean perfectly certain, that you've got it?"

I remember not having a very good feeling about this but Dr. Nhean appears confident. I hang around for a couple more hours just to make sure the patients are stable. The kid seems to be in the clear and the teenager is even arguing with her friends about what had happened. I stay a third hour until the nurses are scolding me, telling me to go home; no further breathing slowdowns, they had tapered down the atropine, so everyone is satisfied. To make it easy, the last thing I say is, "Come and get us through the night for anything. I won't be mad if you wake me, I'll only be mad if you don't." Finally Dr. Nhean puts his arm around me and says something like, "Relax, my friend. I can do this. It's no problem. Now go home. I want to do my rounding." The baby is alive and doing fine. It doesn't have a fever. That was the last thing I checked. When they get febrile, the automatic forces take over. That's what you don't want.

Walking back I was thinking we had overdone it with Nhean. Not good for morale to be so untrusting towards the doctor in front of everyone. This was Asia, so the concept of face was strong and I was only a visitor.

It is Saturday night. Sunday is a day off. Sunday meant freedom. Rob and I took turns taking the Sundays off. A complete full day off every fortnight. We always saved special items for those days, like a drive to the nearby Tuen Kean mountain or a swim at the Srey Sarray reservoir. I remember having a box of dried salmon from British Columbia out there. Saved it for a month until I had my precious day off and ate it with friends getting sunned on the banks of the water. It melted like ice cream in our mouths.

On this Sunday we don't venture very far from home. We spend the morning at the Ministry of Forestry and Fisheries, a tattered former colonial building that everyone called the Men's Club even though there were just as many women around. We sip proper coffee and play boules with the town's dignitaries in the sand pit under the shade of the camphor and thorn trees. The vice-governor sits motionless in a chair while a barber cuts his hair and another attendant grooms his sideburns. Beside him is a caged boa and nearby a soldier in a hammock, sleeping with his gun. No one works on Sundays. Hard to work in that heat any day.

Boules. What a perfectly simple game. Roll a wooden ball along the sand to a smaller white "jack." Try to get your ball to roll up to the jack. If you're closest, you win a cool drink in the shade and a slap on the back.

You had to learn the deferential way to offer a proper salutation. Body bent slightly, outstretched hand ready to shake, head a bit bowed. Even the governor did this. On Sundays the town's elites made appearances at the Men's Club all morning. Business owners, land owners. It was good form. Mogiath came every other time. That day he had good news. The WHO tuberculosis medicines had been successfully rerouted. He called it a success for the partnership between MSF and l'Hôpital Sisophon dans la nouvelle province de Banteay Meanchey. Yesterday's batch came directly to our pharmacy, not via the middle-man. Whoever had been plundering our deliveries now missed his cut.

Dr. Nhean speeds in on his motorcycle, circles and then does a playful skid. He has his helmet off and his sunglasses on. We can't see his eyes but he's all smiles standing before us in a party shirt. Good, I thought, the baby and the girl made it.

Rob says, "Oh ho, here's the good doctor. Everything okay at the hospital?"

"Bahn," says Dr. Nhean, "everything's okay."

"How's the little baby?"

"Oh, that baby *slap hoy*. It died."

"What? No. The baby was fine."

"No, it wasn't breathing well. Problèmes avec le respiration."

"But it was fine. Christ. What happened?"

"It was sick."

"Did you get it to breathe?" asks Rob. He's demonstrating how he should rub the sternum.

"Did you give oxygen?" asks one of the dignitaries.

"No, not oxygen," he says. He's mumbling about how difficult it was with the nurses and that oxygen cylinder. And then he mentions that the other patient died as well. The teenage girl that needed atro-pine.

The infant and the girl are dead, and we are all standing there stunned with our shoulders slumped looking around the compound, muted, everybody in their own world. It reminded me of Picasso's "La Famille Des Saltimbanques." Rob's staring heavenward. My sight's off through the Bau trees. Mogiath's looking at the ground. Nhean, on his haunches, seeming smaller than everyone else, is in the foreground looking straight ahead.

Then Dr. Nhean lets it out. "It was too young. That baby wasn't strong enough. It wasn't even a month."

"You didn't even try to save it because it wasn't a month yet?"

"Yes, and that girl. She wanted to die. It was her wish."

Rob is escalating and he's uttering Dutch profanities. He's so upset he's mixing Dutch, French, English, and Khmer in the same sentence—something like "Ah, idioot, you, pourquoi ne parlez, ott la or chung hoy prap. . . ." He can't make eye contact with Dr. Nhean or any of the Cambodians.

"Why did we show you the . . . why didn't you get us . . . we said come and get us, it was not that difficult to rub the chest. You were giving the atropine fine. Why didn't the nurses do it? Who told them not to? Ah, Christ."

Dr. Nhean doesn't know what to say. In fact, he's surprised that everyone's upset. He's trying to smile to make the problem go away. Again he comes back with "It wasn't a month old yet." Then there is an uncomfortable silence. After a few minutes, he hops on his motorcycle and rides off.

The wise Madame Boran told me that sometimes mothers in the countryside won't make extra efforts to save their own babies in the first month. A moon must first pass through its phases. They wait at home and let it die rather than come to the traditional doctor or bonze or a midwife for help. Better to let Buddha select out the strong ones. Same thing for suicides.

Rob and I get back to the MSF house. Rhee isn't there but she has, upon our instructions, left a cooked meal for us on ice in the red and white plastic cooler, the "Deluxe Supérieure." You had to keep everything on ice in Kampuchea or you would get very sick. Rob and I were being fastidious about it, but we were still spending too much time preparing our food and gathering our nourishment. Rob had been getting tired of explaining to Rhee again and again how to prepare the food, so this Sunday he told me to take care of the instructions. To make sure Rhee understood. But she had botched it again. She had dumped the rice and beef and vegetables into a plastic bag, tied it up, and buried it in the ice. The bag had split open on the sharp ice, fouling everything. Rob makes a face as he pulls up our Sunday dinner between his thumb and fingertips.

"We're eating at the restaurant today," he says.

"It's closed. Today is Sunday," I remind him.

Chuon rounds the corner in the Land Cruiser. Rob asks him why it took him three hours to wash the car up at the fields on the High Road. He asks this because one time Rob went looking for Chuon down at the river's edge where he said he'd be washing the car, but he wasn't there. Rob was convinced Chuon was using the truck for secret taxi rides. A few extra Riels in his pocket for American cigarettes, perhaps? But Rob had no proof. He was watching Chuon very closely, trying to get the facts he needed. The worst day was when Chuon came home at lunch hour to find me swinging in the hammock, listening to Mahler's *Third* with its clangs and clashes. Chuon was looking at the ground, shaking his head as he dragged his feet up the stairs to confess. There had been an incident, a new dent in the Land Cruiser. He couldn't explain how it happened. It was a nice big dent, about what you'd expect a sledge hammer could do to a panel door. Still, Chuon couldn't pinpoint when the accident had occurred. It was all a mysterious act of God. He kept saying, "Don't tell Rob."

18

The Train Station

Sisophon, Cambodia / October 1991

On my way home one night, while the rain is screaming against the walls of the houses, bending the palm trees over as far as they could go without breaking, I open the gates to the Blue House and ahead of me, in the car port, the truck lights illuminate an old woman sitting by herself on a chair. She is sitting in our garage. Who is this? She sits there rigidly in grey robes, offering no explanation for her presence in our house. She has a mask-like face with broken glasses slanting across her nose and she isn't speaking. I thought she was dead or catatonic.

Rhee comes skipping down the stairs. She says it is her aunt who has come to join us. Her aunt is going to help with the cleaning and cooking and she would be staying over during the weeknights because it is too far for her to go back to her village. This is all Rhee's idea.

Rhee says to me: "You explain to Rob."

Every day brought things we couldn't control. And every night, it was the opposite. The nights were the same. Dark at six. We stayed indoors. So every evening we read and read on the balcony. There was nothing else to do. Rob in the hammock, me under the swinging sixty-watt light bulb. Little white flies surround the bulb giving the appearance of snow. I had brought about ten novels, as much as I could squeeze between shirts in my luggage without going over the weight limit. The next thirty books came slowly via IndoSwiss Couriers. The staff at Phnom Penh said, "Why import all those when we have perfectly good books here?" The secretary pointed to all the mysteries and thrillers on the wall, left by travelers and expats over the year. But one book stood out. It was called *The Rattle Bag*, a collection of British and Irish poetry from the last few hundred years, and on the inside jacket cover it was signed by an Irish volunteer from the relief organization Concern. She had left it there amongst all of the pulp fiction.

There are screaming sounds of insects up in the trees and in the pockets of thick weeds, and sometimes they even jump up to the second floor where the light catches them wiggling on the floor. The children have different names for all the bugs.

The children have taken to calling us Om, or uncle in Khmer. We have names for them all. In the mornings, we drape sarongs around us and the kids watch us through the cracks in the fence as we shower, pouring bowls of cool, cool water from the great ung pot over our heads, down our backs. They run across the street to our car port in the morning now. It's a game to see who can swing open the gates first. And Smiles, she's been volunteering around the Blue House lately, helping me sweep and fold the laundry with her tiny hands.

Some days, the propaganda from the loud speakers would start an hour late. We never figured out why. The difference between waking up at five-thirty and six-thirty was restfulness. One more hour to sleep, but the extra hour ushered in the uncomfortable heat, so the bed sheets would get sweat-soaked. The morning announcement began with the national anthem. Imagine a children's band playing their horns and symbols at half-past five. Then there was a curious scripted dialogue between a man and a woman. The dialogue didn't change for about six months. As far as we could tell, they were talking about harvesting the rice, producing children, and learning about the grand history of Kampuchea. There was also something about law and order and how everyone owed so much to the military. At the end of the set pieces, a government broadcaster came on with a live, poorly delivered and significantly muffled message about the news of the day and specific directives from the leaders. We could never make out what he was saying. I asked where this man was broadcasting from but nobody knew. It had to be local because you could pick out the names of nearby towns and he kept going on about Sisophon as the great capital of Cambodia's newest province, Banteay Meanchey. But who was he? "Ott deng," they kept saying. No idea. Where is the broadcast coming from? "Ott deng," they all said.

No one questioned anything. Even more, they didn't mind, they liked it. The locals liked the noise from the loudspeaker going through them. They were comforted by a familiar voice, however loud and incessant. It filled up something that was missing in each of them, the stuff taken away in the Seventies. Better that than hearing nothing and letting the memories flood back in.

One day, Rob asked the government to point the speaker away from our home and my bedroom. He said it had been affecting me in a particularly troublesome way and he even invoked a bit of medical authority for the request. I asked him to. Oh, no problem, they said, and a couple days later it was pointing away, up over the High Road, Sisophon. Things were quieter. Then a week later it was pointed right back at my coffin-like room. Someone must have shinnied up the pole and pointed it my way again.

The noise that came from the loudspeaker had a way of owning you. I bought extra pillows to cover my head but it failed to block out the noise. It helped a bit, but the price of being all covered up like that was being drenched in sweat. I remember making a special trip to a supply shop as we heard that some shopkeepers had a supply of coarse blankets from China. I had a hunch that these blankets could finally block out the noise from the loud speaker and let me sleep in. Rob called them "magic" blankets for the coffin room.

The vendors wanted forty cents per blanket, and I wanted to pay thirty. There were three men, I think brothers, and they had me in the middle, not budging with the price. The one said, "Feel the quality." The other said the dye "won't bleed." The last simply said, "Saart nas"— these blankets are beautiful.

After a while I realised I was haggling over a few dimes and paid forty cents for them. As I left, they had their arms around each other in a gleeful celebration. It had been a profitable transaction. Forty cents each. I had bought five high-quality Chinese blankets for two dollars. I also bought a piece of silver sheet metal from them and had someone at the wood yard in town take tin snips to it. That way the two pieces could cover my window and block out the loudspeaker's clamor. Rob said I'd die of heat stroke in my bedroom. I said anything but the din.

But it wasn't just the haute-parleur outside my bedroom. The Cambodians wanted all kinds of noise. They loved the racket and needed it, and the worst was when they had weddings and parties. There was something about those weddings. They held them on the roadsides or in a backyard and they went on for days. People just sat around in their best outfits beside the speakers, drinking. They played the music so loud it entered you. You could fight it but the haute-parleurs always won. The Cambodian equivalent of a DJ would play off-key music, often repeating a song three or four times in a row. And in between songs, he'd tell stories and make proclamations. These were indecipherable and garbled to me, but the guests seemed royally entertained.

The loudspeaker, and the fact that people wouldn't leave me alone—these things started eating at me. Even after being there for months, locals I had spoken with many times continued to treat me like a freak. Ah ha ha, here comes the foreigner. Let's laugh and talk to him. Let's make him stop and talk to us. Funny, curious foreigner.

Rob wakes up one day to find that Rhee hasn't packed the bread overnight. The ants have gotten into it. Rob has a particular thing about bread. I don't know if it is a European thing or a Dutch thing, but he didn't appreciate what happened to the bread. He had grown up in Holland during the post-war period, when there were food shortages and almost no variety. Typically the family had no meat or cheese or fish or eggs, only bread. To beat the monotony and keep the children cheerful, his mom played a game by cutting the bread into fun shapes like stars and half moons to entertain him and his siblings. One new shape every day.

The same morning that the ants had feasted on our precious bread, Rob saw that Chuon hadn't filled the trucks with gas. Rob was going to have to do it himself and this would delay a meeting, because he now had to change money and go all the way to the National Road gas station to obtain diesel. And he already owed them money—which he didn't want to pay, because he felt they were the ones who owed him for an original credit. There was a disagreement about that. Chuon and Rhee weren't making life all that easy. Rob said, We'll give them each a week to change or we find somebody new.

It didn't take a week.

Exeunt Chuon and Rhee.

They are gone and we don't have replacements. No peace in the Blue House. For the next two weeks we do everything ourselves. We start eating almost every meal at the town's only restaurant, the lousy Lotus. We don't need menus. We rotate between the three passable dishes but because of shortages and the time of year, we'd often go days in a row with the same lunch and dinner. I asked Dee Ling when they'd be getting prawns again, and she just walked away, laughing. Barend from the ICRC came through town every few weeks to see what was up in the province. When he saw me that week he said, "There's the good doctor, getting thinner and thinner."

The kick in the teeth was our proximity to Thailand. The border was fifty kilometers away but you couldn't get to within forty of it because of the opposing armies and the million or so landmines that various factions had laid down over the years. We could almost smell the food coming over the Thai border. We imagined the subtle fragrance of coriander and ginger wafting up over the border to us. Sweet succulent Thai masterpieces floating up over the landmines and bunkers, floating just above the sugar palms, coming in to land on the balcony. We are on the poor side with the poor people. We don't have chocolate. No wine, no cheese, not even milk for an entire year. Nothing from the ocean in months; and there is still only one kind of beer: Viet Namese Heineken. Dutch beer that tasted like it came from Viet Nam.

There was considerable interest in what we were doing up in Sisophon; everybody in the capital kept going on about how bad it must be for the Cambodians—how close we were to the front, how we must have been seeing "crazy things." "Isn't it dangerous?" kinds of comments were common, even though people far away from the real activity based all their surmises on rumors.

So far only the chiefs from head office had come up, and they only did this when a special truce made things quiet. Once a Japanese national from the UN Development Program came by on an "exploratory mission." She was terrified to be up here with us and she brought us French wine and a Gouda wheel to keep us on side in case there was an "attack." Rob told her there wasn't going to be an attack but she was certain. She showed us a huge security brief on it. She lived in fear for the twenty-four hours she was in Sisophon. But at least she had a plan. Our own security was a joke.

We were briefed on the military radio about the possibility of a hostage crisis. Some splinter faction of the KP (Khmer People's National Liberation Front) was making threats about killing Europeans. Rob said he'd never heard of anything like that happening. He didn't think it was real—not Cambodian. I said I was glad for that. I hadn't come here to make the great sacrifice and I said I wouldn't last five minutes as a hostage. Imagine being tied to a tree for a month not knowing the next move. I'd be too terrified to go on—and bored beyond reason.

"No, no," said Rob. "You'd find a way. You would relax, live like them, learn from them. Find a way to be peaceful. You'd survive."

Today we are expecting our first true holiday visitor, our friend Jan, a forty-eight-year-old Dutchman based out of Phnom Penh. He has been in the country a year already, helping to rehabilitate the National Laboratory, a building that looked like a school but had all its windows blown out. With regard to the people living in the south of the country, they all had this intense need to see the north. They wanted to see what was still left of the nightmare from the Seventies because, down in the capital, the outside world had moved in already. People there couldn't see much evidence of the war and on some level, now with all the neon lights and automobiles, it was hard to really believe what had happened. Up where we were, the evidence was still visceral.

Jan had a week off and he thought why not take a little holiday with us in the northwest, be with the Khmer people away from the city and, for once, not have to work with them, just enjoy them. Part of Jan's plan was to take the quaint train all the way from Phnom Penh up through Pursat and Battambang to Sisophon. It was supposed to be a twelve-hour trip. Rob was on the military radio when we heard about Jan's plans. It was Aukeje from head office. She had been in Phnom Penh for a grand total of a month. She had just taken on the communications responsibilities at HQ and she and Rob were speaking Dutch.

"Zei u twaalf? Over."

"Ja, twaalf. Over," she says.

Rob says to me, "They think the train will get Jan here in twelve hours from Phnom Penh."

"No way. It's at least twenty-five hours' driving time in the Land Cruiser. Land Cruiser's way faster."

Rob speaks into the mike. "Het is minstens twintig uren door Land Cruiser. Over."

"...Bent u..." crackling noise, "...zekere..." space sounds droning in and out, "...twintig...."

"Repeat. Please repeat. Over."

"What? Over."

I'm telling Rob to stick with English. I'm saying English is better.

"It's twenty hours in the Land Cruiser."

"Did you say 'over'? You need to say 'over.' Over."

Rob's pointing at the radio, laughing. He pretends to hit it. I tell Rob to say "over" or he'll get in trouble.

"It's twenty hours by Land Cruiser. Over."

"Why are you laughing, over."

"We're not. Over."

"Well, he left this morning, and they said he'd be there by dinner time. Eighteen hundred hours."

I grab the mike. "You forgot to say 'over.' Over."

"Sorry. Over."

"We will be at the Prap Loy Train Station at eighteen hundred."

"Wat?"

"Wij zullen Jan bij de treinpost ontmoeten. We will meet Jan at the train station."

"Wanneer, 18:00?"

"Ja, 18:00."

"Roger. Over."

"Bye. See you later. Zie later u."

"Tot ziens. Vaarwel. Farewell."

Of course Jan isn't at the train station at 1800 hours. He isn't even there the next morning when we knew there is a train arriving from Battambang at 0800.

We stand there at dawn as the sun boiled away the mist hovering over the train tracks and what was left of the ramshackle station. Two and a half hours later, the 1950s train rolls in but it doesn't roll in like a European train; this one was more like a Soviet beauty. Quite a piece of work. The eight-car train is stuck on the tracks two hundred meters from the station, surrounded by a large thicket of jungle green. Even though it is only two hundred meters away, it remains right there for a half hour and nobody bothers to get off. Groups of Cambodians squeeze through the jungle to get to the train so they can sell their fruits and juices.

Still no Jan. We radio Phnom Penh at noon but they haven't heard anything. It's Maurits van Pelt on the radio this time. He says, "Twelve hours? Not by train. It's even double that by Land Cruiser."

I did the fifteen-minute trip back to the Rout Phleoung station at lunch to inquire about trains. "Oh bahn," they all said. "Sure, the eighteen hundred is coming on time."

So Rob and I go back at eighteen hundred. Ho, the train is only an hour late. But it is dark and we're poking around in the crowds with our electric light and they've all got their kerosene lamps. The faces are flashing at us in the dark. Many of them are pointing and calling us "bar rang" and I'm poking my head into all of the train coaches to find him. No other bar rang, just Rob and me. We're asking after Jan and everyone is saying, "Ott deng."

It's too late to radio anyone. We did quick radio calls every day at eight, twelve and four. Protocol. Outside of those times, no one was listening. Rob said we should really tell the government about it, and we didn't sleep well that night. But the next morning we find him. Some passengers escort us over to one of the cattle cars. I remember thinking, There's not a problem with Jan, right? No robbery or assault or something? No trouble for our foreign visitor who might have a relative fortune in his money belt.

There he is lying on the floor, slumped against the steel wall. It's like, "Jan! Hey, man! Welcome to beautiful Sisophon," but he barely moves. He looks up at me through his John Lennon glasses, two-day beard, fucked-up hair and cracked lips mumbling something incoherent. I think he is sleeping or joking and I reach for his hand but it is flaccid and very, very hot.

The scene reminds me of a painting by a Russian named Moissejenko, one of the almost unknown Russian impressionists from the mid-twentieth century. In the painting, a group of soldiers is stationed beside a horse-drawn carriage near a hill, and one soldier lies wounded on his back, propped against a rise in the hill with a sash tied around his chest. He appears wounded but there is no blood. He is very handsome, hero-like, with his tunic and his shoulders square to the scene. Taking a closer look, his face is ashen grey, his eyes fixed, staring off into space. The man has just died.

Rob and I have our arms under Jan's shoulders and, as we drag him out from the station to the Land Cruiser, his feet leave two parallel lines in the soil. He goes "humph" as he collapses into the back seat and Rob almost shuts the door on his dangling leg. Before speeding to the Blue House via the Low Road, we stop in at the hospital and throw saline and dextrose, chloraquine, erythromycin, and paracetamol into the back seat, anything that could fix a fever and dehydration. I remember looking back to see him on his side managing the slightest shake of his head with all those IV bags and medicines jiggling on top of him every time we hit a bump.

Everybody got sick. The Cambodians got sick. The bar rangs got sick. We were like the nineteenth-century English expatriate community in colonial India dropping like flies. One afternoon I arrived in Siem Reap to find Gerome, that six-foot-four Belgian translator with perfect posture I had seen with the meretrix in the MSF house some months before. There he was, standing by the entrance way in pyjamas, still trying to stand erect, his weight down by forty pounds, eye sockets hollowed out as if someone had painted them charcoal for a horror movie. And as I approached, I could see how the hepatitis had yellowed his skin and eyes. Same thing happened to Olaf from Spain, and then to our friend Monique from the ICRC, and then her boyfriend. Stomach problems were so common they're not worth mentioning. And here and there we got malaria, and Dengue and typhoid. That's when the delirium gets so bad you spend half a day trying to tie up your shoes until someone comes home from work and says, "Okay, back to bed with you." And those were just the expats.

Jan slept in Rob's hammock for a day and then the chloramphenicol started to beat up on the typhoid bacilli. That was the thing—Jan had typhoid fever. He spent the next day awake in the hammock with just a quip occasionally, nothing much. Then we took turns walking him around the smooth mahogany floor of our wraparound balcony. We had such plans for Jan. He had the entire city of Sisophon to explore but he said no thanks and, as soon as he was able to walk on his own, we shuttled him off to Siem Reap for the Tuplov flight home.

"Keep drinking, Jan. Keep up on your fluids." That was the send-off for our first holiday visitor.

19

The High Road

Sisophon, Cambodia / October 1991

As we got to the tail end of the rainy season, we knew Rob was going to be gone for about a month. It was in his contract. He got two weeks' leave in Thailand and two weeks back in the Netherlands to see his family. Rob hadn't been back in a few years, so the trip was important. Who knew how many more visits he'd get with his mom?

I asked Madame Boran over for tea. I wanted advice on how to run things while Rob was away. We had two new people helping us in the home. Madame Jewn was hanging laundry and Madame Somath was pouring me lemonade on the balcony when Madame Boran came up the stairs, smiling, wearing an ankle-length purple sarong, and as she took her seat, both of the other madames exited quietly. Madame Boran was always gracious. She had an air about her, even some aplomb.

"Thank you for this invitation, monsieur."

"Well, my pleasure. You're my favorite midwife at the hospital."

"I'm the only one, but I see you knew that when you said it, monsieur."

"Your ward, how is la Salle Maternité?"

"Forty-five deliveries this month already. My ward is going very well."

"You certainly have everyone's respect at the hospital. Everyone thinks you're the leader. I'm telling you."

"You are being very kind, docteur, but you and Dr. Rob are the senior ones. You have made the hospital passable again. It is true."

"We don't know anything. You're the one who tells us what's really happening. Honestly, the place is a mystery without you."

"It has been my pleasure, and the honor of our hospital, to have you here. Everyone is trying so hard now, and of course Monsieur Mogiath as well. Everyone likes the way the hospital is now."

"Even Dr. Sann."

"We agree on that. He has been given the final warning from Monsieur Mogiath. He is to have no more private clinics at the hospital. He does not like this but he accepts it."

"How angry is he about it?"

"Furieux. He is very upset. He came north to Sisophon to start his new life and work after completing training in Phnom Penh. We do not see him at the hospital so much now."

"What do you think will happen?"

"Personally, I believe he will leave, monsieur. I believe he will go back to the capital. But no, docteur, no, you did the right thing."

"Did we?"

Madame Somath sets up a tea service in front of us and pours. She always comes just as I think of her. The green tea splashes into Madame Boran's white china cup, the only cup we have like that.

We are all on the balcony in the shade, under the corrugated tin roof of the Blue House, looking out onto the Low Road. We are halfway between the summer and winter solstices, so the sun is straight up. It couldn't be higher. And it couldn't be hotter. My back and legs are soaked wherever they touch the chair.

"Rob's leaving for a month," I say. "What do you think we should do?"

"Rien. Nothing. It's working fine."

"Well, it isn't working fine. We're just getting by."

"No, monsieur, it is working. We have never seen it like this before. You must trust this."

"I do. I trust you. That's for sure."

"You must trust all of them. There is no medicine missing from the pharmacy any more. The totals are correct. The nurses are following the guidelines. The two boys who died, all of that cannot be helped. When we are hearing about measles and typhoid from the ICRC, the

162

nurses make the changes rapidly now. There have been no further occurrences of the problems. We can try to do more in the camps but that is more difficult, much more, docteur, you see."

"I'm not going to be tracking everything down like Rob."

"Oui, it is better like that."

"D'accord. Okay. It's crazy, you know, us being here. We don't *really* know what's going on."

"Mais oui; yes, you do, monsieur. The hospital is much better."

We watch a horse pull a cart along the road below. When it turns the corner to the hospital we can see a sick elderly woman lying in the back. Madame Boran covers her mouth to hide her smile. "That one is for you, Monsieur."

"Yeah, I know. You only do babies. But Rob's over at the hospital. He'll attend to the lady in the cart, or Bun Thoeun. Get him to see her. He's perfect. We'd like ten Bun Thoeuns."

❧

At the going-away party for Rob, Mogiath gives a speech. It wasn't too bad for a Mogiath speech, but every time he paused someone figured he was done and fired up the ghetto blaster. After this happened a couple times, we just left the music on and he started to dance. Kien Tai, the new government number two, is there. He wants a medicine from Europe to help him stop smoking. He had heard about "a special chewing gum made from tobacco." I tell him about it and what it costs. When he starts converting the price into Cambodian Riels, his hand moves subconsciously for the package of cigarettes in his shirt pocket. Bun Thoeun, the doctor that everyone likes, shows up with his wife. They are going to be having a baby before too long. Everyone is saying it's going to be a boy and they're all giving Bun Thoeun the business, pulling at his shirt and holding his hands. Si Pengthan, the administrator, pulls me aside with a big smile. He's got his index fingers lined up side by side pointing down at the ground. It's a secret symbol. He is showing me his fingers like that and keeping them concealed from the other guests.

He says, "Mean koun?"

"No, I don't have any children. Why's that so funny?"

Bun Thoeun comes over. He's also got his two fingers together like Si Pengthan. Everyone thinks it's funny I don't have children yet.

Kapath says, "Mean bei." He's got three kids himself.

Then they call Rob over and start bugging him about the same thing and all the men are utilizing the secret two-finger signal. They figure Rob should be married by now and they have a few women in mind. Bun Thoeun has one in particular in mind.

Rob is saying "Oh no, no, no," but Bun Thoeun is saying this woman is very special.

"Sahat nuh. She's very beautiful."

"Really?" says Rob.

"Oh, yes. From a wealthy family who have a rice farm."

"Hmmm," thinks Rob aloud. He says he doesn't really care but wants to know more.

Kapath Rang is shaking his head. "Oh, that woman is very beautiful. Her family has many, many cattle. Many oxen." He toasts Rob, telling him he must drink a hundred percent of his drink. "Cent percent!" He toasts Bun Thoeun too. Then he's off to the red and white cooler to find a good-sized piece of ice for his cream soda and brandy.

"I thought it was a rice farm?"

"Oui, rice farm. Kapath doesn't know her," says Bun Thoeun.

"And many, many cattle," shouts Kapath from the cooler.

"What does she look like?" Rob wants to know.

"Oh, sahat. Most beautiful one in Kampuchea."

A few of the others come around and we do a toast to Kampuchea and then we do one to Rob. Everyone's trying to shout "bon voyage" and "som lea hoy" over the music. Rob's got his favorite premium rum and Coke going, real Coca-Cola smuggled in from Thailand, and amber Bacardi. The border is loosening up just a little bit these days.

Some of the kids from the street tiptoe up the stairs. They are watching the bar rangs dance. They've never heard music like that but they like it. Some of them try to dance Western-like. Especially Smiles and her sister Genius, but not little Monster-boy. He's the youngest and he's scared up there with all these strange adults, way down the street from his mom and dad. He starts to cry so Smiles puts the boy on her hip and rocks him. No problem, she will take the little boy home. That little Smiles, always the one helping out.

Everybody's having a good time up there in the Blue House. Rob gets me to notice Kapath and the nurse Monsieur Min Loew. They had been having some kind of disagreement at the hospital, refusing to work together in the past week, but there they are, arm in arm toasting each other, swaying to rock and roll, shouting "Cent percent" as they drain the glasses. And Sok Samuth is dancing with the kids. Great fun seeing him so juiced with his guard completely down. Rob's asking people not to smoke inside. He's pointing out it's a wooden house. A tinder box. So they all go to the balcony. Orange cigarette butts spinning off into the night air.

Towards the end of the party, when the music is peaking and the Cambodians are doing their most fervent twists and shakes, Rob pulls me over to the corner. His eyes are bugged out and he's got his hand over his mouth, pointing to where everyone is jumping on the worn mahogany. The floor was bowing up and down.

❧

Our party was a success but it wasn't out of control. Not like the debauchery I had once seen at an outdoor market in Moscow, in the days before the reforms had taken hold. Not by a long shot.

Taking advantage of the exchange rate, I was on a spree. Water colorists and photographers offered up their finest works, for little. Families sold their collections of brass objets d'art, samovars, dark tapestries, Rembrandt-like near masterworks, whatever. Everyone was stoic. Many emotionless Slavic faces going about the day's sober business.

By October in Russia already the light at that latitude had taken on a winter's wan silver and as the sun was setting, the temperature plummeted and it snowed. Then vodka bottles appeared from car trunks, out of bags, from inside coats. The formerly rigid artisans and vendors began slanting and tipping, bumping their goods off tables, bumping into each other. Here and there you'd see someone curled up on the grass, another standing with the clear vodka mini bottle pointed to the sky like a trumpet. The whole scene transmogrified into a mess unleashed by the coming darkness where all of this debauchery could be hidden.

The night we had our party, up on the balcony, after the guests left and after Rob had retired, all the insects and frogs were shrieking away in the trees and bushes and there must have been a moon because I was writing in my Grumbacher without the swinging light bulb. No light bulb because the music had used up all of our battery power by about ten. No flurry of white insects around the bulb to give the appearance of snow.

Rob was departing and I was going to be running things for a while. For twenty-six days, to be accurate. Kind of a neat feeling. A little bit like the first time you practice medicine on your own. No senior resident to check your work. No staff physician to co-sign your orders. Just you and the patients.

The first day I did this in Toronto I had the ICU to myself at Women's College Hospital. A patient was lying in bed with all the usual wires and monitors hooked up to his chest and arms. The man had a nice Somerset-type accent. Looked like he could be a Shakespearean actor with his wavy grey hair and aquiline nose. He winked at me and told me he knew his heart wasn't going to let him run many more races.

He wanted to know what I wanted out of life. He had been a career diplomat and the Foreign Service had put him in "stupefying" places like Cairo and Japan. His last and longest posting was Barbados, where he was Honorary Consul. "Ah, the functions and the daily etiquette." He used to wake at dawn, take the morning papers to the terrace over the Caribbean Sea and drink ten cups of coffee to "wake his heart."

I looked at his cardiac monitor. They were the craziest rhythms I'd ever seen.

"I'm done for," said the man smiling, being brave about it and proud for the life he had lived. He knew I wasn't made for hospital work and the last thing he said to me was, "Get out of this place, my boy."

That's how good it gets, I suppose. Kind of like Ulysses, ancient in bed, surrounded by all your friends and family, reminiscing about all the great battles you fought. Better that, than dying when you're in your twenties or teens like all those soldiers Robert Graves and the other war poets wrote about. Better than dying in childbirth—or, worse, as a child. No, I'd much prefer the Norman Lewis approach, a travel writer, maybe the greatest, who was ninety-five when he passed. Imagine that, almost a century, many books to his name, an acclaimed place in the literary arts and an infinite count of rich memories to replay in bed as you weaken and get ready to go.

I found one of his books in the most scripted but unanticipated ways. On the way to Cambodia, I had a five-hour layover in London and made a mad dash downtown, did the Tate, had a ploughman's lunch at the Cittie of Yorke, and then went to shop at Covent Garden where there were stalls filled with out-of-print books. In one of the first piles, after perhaps one minute of rummaging, I pulled out Lewis's *A Dragon Apparent*, an account of his travels to Cambodia and Indochina around 1950. I could have gone to twenty bookstores and never located this rare, out-of-print edition.

He said Cambodians were people living in monastic retirement, followers of a contemplative and renunciatory religion in the march of progress. Fair enough. He pointed to some massacres by the Foreign Legion and how the French air force bombed Cambodian villages off the face of the earth. Why did he pick that? That was 1950 and it felt like I was reading about the Americans in the Seventies. It was as if he were seeing the future, and he said that the country people were turning to communism. Lewis had been everywhere. He said, "I believe in pure travel," and he toured all over Kampuchea and even met the King but he never made it to Sisophon. It's right in his book: "Somehow we missed Sisophon."

Two weeks later, Rob has long left the country. I'm on my own in the late morning with the massive thunder clouds darkening. Nothing unusual in that—no sightings of ghosts or anything unnatural. The staff and I have put in a pretty good morning on the wards. I feel I was experiencing some unusual energy. It is a strange liveliness and it is nagging at me. Sok Lou suggests we go for coffee at the new coffee house. Well, it was more like a shack, a block west along the Low Road away from the hospital. As we cross the road a truck barrels around too fast and clips a dog. The poor dog is yelping, doing circles in the dirt like it's trying to bite its tail. Then its legs straightened out and it fitted for a minute and lost its urine before quieting. There it lay, panting on the roasting road. A man—I guess it was the owner—came up to the dog. I am feeling that strange and unusual energy while this is happening and keep thinking it better rain. There is a pressure in my head. It is like the thunderclouds were so ripe and full of water that I couldn't take it. I keep thinking it better goddamn rain. Why isn't it raining? The dog's owner picks up the dog and, because it is in pain, turns the dog's neck in a circle until it snaps. That's when I feel the first drop of rain. The owner then marches with the limp dog in his arms off the road, away between some houses.

Sok Lou says it couldn't have happened like that. I can see him there, shaking his head at the ground, trying to convince me. "Buddhists don't kill." He says the man must have been struggling with the dog and I saw it wrong.

He offers to buy me some of those X-shaped chromosome-looking sugar pastries to go with my café kmau but I can't seem to get my coffee ready. The weird energy is taking over. I pour a spoonful of sugar directly onto the table, missing my cup altogether. I laugh it off and mumble something like, "Am I stoned?" Then I line up the cup and miss it again.

A couple of people in the restaurant notice this, covering their mouths as they laugh at me, and then the café seems to slant and everything has shimmering edges like a migraine aura. I take a deep breath and close my eyes. Open them: everything is still fucked up. All the chairs and tables and people seem too big or too small. The plantain tree above us seems monstrous. I'm not in pain. Stomach feels all right. Sok Lou tells me I look okay but he notices pretty quick that I can't seem to get up from the chair so he takes my pulse. A lot of good that would do. He calls for a horse-drawn taxi. I am slumped in the back while we move amazingly slowly along the Low Road. People are walking by. They all look in and say, "Bar rang." I roll around in the back trying to feel whether I have the 20 Riels to pay the driver. I don't have the strength to push my hand into my pocket, and I can't seem to find my canvas bag.

It is really raining when we arrive at the Blue House. Our new maid and cook come out all concerned. Madame Jewn has her palms over her cheeks—straight out of an Edvard Munch oil painting. I'd never seemed to notice before how big her front teeth are or that she has a bit of grey hair coming in. Perhaps she lied about her age. Maybe she thought we wouldn't hire an older person. I am soaking with sweat as she and Madame Somath get me out of the cart with some help from Sok Lou. The driver wants his pay, but both madames just scold him as he stands there, laughing and spitting at the ground.

All the while I am trying to figure out whether there are any other expats in town and worrying about who is going to run the hospital if I'm sick. But then I think, Who's going to come and help me? Who around here is going to give me the correct intravenous solution when I need it? I could feel the dull needle going in. The hypodermics they all swear are clean. Maybe that guy from Concern was still in town. He could get one of the ICRC docs. Or perhaps Barend would make one of his bimonthly visits, just in the nick of time; he'd come and check in on me. Or Andrew Thompson, the Kiwi medic, he'd be perfect right about now. For sure nobody else was within a hundred miles and I didn't want some kind of local treatment for whatever this was. Dengue? Shigella? Could be Shigella, that's the one with nice neuro effects like the double vision that made me pour the sugar onto the table.

Or botulism; that would be really good. I remember Rob saying the only botulism antitoxin was in Bangkok—three days away. I'd be dead in the morning. But what else could explain the slanted and shimmering café? Anything but malaria. Please. Not paludisme cérébral. I kept thinking about that big possibility: I've got cerebral malaria and it's going to turn my grey matter into paste. The same thing that killed the man in Pursat, who got the wrong perfusion: saline instead of dextrose. I am about to faint, fading in and out, with Madame Somath holding me by the shoulders, my head listing to one side, and Madame Jewn giving me one awfully worried look—and all I can think about is that man, my own Cambodian ghost. The one they all laughed off, patting me on the back, telling me how innocent I was and how it's all just part of the way it is here. I killed him. Now it kills me. How do you say sorry to a ghost, someone already gone? I don't even know what the man looked like. Just a faceless death in the countryside.

20

The Second Floor of the MSF Blue House

Sisophon, Cambodia / November 1991

The women can't lift me, but manage to push me under the overhang so the rain isn't directly falling on me. I actually preferred the cool rain, but never mind. Some man I don't know just picks me up and carries me up the stairs to Rob's bed. I keep telling them to leave me there in the bed, that I don't want to go to the hospital. They shroud me in the frosty mosquito net. I have no idea who the man is. I guess they just summoned him from the Low Road. He and the madames are conferring. I don't want him there influencing the madames. I don't want to move. Then Madame Jewn puts her face up to the netting.

"I don't want to go to the hospital."

"Oui, monsieur, but wouldn't it be safer there?"

"I'll sleep it off. I need something for the head aching."

Pointing to my head, I try to explain what kind of tablets to get, but all they understand is "comprimé" which means tablet, not what kind.

I say, "Get Boran. Get Madame Boran or Bun Thoeun."

The mosquito net has a hat-sized white ring fixed to the ceiling. The fine lace-like netting flows out of the ring in all directions, shrouding the bed. The breeze puffs at the mosquito net, indenting it in slow motion. But I can't feel the cooling breeze; the netting traps the heat. It's a stifling microclimate inside the net.

Time is distorted. It feels simultaneously like a day but only a minute later that Bun Thoeun arrives, all serious in his white smock with his stethoscope around his neck, a custom we taught him. I remember Rob pretending to knight him, taking out the stethoscope, holding it up in the air like Apollo, the Sun God, and then draping it around his neck. I was so used to seeing Bun Thoeun smiling that he is scaring me now. Come on Bun Thoeun, start smiling. Let me know we'll all be laughing this off soon. My head was earthquaking and I couldn't move or speak or concentrate. He starts to examine me but there is a small crowd all leaning over to see, so he asks for some privacy. Then he peeks under my socks and frowns.

"Les capillaires sont fragiles. You have some bruising. Maybe it's Dengue."

"Dengue fever?"

"Maybe. Peut être."

"Oui?"

"Peut être. Je ne sais pas."

Then he notices I am having trouble concentrating and that even French is difficult. So he speaks in English for the first time. "I don't know. Very hot but you okay, be fine."

It is odd listening to him speak a new language. It's as if he has become a different person. Some gentle and honest stranger beside my bed. Bun Thoeun the Kind.

A couple of the nurses show up a little later. They are saying that maybe it is Dengue. That wouldn't be too bad. Nothing to do for Dengue-infected people except give them liquids and let them feel miserable for a few days. Just wait it out. Take stuff for the fever, something strong for the headaches. Make sure nobody exsanguinates. But that really never happened to adults, just the kids under five. But why did the café go all funny? I ask them to bring our textbooks into the bed. We had *Harrison's Principles of Internal Medicine* and *Cecil Textbook of Medicine*; that was the extent of our medical library. Two books. I was checking the symptom lists in *Cecil* but I couldn't focus. I couldn't even lift the book. I ask one of the nurses if he thought that it might be Dengue. He put his palms in the air, maybe. I would have gladly had them inject something into me to make the aching in my head stop. I'd gladly take one of the clean but dull needles we used on everybody, morphine even, but we didn't have anything like that around. It was only available up in the market and I wasn't going to trust that. Up in Sisophon, pain relief was considered nonessential even if you were dying of cancer. And they both shook their heads at the idea of a perfusion. Not necessary, they said. And I wasn't thirsty, not yet.

The loudspeaker blares its announcements. The noise penetrates me. It's trying to get me. Madame Somath shows up with a glass of ice chips for me to suck on and a full meal. The madames have learned how to make pommes frites and steamed vegetables, and, depending on the day and the market, beef, pork, or chicken, all done up in a sweet sauce. She places a tray of her best cuisine on the bedside table. The cutlery is wrapped in a serviette just like in a restaurant. I stare at it. The pork has the sweet sauce dripping on to the white plate and the heat rising off the eggplant swirls in the air. It looks like a desert mirage. There are three baby chicks fried up in bread batter and a rectangle of butter is sinking slowly into the miniature mountain of white rice. When I look again, the steam has stopped and the ice chips have melted. Finally Madame Somath takes the untouched meal away.

I feel like I am on a boat or a spaceship. The bed is way too big for the room. The window is too far away and the fever won't let go. The night comes and goes, and in the morning I am just as bad. Bun Thoeun says, "Oui, I am not surprised. It will go soon. But you must drink."

One of the madames puts the military band radio up to my ear. I don't remember asking for the radio, but we were surely behind on our thrice-daily security check-ins. I figured it would be Maurits calling about my delinquent radio calls, and maybe prodding me to focus on my work again. But it was Coen Albers, the surgeon who was stationed in Svay Rieng in the south of Cambodia, one of my favorite people. He sometimes radioed over. We had met in Mozambique when I had taken that month off at Harvard to see MSF in the field. That was a year or two before coming to Cambodia.

The fever's got me confused. I'm getting my dates mixed up, so I ask him how it's going over in Cuamba and he just laughs, saying Cuamba's in Mozambique. The conversation doesn't make sense but when I hear him say, "Keep your head up, it will all pass," I feel better.

What do they call it when you're febrile and having those strange fantasies? Deliriums? Waking dreams? One had me sneaking out at night barefoot under a moon, walking up to the Vanishing Temple where the local orange-robed Bonzes lived. Another had me shivering in ankle-deep ice water on the floor of the ice factory at the edge of town.

While the factory was real, ice water was a hopeful fantasy. The closest we got to that kind of cold was the five a.m. dollop of water from the great ung pot in December. Here I was stuck in the heat, sweating. That might have been it. Confusing the ice factory water with the drenched sheets in the cooler wee hours. Sisophon never did cool enough. Never in the daytime. Not in those lowlands at the equator in Indochina.

But what transpired with the monks, going up the Vanishing Temple, barefoot, that was true. These monks, the Bonzes, were kind and spiritual but also peculiar, odd in an other-worldly way. They were harmonious clerics floating through the day. They'd walk by us in Sisophon not making eye contact, only responding if you voiced something their way—a smile and maybe even a wave and some words. It was the way they just stood on the street, detached, in their flowing robes waiting for alms. The older ones, however, had the true enchantedness. They were real, both unearthly and right here with everyone else. Present. Able to belly laugh at a subtle joke and aware of an adjustment in someone's breath.

Not long before I got sick, I walked in barefoot off the sandy Monkol Borei Road past the gatehouse, through the garden to the sand in front of the main Pagoda of the Vanishing Temple. One of the monks was sleeping in a hammock. I thought someone was by a cooking fire but as I was trying to see into the room, two dogs came out and their tails were rigid and down. Noses lowered, they were taking neat little steps faster and faster towards me, on the verge of running. I was fifteen feet from the Wat and it was one of those situations. If I kept the same calm pace, I might beat the dogs into the temple. If I run, the dogs will spook and charge even faster.

I thought maybe I could beat them inside. But what was inside?

Then someone whistled and the dogs turned away. I walk in. Two monks are on the floor, cross-legged, having tea. No foreigner had been in the Pagoda for twenty years and it didn't faze them. It was like, "Oh, hi. Here, have some tea."

We were trying to exchange ideas in Khmer. It's a weak conversation on my part. I used up my standard lines about where I was from, what I was doing, how old I was. There was incense and candles burning, no chairs or tables. The sun was laying down slanted light on the floor. Same worn mahogany floors as the Blue House. I gave them a few Riels. They treated the money like it wasn't theirs. In it went to a pot. What I gave them was ten times greater than what was already in the pot. They rolled out a reed mat. I was to sit in the middle. These monks are fifty, maybe sixty, and the one with glasses looked physically strong, like he had walked many hundreds of miles in his life.

He was sitting opposite me, a foot away, and the other one was there on my right. They started chanting and they were doing it in the tonal way with those mind-blowing harmonics, only with the one guy in front of me and the other to my side, they were basically hypnotizing me. I couldn't help it. I started humming. It was very hard not to stay in pitch with them. It carried you along. Their song was probably a thousand years old. Any song a thousand years old lasts because its value is so great and deep.

The light outside the window seemed to flicker like the wind had pushed at the window slats to scatter the light, only there were no window slats. The light looked silvery and I can't tell you how long they kept doing their trick of deep meditative trance or divine beauty, whatever extraordinary gift it was they were handing me.

That silver light. I saw it at McMaster University one afternoon. We were seated at the Faculty Club for lunch, me and my dad and some others, and we knew there was going to be a solar eclipse. A solar eclipse is rare, but as we dined, we weren't paying much attention as the moon floated in the way of the sun. Same silver, unnatural light. And when it happened, a squirrel actually tried to run right through the window into the Club and two seagulls who landed on the terrace were flopping over sideways as if they were drunk. They could barely right themselves, and one clipped a table as it flew away.

When the monks were done and the silver light had passed at the Vanishing Temple, I was really confused about how long I had been in there with them. Between five minutes and an hour? Time had been suspended. When it was over, I left in a state of cool tranquility, feeling light and cleansed, like everything was easy and it all made sense. Us being there in Cambodia. The way the people were. The war and what had happened.

&

Still feeling derailed, finally sometime during the stretch of hours and days in the feverish bed in the Blue House Madame Boran arrives. She apologizes for not coming sooner. She had been with the Bonzes and they were initiating her into a new status reserved for only the most respected women in society. When she is with me there, I can't seem to carry a conversation and I can't understand her French. I am over to one side of the bed, looking away, and when I roll over, I feel like I am going to slide out of bed into her. Her face looks monstrously large and her teeth are all red. They were red because the Bonzes had instructed her to use the red Beetle nut as part of her rite of initiation. And so she sits beside the flat bed with her face and red teeth an inch from the mosquito net, me with clenched fists digging into the sheets and mattress thinking I am about to slip and fall from my flat bed.

I don't know what she is saying. It is French, probably simple enough French but with the fever like that and the feeble thinking, I start to wander all over the clouded landscape, in between false and true memories of a conversation weeks ago. The conversation was between the two of us, and it was a window into what happened under Saloth Sar in the Seventies. Very valuable to hear first-hand what happened, how something like that could ever have happened. It was the closest I got to authenticity. That's because when I asked the others about what occurred, I always got muddled stories. Facts were given but there was no context to make it resonate and their accounts didn't seem real. They all laughed it off, saying, Oh, yes, bahn high, you're right, it was very bad back then, they killed my brother, terrible for Kampuchea, many people starving, very bad, yes.

But sometimes they opened up and talked about life under Saloth Sar—it sounds like a Tolkien character from the dark side, but that was his birth name. The name he took for himself later became infamous and legendary in an inhuman way: he was Pol Pot, the architect of what happened here. And when people mentioned his name, they spoke in a drone, often going into a trance, into a fuzzy, nearly unconscious place that even the Bonzes couldn't enter.

A man named Ieng Phuon living two doors from the Blue House opened up about it one afternoon. He said: "Soldiers everywhere. So many soldiers. They come after us and you can't run away, even at night. You cannot talk to each other. Just work. All day. At night you are exhausted and sleep on the ground under a plastic sheet. When we hear the shooting, we run. We don't stop. We drop everything and run. Run without my family. Maybe we don't see them again. I lost my father like that.

"I don't know where they got their ideas. I don't know politics, just people. I really don't know where they got their strange ideas. I can't explain it. They were very bad people. Very bad. Horrible. There was no food. Just work. I was exhausted. Tired and so skinny."

Madame Boran kept saying it wasn't so bad in her district. I guess that was true. Someone else from her district said the same thing, that some places were not persecuted as harshly. She said the day she knew the change was upon them was the moment strange-looking soldiers blocked the main road and closed down the market. Everybody had to stop what they were doing and come to town. They had done this before, but this time they laid big trees across the roads. More outsiders came in and made speeches for hours and everyone in town had to stand there, even the elderly. They couldn't believe what they were hearing. No water for hours, just directives from the cadres—new rules for conduct.

She told me at first that it wasn't so difficult to live. Not so bad compared to the south and near Phnom Penh, where there had been mistakes with the planning. I think she said they shot the mayor and some other men as well as a woman that afternoon. Others were arrested and taken away. This was after hours of the new people speaking through the loudspeaker at them, everyone standing in the heat. She said that some of the people truly liked the ideas, especially the farmers. But when they shot the woman, that's when it became deeply disturbed. No one had witnessed anything like this before even though they had heard rumors. When they woke up, some kind of hex suffused the community. She began to go along with them. She called it a spell.

Months went by where no one saw any of it again. There were rumors of this and that but they didn't see it and maybe it's true, that it wasn't so bad in her district. I don't know. She stayed almost exclusively in the countryside farming rice and root vegetables, some fruits in the dry season, only a few animals. She became a self-sufficient farmer with the others she was billeted with, whoever they were. She had tears in her eyes when she told me of her family lost to famine and executions. And in the same sentence she said she was so happy Rob and I were there to help. The next thing she said was a blur to me. She started to speak about her husband and I don't think she meant to let it out but she called him a different name. At first I thought I misheard. We all knew her husband. He'd come to official events now and again. But this was another man, the one she called out for, and he wasn't around anymore. He must not have survived, and I remember asking about it and meeting a wall, a memory shield, some kind of impenetrable stone wall just like the ones Suryavarman II used to build the temples in Angkor. I was not to ask about it.

21

The Balcony at the MSF Blue House

Sisophon, Cambodia / November 1991

Who knows, it might have been Tuesday or Friday. The two madames helped me to the balcony. They figured I needed a change of venue, out of that bed, and they needed to change the sweat-soaked sheets again. I remember telling them several times that I wanted to stay in bed, that I didn't want to go to the balcony, exposed to the light and the curious children below. But they insisted. They made a little bed of cushions up against the wall so I had privacy and was out of the direct sun. But after a while my bones sank through the thin cushions, pinching me against the floor. Madame Jewn went to the market and brought back four new pillows, which helped me prop up my head so I was just able to peek over the balcony to the street. That was better, but man, had I lost weight, and still the freaky fever was there and all the distortion. The Blue House was seemingly massive and too tiny all at once. It sounded like people were talking in Rob's room but the whole second floor was empty. How many days are you supposed to have fever before those effects seem like they're becoming permanent?

The highlight of the morning was inching all the way around the smooth mahogany wrap-around balcony and down the stairs to urinate. Same highlight for the afternoon. All the time waiting and waiting for six o'clock when the sun would go away and the reception on the shortwave was good enough to pull in my channels, any of fifty different broadcasts. A feast of voices and music, however garbled it was.

Up over the balcony wall—how can I describe this wall? It was blue and made of metal. We were on one side; on the other, it was like a movie set, everyone in costume holding props like machine guns or riding by on horse-drawn carts. A huge Chinese man, shirt undone, smoking konch chhar, is pushing a fruit cart through the mud. That is followed by a blind water delivery man. And then a woman in a full-length lavender gown. All day I had been watching these actors come along the Low Road. Short ones, old ones, robed ones, naked ones. The poorest kids were often naked. Why not, in that heat?

Then someone comes along who is looking completely different. It's a woman, thirty or forty, quite pretty in a different way, and she's got six or seven kids in tow. She's talking and everyone on the street is noticing how loud she is. Every twenty paces she sits down on the dusty road and the kids form a circle around her. She tells them stories and her hands are gesticulating as she describes wondrous events and amazing occurrences. The children are giggling, and the older ones are eying each other because this woman is more than they are used to. She is un-us-u-al.

Ho, she's up walking straight away down the dusty street, right hand pointing up to the sky. You don't see Cambodians pointing like that but this woman is not like the others and she'd be the first to tell you she has very special things to think about and share. There, she stops again, sitting cross-legged right below the balcony. She waves the children around her and it's some new story. She has such authority. This time she's playing the roles of different characters and the older kids know that it's not the story that's funny, it's the teller. Maybe they shouldn't be laughing at her. They know it's not right but they can't help it. There's something very infectious about what she's doing.

I notice she looks very, very poor. I guess this because of how dirty she is and how her clothes look. Then Sim Sok comes out from her home on the Low Road. Sok always kept an eye on all the children in the street. All the adults did. Everybody raises everybody here. She isn't happy about the goings on, telling the woman to be on her way, but the woman is only going to move along when *she* is ready. The children want more of her entertainment but Sok knows this is a sadness, not the happiness the children are feeling.

Uh huh, the woman is pointing up at the sky, but the children don't see what she sees up there. The woman has a sudden idea. It's time for her to leave. She must go away from Sisophon. This must happen right away and the children must not follow her. She's giving her reasons and I think weaving in bits from the stories and Sok is saying, Yes, yes, you're right, good idea to leave now, you're wise and kind to have decided that and thank you for the wondrous stories. I'll just keep the children here and they won't slow you as you leave here, hopefully in peace. That was the word Sok was using again and again with the woman. Peace.

When the woman marches away along the Low Road, she is Queen of Sisophon. She is full of wonder and vitality, just like Newton and Darwin, and Gauguin and Chopin, when they too were manic, walking the earth with their immortal gifts. But there's always a debt— the devil tells you that. Some kind of eventual letdown from the heights where you'll find that energetic story-telling woman no longer marching along the High Road in Sisophon. No, she'll be slumped in a corner somewhere. No more stories, no more vigor and maybe something bad has happened to her. Something taken from her, some abuse perhaps, exacting a price.

There was a job I had for a while up in Penetanguishene in the near north of Ontario. It must have been just like the work my grandfather Arthur Doyle did in the provincial mental health centers. I used to go up there with Carrie. They gave us a house to live in with a view of Georgian Bay, and for my services they handed me an average Cambodian's yearly salary every eight hours. No one else wanted the job because it was up north and it was in a place people used to call the insane asylum even though it was idyllic; the high Georgian facade was framed in grand oaks sprouting out all over the generous meadows.

There was more than a little bit of mania up there. Beyond-belief stuff. But it would be wrong to think of it as an insane asylum. Such a barbaric term, one that doesn't do justice to the people trying to help and the patients who are trying to cope. But when someone did something really crazy, the doctors sent the patient to a typical big-city hospital psych ward. If the case was too much for a general hospital, they sent him or her to one of several provincial mental health centers. And if the ghouls slipped in, the ones that could control your movements and tell you to do something unthinkable, those patients went to Penetanguishene, as I say, an aged edifice cloaked by those ancient shadowy trees marking spots in the soil.

I'll never forget Johnny Starrs. One day he's kind and gentle and normal, apologizing for any digression or altercation "even if it was imagined." "And one more thing, doctor, only a minute; I do hope you can put in a good word about my smoking privileges. Such a dreadful mix-up the other day. Quite impossible to explain that one away, as it were. I am indeed having my difficult moments here. But it's not as if the boogie man is real, like I might have said, and thank you so kindly for whatever you might do."

Really, he had a grand civility, but the guards knew. They've witnessed what he becomes. The next day, he's juiced up on some kind of fuel, yet no one slipped him anything. It came from within. He is Mr. Boisterously Happy now, an infectious man, a bit too happy for someone triple-locked behind an iron-barred door. He's got a whole bunch of things to say, many, many things, most of which are hilarious and vital. He wants to include everyone in the telling and he's asking about the others on the ward. It's essential to him, and humanity, that all patients are enjoying their lives there on 2B. "Would you be so kind as to get Mr. Parks a cup of tea. Please do so immediately. I can tell he's thirsty. Thirty. Thirty thirsty. What? Thoroughly thirsty at age thirty. Did I say that? And let's not forget Mr. Humphrey's birthday. Birth. Day. Why, the day he was born, of course. But I can't remember if it was today or last week today. Same time, same sweet birthday cake. Birthing suite. Isn't that funny? I've mixed up the days."

Then on the third day, when the gas is running out, sitting at the dining table of life, he flipped over the dinner tab in that very luxurious restaurant called Ward 2B to find that there was a price for all of this rich food. That was the day his face changed, white-knuckled, holding the inch-thick steel bars, white freaked-out hair, no eye contact until he's pulled you in close. He's truly the bad thing now, a monster roaring at you through the steel as his saliva hits you in the face. And he's crafted a perfect insult, too, letting it hit with precision. He's telling you what he will do and how it will get you when you aren't looking. Here come the male nurses with their syringes. He's got those same wild eyes as the soldiers in Africa, but they are fading, and the next morning he is slumped in the corner, open mouthed, a long strand of saliva not quite touching the floor, eyes fixed on a cinderblock. Quite crazy but not stupid. I remember one thing a professor made clear: no matter how psychotic they get, they remember everything. "Careful what you say to a mad man," he said, "even if they are bouncing off walls."

In Penetanguishene, there is a pleasant walk that takes you down by the Georgian Bay Inlet, past an Anishnabe Indian site to a clearing behind the old hospital building, what used to be called the Insane Asylum. In those days, when people were floridly psychotic, there wasn't any calming medication for them, nothing to slow them and offer a peaceful chemical restraint. All they had back then were padded rooms and straitjackets. Those patients, so sick and terrified, impossible to manage and simply dismissed by their families. Behind the main building there is a plot of grass and every few feet you find a simple headstone about the size of a brick. On each of these there is a number. No name, just the case number, the number you'd find on their medical chart. Here lies 7194-2.

I lost a day or two. It was Monday in Sisophon when I got sick and next it was Thursday. That floored me when I heard it. I said, "Nah, can't be." And they said, "Mais oui, certainment, il est jeudi."

Enough sleep. I had been trying to force myself now. The shortwave is coming in pretty good for midday. Sometimes the midday ultra high frequency for China Radio International brings interesting news. The first story was about how the world Ping Pong champion lost his number-one ranking but, with great confidence, he was explaining why he could regain it again after a four-year absence.

Somewhere in there I manage to wrap a sarong around my waist and inch down the steps to the great ung pot. I want to wash away the days of sweat. No one else is in the Blue House. Take the tin scoop. The silver fish darts away every time the tin scoop dips. Put the cool, cool water up over my head and let it fall through my hair and down to my feet. The red rock before the ung pot darkens.

I think I notice a dawn bat in the kitchen rafters. There is the feeling that someone is watching me. At the slatted wood fence, I catch a short shadow but when I looked directly at it, it freezes. It is our neighbor, the little girl, Smiles. I guess she had been watching for a while. She is looking at me through a knot hole in the fence. You can just make out a brown eye.

"Sok sa bay, Smiles?"

"Sok sa bay," she says. The little girl is fine.

"Ott tao rean te?" Not going to school?

"Ott tao." No, she's not going to school today.

"Ott chong?" You don't want to?

"Chong." Oh, she wants to, all right. It's just a question of competing interests. She wants to learn, but she also wants to watch the foreigner. The foreigner is very interesting and she's still shy with him. There. She moves sideways just enough to show herself through a gap in the fence. She's wearing the school uniform, blue shorts and a brilliant white shirt. What peace and contentment she carries. She has the prettiest smile in Sisophon.

I pour more of the cold water through my hair and it gives me a chill. I am feeling too cold now. Not feeling good. There are some of those big white clouds going by. When they get in the way of the sun, it is cold standing there in a wet sarong, so I have a seat on the steps and tuck my legs in.

"Skorm," she says. She thinks the foreigner looks too thin. She knows he's been sick. That there's been a problem and she's worried about it. She heard the adults talking. She knows it's serious because there haven't been any balloons in a week, no other treats or little pastries from the balcony.

Smiles has her fingers poking through the slats. She wants me to play the game with her. The one where she keeps her fingers in the hole in the fence and I sneak up and just before I can grab them, she pulls them away. She always wins the game but I'm sick, Smiles; we can joke around another time.

Here comes another little one. It's her younger sister, the one we call Genius. She's wearing a blue and white uniform too, and carries books in her bag. The bottom of the bag is at her knees, the top is at her shoulder. She's smaller but bolder than her older sister and comes right up to the fence.

"Om, khnom chong ban petpong." She's got her hand through the gap in the fence asking for a balloon. Smiles slaps at her arm and tells her the foreigner is sick. It's not right to ask for a balloon when the foreigner is sick. But Genius doesn't believe it. She's a bright little girl and can't be tricked. She knows she's bright because we taught her to count to ten in French, English, and Dutch and she learned it faster than the others. Faster than Running Boy, Monster Boy, and Monster Man, the sons of the blind water delivery man. I'm sitting on the steps with a towel over my shoulders, shivering.

"Trorchak," says Genius. She wants to know why I'm so cold. Smiles grabs hold of her sister, gives her a swat and tells her not to bother the foreigner. She freezes her little sister with a stare. Then they both can't hold back the giggles.

Genius breaks free and goes to another hole in the fence. She's asking for the Frisbee now. She wants either a balloon or a Frisbee or something of similar, equal value. Smiles chases her away. She's pretending to hit her with a twig. Genius plays along like she's been caught and has to take her punishment.

Then some little friends arrive and everyone is laughing. Where do they all come from? There are a dozen or so by the fence. Some of them are using the "skorm" word. They have a second sense about what is healthy and what isn't. But they are kids and these younger ones don't really know they were being offensive.

Now there are some bigger kids at the fence, older boys, teenagers I suppose, and as they approach the other kids step aside. Never seen them before. They don't seem as friendly. They're asking for the balloons and one of them wants money. It sounds like they are making fun of the foreigner by the way the tallest one says something, and then all the others laugh. All except the shortest boy.

He's the one boy taking longer looks at me. He's wondering what is the foreigner doing here. Why is he speaking Khmer? Smiles had moved back behind a Bau tree and her sister has crossed the street to sit on the neighbor's porch. Nice safe distance. Let the older boys pass. More "big" words from the tallest kid. He's directing it right at me through the fence and the other boys are laughing along, all except the shorter kid. They think the foreigner doesn't understand. They think he's beneath them.

I don't say anything there on the stairs. That shorter boy is looking at me, trying to figure me out. He'd be the one in the group who didn't respect the tall kid but knew that the tall kid respected him. I wait until only he is looking and then I wink. I just give him a simple wink and it stuns him. I don't think he's seen that before. The foreigner shouldn't do things like that. It wasn't natural. He looks around to see if anyone else saw what the curious foreigner had just done. No, no one saw. Maybe the foreigner didn't really do it. I do it again and this time he's got his hand over his mouth to cover up the smile. He's telling the others what happened and for once the tall boy is silent. They're all looking at me and they're waiting for me to do it again.

Now everyone takes a big step back off to the side of the road. Here come the even-bigger boys. The ones with guns, wearing fatigues. And right behind them is an armored troop carrier. It's full. Here comes another one. A whole platoon is coming by.

The teenagers walk away. They've had enough of the foreigner. Time for school, anyway. But the shorter kid, I watch him look back but he can't find me for all the dust. Smiles wants to come back to the fence but Genius is dragging her away to school. Everyone is off to school or off to war or whatever obligation they have been signed up for.

I drag myself up the stairs to the balcony of the Blue House, on the Low Road, Sisophon. Maybe some of Madame's cooking would hit the spot right about now. I wipe my mouth. Hey, I feel a bit of a beard.

I remember standing on the steps when I realized the fever had broken. Leaving a serious illness is heavenly, and when a fever breaks, you know it. The first person who told me this was Craig Lapp, older brother of my friend Tim. Craig was something else. Still is. He wrote a thirteenth chapter to Lewis Carroll's *Alice in Wonderland* as a university essay and got an A. And before he went off to Europe with only a few hundred dollars, tiny backpack, and a 35-millimeter camera, he got the shortest haircut any of us had ever seen in those late Seventies. He instructed me to always read with a dictionary and that was around 1980. He said, before you can write, you must learn how to read. And before you can photograph or paint, you must learn how to see. Pretty much me and basically nobody has seen him since.

I felt my forehead—yeah, no fever. But I sure did have a beard. Haven't had one like that for a long time. Way too hot for a beard in Cambodia. Going to a barber now was going to be painful. Five cents for a shave, an extra quarter if you wanted a new razor and, for sure, you wanted a new razor. Some power surge had blown out my Philips, so I think I'm doomed. I think I am going to end up at the painful barbers. There are three or four barbers in the thatched hut waiting for the customers to come by. A couple of them would be sleeping and the others would be smoking, discussing. They shaved their customers with hot towels and no shaving cream. There just wasn't any. They did it by taking a razor, stretching the skin taught and making neat cuts chopping at three or four roots at a time. Then they'd wipe the blood away on a white towel. Halfway through, everyone pauses for a cigarette and brandy.

It was seeming like such a crappy impossible life here in Sisophon, and even if the fever is gone now, I still have no energy and little interest in anything. The past two days I've gone to bed with the great intention of waking and making some energetic humanitarian contribution in the morning, but the place has a way of defeating the plan. It puts sandbags on your shoulders. I awake, stuff the stethoscope into the canvas day bag, push some Riels into my pocket, pull a cap snugly on my head and get ready for the walk to the hospital. Then I feel weak, have an epiphany about the utter uselessness of it all, decline to go, enter into some slumber and shortwave, and chew on a cigar. Then I'd just stay at home for the rest of the day.

I'm trying to go back to work but can't. What is going on there? Bun Thoeun came by the Blue House to see me several times, and each time he said everything was fine on the wards. He went over the patients once or twice with me but it's awful hard to concentrate in that heat.

You could call it a blue funk, a mild depression, not the real thing. The real thing was reserved for people with chemical imbalances, something like an air-gas mixture in a combustion engine going wrong. We for sure saw the real thing up in Penetanguishene. Plenty. The worst ones were the psychotic depressions. You didn't want that. There'd be one corner of the cafeteria where they sat, the patients with that kind of depression. It was a kind of Blue Period painting. Some upright nodding as they smoked ten cigarettes in a chain, focused only on some mark on the floor. Somebody else would be slumped forward on the table, head tilted sideways, mumbling. Others watching the nurses as they moved around, staring at them like they were guarding something unmentionable. Many of them had special powers and a few could put thoughts right inside your brain and even control you. They could do this even though they have been mute for over a year.

I remember watching Mary Sinclair walk by us at the nursing station. She was already sixty, in and out of the ward many times. She has been walking, following her usual pattern. Around the inside perimeter of the ward, past the fountain, stop, look over to the nursing station with those intense eyes, walk past the bay window, the one with the view of Georgian Bay, and then in and out of the smoking room, before going past the nursing station with those eyes before sitting. Count to one hundred and then do it again. All morning.

"Mary?"

"Yes."

"Are you all right?"

"Yes."

"Do you need anything?"

"No."

"Not thirsty or hungry? Not feeling anxious today?"

"No, I'm fine. Thank you, dear."

"Can you tell me what this place is? Where we are?"

"This is the hospital."

"Do you know what day it is?"

"Thursday."

It was Monday.

"Can you tell me when you were admitted? How long have you been here, Mary?"

"Five billion years."

PART V

22

The Low Road

Sisophon, Cambodia / November 1991

Bun Thoeun came to the Blue House that afternoon. He comes up the stairs smiling, white smock perfect as usual, with a stethoscope resting on his shoulders. Never a drop of sweat on Bun Thoeun, not even when he's directly under the fierce sun. He says everything is fine on the wards. There is nothing to worry about. Nothing at all. But he is indeed expecting me today. Madame Boran and Palek, the nurse, told him I was coming back. They even had a cake and a card. It said "Get Well Son" in English. They all loved English and they all thought English was going to be way more important than French. The world was coming to Cambodia and it was going to be an English world.

I ask Bun Thoeun to tell me about the patients and the protocols and the supplies in the pharmacy, but as soon as he starts telling me this, I don't care. I'm noticing one of those kingfisher birds on the pole by the welder's house across the street. It's pecking away at the wood. Maybe there's a grub in there. Rob operates on the assumption that anything made of wood is infested with insects, except the hardest hardwood. You never heard it in the daytime, but at night, around nine, when most of the town is beginning to sleep, that's when the chewing sound began. In my room, it sounded like termites nibbling through the floorboards up through the bed legs to my ears. Every night the noise seemed louder and a little closer. Maybe this was a false memory because in the morning, when I shook off the fog of sleep, the sound was always gone. Then the next night, there it was again, that terrorizing gnawing.

"Doctor?"

"Sorry, Bun Thoeun. I'm not all here yet. What did you say? No, you don't need to repeat anything."

"We need some help with the supplies."

"I don't think I'll come today. Tomorrow for sure."

"That is okay but we are very low on supplies. They need the money."

The next morning rolls around and I make it over to the Lotus restaurant. Everyone's happy in the kitchen. I'm back at it and I get my breakfast free. There's brilliant sunshine splicing through the lattice work making squares over the cracked tile floor. When the wind gusts, the squares move. I've got my Grumbacher notebook and a novel. All the protagonists are nihilists lately. Can't blame the writers for doing it like that. I'm sure some of the older ones were living in places not too dissimilar from this one. A war comes through, thousands and thousands die. The diseases get many of the rest. Corruption, ineptitude, and ennui. What's the point of trying? We didn't really have a clue about how to move in and change things. Almost everything we did didn't work well. Or they told us it was working but it actually wasn't. And when we leave this place, everything still might fail.

The novel in hand is novel number twenty-five for the year. They're all on a shelf, squeezed up against the ceiling in my coffin-like bedroom. How pleasant it had been in the past months, reading away the evenings up on the balcony under the light bulb. It's all copasetic and cozy. The Dutch call it gezellig. Read, make notes, sketch something, write a letter home. Have a beer and something to smoke.

That was funny. Since I got sick, I hadn't had a single cigar. I still had plenty left and normally I was rationing them because they're impossible to get in Sisophon. I was hearing you couldn't even get the cheap Cuban ones at the Russian market in Phnom Penh any more. Apparently there were big problems with Comecon, the Russian-based trading system that let us have some treasures for practically nothing. Things like tinned caviar for thirty cents. Rob was saying the Soviet Union could collapse and that it would mean the end of the Cuban cigars forever. Nobody believed him.

That was the other thing. I hadn't read anything in the two weeks since the café went slanted and everything had shimmering edges. I'd been unable to focus. So now, for the first time in a while, I was making my way through a novel, a little slower than normal but glad to be in fiction land again.

As I'm reading, people are flowing by on the mud-packed Low Road. I'm trying not to hear it when they say "bar rang." But I couldn't help hearing the word "skorm." Such an ugly word. It cut through. Who do they think they are—that they can walk by, look me up and down, and then pronounce it to my face. "Skorm. Hey, bar rang, you're all sick and skinny."

So when that happens, it puts an end to my plan to return to work. Palek and Bun Thoeun come around to check on me, and luckily everything is still okay on the wards. It is midweek, I think Tuesday, so I simply tell everyone I'm not ready to come back yet. That I'd be there at the end of the week.

I remember thinking, I sure hope nobody dies, as I went up to see the monks at the Vanishing Temple. I had been there a few times now, trying to gain some mental sustenance from them, and this time the dogs were friendly, wagging their tails and letting me pet them. Such healthy dogs too, not like the ownerless canines that roam the streets hunting for scraps, dodging rocks. The monks were giving me the treatment and teaching me how to see that silver light on my own now. Every day I got a little better at it. And when rising out of the Lotus position, I felt lighter, more positive about Sisophon and what we were doing.

I march over to the market one morning and acquire a new T-shirt and pants. I buy a case of soda pop, some coffee, and Chinese cookies, and take a horse-drawn taxi to share the bounty with the hospital staff. I'm finally back on the wards. Bun Thoeun does indeed have it under control. Way better than the months before when Rob and I arrived and every patient was given every medicine to cover any number of illnesses, so long as they could afford it. Mogiath is very, very happy to see me. He takes me aside and shows me the sad state of the surgical stockpile. We count up the boxes. Our stores were depleted. Rob wasn't going to like that. But where is Sann? The nurses look at the ground. Is there some problem with the surgery ward? Then Mogiath speaks up. Sann isn't working here any more. Something about the government granting him an exception to his placement and an "étude supérieure." But really, it was simply that he couldn't make money like before. It wasn't worth it for him. So he left. Rob was going to like that.

On the pediatric ward, the walls are now a brilliant white, and in the nurses' office somebody put up posters in bold letters with all the treatment protocols. The staff did it themselves. Lok Loun brought the ward and district data to me. We had taken such a long time figuring out how to collect it. For sure we have the only data like that in all of northwest Cambodia. Wouldn't want to lose it.

Mogiath, Dr. Nhean, the accountant, and Kientai from the government, all of them wave me over to the bureau d'administration. They needed to discuss the fiscal situation in the hospital. We sit under a framed portrait of Hun Sen and everybody fills the silence with unnecessary platitudes, signs of their nervousness. Mogiath keeps jerking his chin foreword and he reminds me that the monthly medicines from Phnom Penh are late and the existing stock will run out in less than a week. The accountant, Si Pengthan, keeps tapping his knee. He says we are out of funds. He accidentally breaks three toothpicks as he picks his teeth waiting for Sao Sim.

Short Sao Sim with his substantial girth arrives at the door, but we had heard his grumbling laugh coming up the road. It is how he announces himself. He approaches with his handshake, the one with the wiggling finger in the palm. But before anyone says anything, I pull the envelope out from my bag. Eight hundred thousand Riels, about a thousand dollars—enough to pay for the supplies everyone had been borrowing on credit while I had been sick. Even more than they had been hoping for. Such a fortunate exchange rate lately. The volume goes up in the centre d'administration and everyone wipes their brow. Mogiath stands up and delivers a speech but everyone is talking over him saying how great MSF is and that it is such a wonderful partnership. "A partnership for all of history," is how Mogiath puts it. More of the wiggling finger from Sao Sim; he's even got his arm around me. The accountant takes a bottle out from his desk—what a nice 1960s touch—a bureaucrat with a bottle of booze in his desk. "Glasses," they're yelling.

Such a great occasion for l'hôpital Sisophon dans la nouvelle province de Banteay Meanchey.

And right then, in comes Rob Overtoom, just back from Europe and through our gates. Big happy welcome for Rob. He's got some of the nurses coming up to him. They've got their hands pressed together in prayer-like fashion and they are saying, "Choum reap sour," and Rob is saying, "Sok sa bay, sok sa bay."

We all spill out. Rob is laughing because we were all a bit soused. "What's this? There's the good doctor. Oy yoy yoy. They told me you were sick, but oy yoy. How much do you weigh?"

"Welcome home." We are all back-slapping him.

"It's good to be home."

Rob's laughing at my face. He touches my beard. "U hebt een baard! How old's that?"

"No idea. My shaver broke."

"What's wrong with the barbers?"

"Are you kidding? I don't want to bleed to death."

"Greetings from all in Phnom Penh."

"Thanks. I'm looking forward to seeing them."

"Maurits said he was worried about you. What was it? The Dengue? How's the depression? Don't you worry, it passes."

"I don't know. Not sure it was Dengue. My neuro system went sideways. You should have seen that new café you like."

Mogiath is going on and on about the great job I have been doing. He was explaining how there were no unexpected deaths on the wards and that the hospital had been functioning superbly. He says, "Système impeccable." Rob is winking at me, saying he's certain there hasn't been a single problem for the whole month while he was away.

And Mogiath is inviting us all out for dinner to guess where, the Lotus, and I think he then followed it up with, Of course, we'd all have to pay for our own meals. There was no extra money in the budget, unfortunately. Just for fun we hail carts. Why walk when we can be chauffeured in style? We're lying in the back, Rob in his cart with his luggage, me in mine, this time no fever. I'm wondering if Rob's brought any goodies from Holland, maybe a Gouda wheel, as we clop along the Low Road in lovely Sisophon.

Rob says, "You're buddy's coming up."

"What?"

"Your buddy's coming."

"Who?"

"Ian Small."

"Are you kidding? That's impossible. He's in Amsterdam."

"No, sir. He's in Cambodia, now."

"That is amazing. He's coming up for a visit?"

"No, sir. Ian's coming to live here."

Ian Small was younger than all of us. The first time I heard his voice, he was calling from the bush in British Columbia where he had been tree-planting. It was a bad connection but what he said was very clear. He read the article about MSF in the *Globe and Mail* and said he wanted to work with us. He said he was willing to stop everything to come join us.

Last I saw him in Canada was in Collingwood, at Jim Lane's chalet at the Osler Bluff Ski Club. The three of us were engaged in our usual revelry, when a north-western gale slammed into the mountain and dumped a foot of snow on us in an hour. We were trudging through it at night, snow blanketing our shoulders and touques, our footprints disappearing behind us.

Ian had been helping build the fledgling MSF office in Toronto when we went on mission in Iraq together, up in the Kurdish area near Zhako and Dahouk. That was before I came to Cambodia for the year. He had been spending time in Amsterdam, and now he was in the south of Cambodia, in Kampot. Rob and I needed help, so I guess Maurits finally gave in. But before Ian made his way around the Tonle Sap all the way to Sisophon, we had another visitor. It was Katherine, from Phnam Penh, a nurse and the wife of Dr. Eric Goemaere.

She rubbed Rob completely the wrong way. From his point of view, here she was, up in our project for a week, behaving like she was the one with all the experience. Well, that was a toss-up. She had a lot but not more years in the field compared to Rob, and all of hers was in Africa, mostly in Chad where her husband Eric had found her "wandering

around the desert as a teenager, barefoot after running away from home."
Well, that was the rumor. I never asked her. For sure Rob had way more
Southeast Asian experience, and he was miles ahead with his Khmer.
Rob pointed out numerous times that she wasn't even a doctor, and yet
she kept making medical inquiries and putting forth theories about phys-
iology, for example, why a glass of Coca-Cola would dehydrate you even
though it was liquid. As far as Rob was concerned Katherine was there
to do one thing—assist with a measles vaccination program in the big deplacée camp outside Sisophon. But she reminded Rob that she was also
here to make sure the project was going well. She was evaluating us.

I quite liked Katherine's stories. What a tough francophone. The
book she was carrying was titled *Why I Ate My Father*. Here she was
up in the war zone while her son and daughter were back in the capital
with an au pair. We spent hours talking about MSF, speculating if it was
a cult or not and how Madame Boran was a grand woman. Katherine
had a lot of opinions about what she said was France's dirty role in
Cambodia and even dirtier role in French Africa. My lasting image has
her moving barefoot through ankle-deep mud in the deplacée camp, a
Cambodian child on one hip, a clipboard under her arm with four or
five Khmer nurses and helpers following, not wanting to miss any of
her orders.

One evening I have a Romeo y Julietta number 2 going. I have 1s
and 2s, a glorious box of Upmans and about eight Churchills left.

"Let me try one of those," she says.

"These? You don't smoke cigars."

"They smell very nice. Ça sent bon."

"You're not supposed to inhale them."

"How is it you blow rings? Comme ceci?"

"It's tough in the wind, mais on doit faire un petit pousse comme
ca et voilà."

"Ah oui. C'est tous simple."

"Here. More like this. Regard."

"Like this?"

"That's it. Now you're a cigar smoker. Congratulations."

I tell her how I got them into Cambodia: "One day I arrived at
the House of Hajenius; that's the hundred-and-seventy-five-year-old

tobacco shop on the Rokinstraat in Amsterdam. The man behind the counter rolled his eyes as soon as he saw me. That had to be due to the mix-up that had occurred with the VISA card payment the last time. Anyway, that got cleared up, but the Dutch don't like loose arrangements and the extra hassle of tracking things down. It seemed to bother the man and I would have gone elsewhere, but it was the oldest shop in Amsterdam and I felt like a big shot going in there. So this time I had cash, and he was now very accommodating. I was even given twenty little "quick ones" for free. They were just Indonesian tobacco, but still, I was grateful. The bulk of the five hundred I spent went towards the Cubans, mostly Upmans and Partagas."

"Five hundred Guilders is a lot," says Katherine.

"Dollars. It is a lot. You're smoking a fine cigar. Anyway, I've done this before. I tell him I want the boxes sent to Cambodia and I want it sent not today but in a couple of months when my first supply will have run out. That way everything stays fresh and humidified. He's not that happy about it. They have no 'system' to delay a delivery. Says there's charges. I say I'll pay and I give him my credit card. He still says it's a bit inconvenient but whatever, he does it.

"Two months later I get a box of number 1s and two boxes of number 2s. The 1s, my favorite, are ruined. They have some kind of fungus in them. The tropical humidity spoiled them. I had actually smoked a couple of them with the fungus before figuring out something was really wrong. So I send them back and ask for a replacement. Big upset. You should have seen the curt letter. They said it was the improper handling in Cambodia that did it and that's where the fungus came from. Well, two months later there's still no replacement box in Phnom Penh and my friend Jim Lane back home, he's been watching my accounts, he says they've gone ahead and billed me for it anyway. I forget how many Guilders. For nothing. That's when I got Roeulf Padt involved."

"What's Roeulf got to do with this?"

"Roelf is famous at Hajenius. They love him because of his presidency at MSF in Holland. He calls cigars his 'old Dutch habit' and I asked him to say hello and straighten things out. I haven't a clue what he said but two weeks later Indo-Swiss delivers a box of twenty R&C-U-J Churchills in aluminum tubes, all in perfect condition. And by then I had one of the local tinsmiths here make me a humidor so the mould wouldn't get to the cigars. You're actually smoking one of them."

We recline on the smooth mahogany floor of the balcony blowing smoke rings, talking.

But that was the fun side of Katherine. I'd seen her change into something else, too. One morning, a pleasant-enough man approached our home. He was maybe forty-five, slight with glasses, speaking Parisian French. He said he was just passing through. Passing through never happens in Sisophon. He may have been only the tenth foreigner I had seen up to then, and Katherine knew exactly who he was. I think she called it a branch of the French government: Le Ministère de la Culture et des Communication. That ministry sent these people around to keep an eye on the former colonies, she said, to look for opportunities—places where the French government should place a little extra emphasis and influence to keep the French language and culture alive, give it some advantage. It was supposed to be about business and passing around favors. But Katherine felt it was much more. That it was linked to the DGSE, the secret service and military. It was the French version of the CIA, and Katherine had seen how the French undermined West African politics. She had seen way too much suffering over there.

This slight man had come from far away. I have no idea if he really was those things Katherine was saying, but nobody comes all the way up to Sisophon without some trouble and effort. The man walked up expecting to be welcomed to our balcony for tea, or maybe even a beer on ice, but Katherine snaps into a different mode. She demands to know exactly what he's doing here, what his agenda is, and who he works with, and tells him that this is MSF and he's not welcome. It was like it was her home, and she was deciding who could enter or not. I remember the man being dumbfounded, and every time he tried to explain, she tore another strip off him. Katherine said if he didn't understand what the upset was about, he should ask his superiors. She said something about having nothing to do with France. That MSF was independent. Fiercely so.

Rob let out an "Oy yoy yoy" when I told him what had transpired.

23

National Road #6 from Sisophon to Phnom Penh

December 1991

The new driver, Wi, is cleaning the headlights of the Land Cruiser number two. Rob and I, and the two madames, we're enjoying the gorgeous morning. Brilliant sunny day, six a.m. with the eight-foot-high gates of the Blue House opening onto the street, and the Land Cruiser is pointed out ready for me to go get Ian in Phnom Penh. We had packed it the night before. Stuff that head office was going to deal with: a box of paperwork about the mission in Sisophon, a broken autoclave, a broken radio adapter, and a broken typewriter. There is the red and white plastic cooler filled with ice, cheese, and bread, as well as Cokes and beer, because I was on holiday. Lots to nibble on during the fourteen-hour ride. Plus I had got my silver Zero by Halliburton, with all my clothes folded neatly, days earlier, and my personal effects like the Sony SW 1000 and the last unread paperback, J.M. Robert's *History of the World*, an utterly expansive review from Mesopotamia to Gorbachev.

Somebody called the Zero the world's best suitcase. It was built with aircraft-grade aluminium, designed for an oil executive who needed something sand- and weather-proof for his jaunts to the Middle East in the Forties before that area had opened up—before there were spectacular airports and roads built from all the unimaginable fortunes they pumped out of the ground. I found the suitcase at Henry's camera shop in Toronto. It was mint, no scratches and not even a dint, returned by a photographer who had to "liquidate in a hurry."

There is a three-digit brass combination lock built in by the handle of that Zero. The staff didn't know the combination number and they couldn't open it, so they sold the case to me for a hundred dollars. They didn't figure it out. I found the number after spinning the dial for only a few minutes. The magic number was 420. Only a hundred dollars for a case I had seen for twelve hundred at Gold's on Queen Street in Toronto. There it was all dented now. More like art that way, or at least something with some history to it.

The night before, Rob said I could choose the number one truck with the air conditioning or the number two with the stereo. That was the choice, and he said it was up to me—he wouldn't be mad either way. I chose number two with the music, and he said, "Ah, you bastard," in Dutch.

There is a different kind of freedom over here. I love these long trips. As hard as they are, at least we are traveling. Moving. Going to a new place to discover something. Just a change. Keep moving. Sharks have to keep moving or they die. Most living things do. I think it started way back in the pram when my Poppa Roman used to push me for miles all over Hamilton.

I sit in the front with Wi, pass a couple of hours with half a dozen cassettes, looking forward to purchasing new music in Phnom Penh. I have Rob's map of where to go and whom to talk to. After a while I crawl through to the back and get a few more cassettes out for the stereo. Had a first ice-cold Viet Namese Heineken. That's another thing. Rob said there were all kinds of new luxuries in Phnom Penh. He made a list of all the different beers you could find in Phnom Penh. Touborg, Amstel, Kronenbourg, Singha. He said there was a pub they were building that had air conditioning and pizza. Jesus—pizza! It was on the map, too.

Wi was perfect. We asked him to wash the truck, rotate the tires, check the pressures, change the oil—and he did it all. Both gas tanks were full and even the spare tire was checked. He did it right the first time. Not like Chuon, even though I missed having him around. And I don't know where Wi learned to drive. He was a slight man of very few words. He was one of those people who says almost nothing, so you think perhaps he's a bit troubled, or slow, or just very shy? Some were hurt so badly by what they witnessed in the Seventies that they walked around unconnected to people. They were walking ghosts.

But Wi, out of the blue, he'd go on about something, quite confident, all loquacious and normal. Maybe he was just shy but this is Cambodia and that meant anything may have happened in the past. Truly anything. But, man, could he drive. I've been with him going seventy on the dirt roads. He had mastered the trick of keeping two wheels on the road and two off the side so the pot holes didn't make the shocks bang so violently. He was better than me and I was better than Rob. The thing about his driving was he never faltered, even after ten hours of continuous driving on those roads. Cool concentration.

I had been enjoying myself in the back having a little bit of a party, watching the dusty Cambodian countryside, all those traditional arches and dunes and rice fields. I guess I was a little more excited than I realized—on holiday for the first time—finally, finally getting away from Sisophon. We get out of the truck by some gate to a farm. Some of the stupid empty beer cans fall out on to the road. I am mumbling to myself something about not polluting the countryside as I try to reach under the truck for the one that was just out of reach. I couldn't get it so I slide under head first onto the road. Wi gets it for me.

"Why don't you let me drive, Wi? I can drive, Wi. There's no problem. Are you sure you want to continue, Wi?"

"Yes."

"Not tired? Here, why don't you just give me the keys for a while. I feel like making this truck hum."

"No."

"Come on. Gimme the little keys. I wanna drive."

"No."

He shrugs. He's waiting for me to say something else but I've got nothing. No more jokes for Wi. So he opens the door to the back and inside I've got the seat down and the pillows and blankets arranged. It's all business class.

After a while I wake up. We're stopped by the side of the road in front of a bridge that's out. Wi is up on a high hill, a kind of dune or something. He's looking out to the horizon way left of the normal road. Up there, he's showing me how the next set of little bridges are all out. He's saying it's the Khmer People's National Liberation Front, the "KP," who did it. Normally we would have been radioed this information.

They were pretty good in the capital about keeping all of the NGOs aware of the security situations, such as where they were finding new mines and sighting the rebels. They didn't radio us because this must have just happened. We were the first to see it. The KP couldn't be far from here.

I'm telling Wi to go off-road over to the east. I'm pointing it out on the map in his hands but he's politely shaking his head, something about mountains in the way. So I make up a route further east but he laughs and shows me the Tonle Sap Lake is right in the way. I'm watching Wi. I've never seen him like this before. I say, Let's do this, and he says no. No hesitation. I suggest, Let's just wait it out, and the government soldiers will arrive with their trucks and fix the bridges and clear away any of the mines. No. Anything but all the way back to Sisophon. I couldn't take it.

He puts his hand on my shoulder and pushes me down. A few hundred meters away, there are two trucks turning off our road and receding in the distance. We hadn't seen them. KP? Maybe they're laying a few more mines before going overland west. Wi gets us back in the truck, gingerly turns us around and we go back the way we came. His eyes are darting around and he's way more careful about going off-road where the KP lay mines. Half a dozen times he stops, gets out and inspects the road on foot before continuing. We turn left instead of going straight back to Sisophon. Thank the gods for that. I couldn't take going back there. The shark in me says so. Keep moving forward or die. That put us on an unkept road overland for an hour, but then it links up with a fairly decent road at the turn to Pailin that even has some paved sections. An hour later we are in Battambang. We didn't expect to be here but Wi knew exactly where he was taking us.

Battambang is Cambodia's second city. It was at one time an industrial center, but Saloth Sar obliterated everything and it still looks like a ruined place, dark and depressed even in the sunlight. Here and there are splashes of new color. A Fanta billboard. Some new-looking place to get truck parts. Navigating the roads is all a mystery to me, but not to Wi. He grew up here. Two left turns, one right, two more left and we are at the town's best hotel, done up in fresh white paint, not decrepit at all, and the hotel lobby has French doors which open to a café area with metal chairs on the sidewalk. There is French cuisine on the menu. Well done, Wi. We eat and drink, only Wi doesn't drink. As we're waiting for dinner, I stand up and show him how my legs are still shaking from the crazy twelve hours in the truck, slamming in and out of those massive pot holes.

The telephone in the lobby actually works. It had been a few months since I had made a phone call. All we had in Sisophon was that lousy radio and the "Over." Head office was surprised about the bridges but glad we called in our delay. They hadn't heard about KP movement and they radioed Rob about it. Rob was surprised. He had just driven through that area a couple days earlier on a trip back up to Sisophon. The Agence France-Presse correspondent asked me all about it when I got into Phnom Penh. She said she didn't think it was the KP after all. There is a new faction that has broken free, calling themselves something like the white party for freedom and democracy. They were trying to carve out there little bit of territory near Pailin, their little bit of paradise with all those gemstones under the ground, not to mention the thick timber. One new rebel group every season in Cambodia's northwest, twenty or thirty new landmine explosions every week.

The wind is kicking up a lot of dust on the National Road # 6 as we approach the outskirts of Phnom Penh. We have to slow down for other cars. It is no longer just trucks and Land Cruisers from the few international NGOs out in the countryside. There are family cars, trucks delivering fresh produce, flatbeds full of boxes and bags, and luxury cars driving wealthier people to and from the city. There are so many cars they are jamming up. We are in a traffic jam! Way more businesses and larger buildings. Here and there were some brand-new structures and an ultra-modern gas station with four pumps and cars waiting to be topped up. The attendants even wore uniforms with an insignia of Gaz de France above the shirt pocket.

I had forgotten what the city looked like and how big it was. Hundreds of people on the streets. Not just peasants in their grey-brown clothing anymore. More of the middle class here, still quite a few monks in the orange robes, but others in suits, and tourists. Tourists in Cambodia. I hadn't seen Europeans for so long and whenever I did see them in Sisophon I knew them personally. But here in Phnom Penh, every time I saw someone from the west, there was a kind of automatic recognition factor: I thought it must be someone I knew—but of course I didn't. It was a trick. Still, it was reassuring to see other Westerners and pleasing to see women from Europe. No "Dutch Masterpieces," as Ian Small called them, but welcomed after such a long isolation.

We pull into the MSF HQ by way of Sihanouk Boulevard. There is Serei King, the chief mechanic, working on a Land Cruiser. Six white Land Cruisers all side by side and four or five pickups. A big operation. They all have the MSF logo emblazoned on the side, same for the steel entrance door. That logo, so familiar now. Here comes Maurits van Pelt. Handsome Maurits with his perfect front teeth, in slippers, smiling away. He's pointing at my beard, shaking his head.

"Look at you. Mr. Development Worker. Welcome back. Oh, you're classic."

"This is Wi. Best driver in Banteay Meanchey."

Maurits says, "Pourk yeng tha tveu dom neu tam phlao mean ka pibak neng mean kraob min nov knong dey. Orkun chren nas dael mork dol tinis daoy sovattapheap."

Wi says, "Vea kruan te mean kar pibak tam phlao krao khet Battambang pon norse krao pi nous phlao srourl te."

There were twenty-story apartments and massive pagodas with their ornate roofs towering over us. This is Indochina, Bhudda land. Time to cool out. I am looking out the compound's entrance way to the street and I see a man with no hands stop to light a cigarette. The poor guy has got two stumps where his hands should be. Those landmines. But wait. He uses his mouth to pull a cigarette out of the Pall Mall pack in his shirt pocket and then rearranges it in his mouth with his lips. He then squeezes a lighter between the stumps and makes a rubbing movement until the lighter is going. He bows, and lights the cigarette.

Now out comes the rest of the MSF staff. Aukeje, the pretty Dutch administrator we'd been having the radio calls with; she's followed by the secretary, the accountant, the man who makes tea for the staff all day, and Madame Leanne, the receptionist who kind of reminds me of Madame Boran, only she stayed in France with her relatives while Saloth Sar was killing everybody here. Everyone's hugging and doing the three-sided kissing and shaking our hands. I'm so glad you're okay, says Leanne. She's kind of half-hugging me, patting my arms and torso to assure herself that I'm still in one piece. Everyone is shaking their heads at how dangerous it must be up in Sisophon.

"There's more risk from a car accident or from the bad food," I say, and they all think I'm joking with them.

Another Land Cruiser comes squealing around the corner. Maurits is annoyed at the irresponsible driver. He's getting ready to scold whoever it is; this is Maurits's country. He's in charge, after all.

But he doesn't get the chance. The driver whips open the door and jumps out, yelling, "Dick, Dick!" It is Ian Small.

"Don't call me that name. I hate it."

"Dick. Ha, ha! Whoa, Dick-man."

I can hardly breathe from his hug and my feet are an inch off the ground.

Maurits is shaking his head. "I knew I shouldn't have agreed to send him up to Sisophon," he says.

"Dick," says Ian. "We're going to do it, man. We're going to save the country."

"Better start with Banteay Meanchey," says Maurits. "Now let's help him with his bags. Let him rest a bit."

As we go into the office, Ian tugs at my beard and rolls his eyes. Then he shows me his shirt pocket with a wad of Cambodian Riels. He says he's got cold beer in his truck too. And he wants to talk all about MSF back in Toronto.

"Oh, I've got it all planned, Dick. Just you wait."

His plan was simple: celebrate by indulging all night in the finest restaurants in the capital.

But first we go to one of the many places called the "Mekong Café." This one has a picture of the moon at the entranceway. We sit in wicker chairs and Ian tells me about all the Canadians in the field now, waving his hands as he talks: "We are real! MSF Canada exists."

I tell him how the head office has been coming down on me, telling me in their words to "focus on my work in the field." I ask him if he's heard anything. He says everyone's cool about MSF in Canada. All is well with the French now, not like before when they told us "non!", and Luxembourg and the Swiss too, no problem. Same with Josep Vargas and the Spanish. Everyone was with us.

But I think for a minute. Maybe the Dutch aren't really with us like they say. Maybe they don't want Canada to have an independent section. Perhaps they're trying to do an end run around us, keep Canada on some kind of a leash and keep all the nice funding and healthcare workers from our country for their own projects.

"Hmm" says Ian. "Either way. We're real, we've done it. MSF Canada exists."

That night Ian and I and half a dozen others went out, all over town. We started at five and had dinner at Lumiere on a busy boulevard that felt more like Buenos Aires than Phnom Penh, and we kept it going until three a.m. when we closed down the King Fisher boat bar. Coen Albers, the Dutch surgeon, was with us. At one in the morning, we banged on the door of the Reunion Française restaurant because Ian swore it was open and he saw someone moving around in there. We kept banging on the door and kicking until some dogs started yapping. Phnom Penh was owned by the dogs at night and finally someone woke up and came down. Not all that happy about it until we gave him ten dollars to open up the restaurant to serve us dessert. We wanted the crème caramels. Everyone talked about them. They were the best in Asia. There were about ten of us there, eating in silence with the restaurant owner and his wife and kids watching us from the shadows in the back.

At two a.m. the streets were already quiet but we found some cyclo drivers going home and hailed them over. These cyclos, they had two bicycle wheels in front and between the wheels there was a spring-loaded seat big enough for three. The driver sat behind the passengers, up high on a wide leather bicycle seat. It was an inexpensive way to be chauffered around Phnom Penh. That's how everyone did it. Amsterdam had city bikes, Manhattan had yellow cabs, and Phnom Penh had cyclos.

We asked the drivers to switch places with us. We paid them off to let us drive *them* around. That was new. When we sat the drivers up front in the spongy seats, cars stopped and people came out of their homes to cheer us on. It was a little out of the ordinary to have a group of expats pedaling the cyclo drivers around the middle of the Monivong Boulevard.

After three a.m. the streets were hushed, dead, even, and the only ones out were the police walking their beats. No wind was moving the banana fronds. No cars or children. You might see a cat tiptoe around a corner, nothing more. Carla, the nurse from Svay Rieng, and Dirk, a Belgian logistician, walked me back to house Number Four, the one reserved for the field workers coming back to the capital. It was a simple house, with working faucets, a toilet, and shower, things I hadn't seen in months; there was even a couch and a proper bed with a new mosquito net. The bedroom was many sizes bigger than my room in Sisophon.

Dirk called himself one of the "silly people" and he'd invite you to play along with his jokes and fantasies. He'd carry you along in them. After a full night of what we had all been doing, we had an imaginary bowling match on a hushed residential street. He'd roll the imaginary ten-pin ball down the road and wait for the pins to fall. And then magically, the ball would come back along the track, automatically popping up for the next shot. Those streets near the Independence Monument all looked the same at night. In fact they looked the same in the day, but at night all the houses looked identical. Impossible to tell them apart. All bungalows behind a wall, one or two sugar palms, one or two banana trees.

We were trying to get back into MSF's Number Four House to retire for the night. Time for a cool shower and a sleep—we needed it after the night of substantial jocularity in the capital. Of all things, the key didn't work. We started cursing the receptionist at headquarters because, with the wrong key in hand, we'd now have to walk all the way back there, ten blocks away, and it was late and there'd be the dogs barking at us. What a bother. So someone gets an idea, I think it was me. Let's just hop up over the eight-foot-high wall and go inside. Why bother with the key? There was a way of getting over the wall by using a window ledge and a piece of bamboo to boost yourself up and over. Only thing was you had to be really careful about the jagged glass. As an extra security measure, along the tops of all these walls, they had cemented in hundreds of shards of glass to dissuade criminals and other irresponsible riff raff from doing—well, exactly what we were doing.

It wasn't much of a problem for us to climb over and we managed to do it without getting any cuts and also without making any noise. We thought our antics were pretty good and we were accusing each other of breaking and entering and how ridiculous it all was. Then I went to the bathroom and for once it was a fully stocked bathroom with toothbrushes and shaving cream. There were new posters and calendars on the walls and the furniture looked different. Even the kitchen looked all new and totally impressive. I thought the office team must have brought in all this new stuff during the day when we were downtown. Nice of them to spruce it up like that. What a nice gesture. We reclined on the comfortable couch admiring the handsome home and all of the new fixtures, then continued our tour around the house and looked in one of the bedrooms. There was a man sleeping under a mosquito net, which was strange, because nobody else was supposed to be there. So, as I was getting a closer look, we realized we didn't know the man and that this wasn't the Number Four House after all. It was somebody else's house. We had climbed into the wrong house.

We tried our best to stifle our laughing—didn't wake anyone and climbed back over the wall, out onto the street. Got our bearings and made it over to the right house where the key actually worked, had one final beer on ice, and slept till noon.

24

The Cambodiana Hotel

Phnom Penh, Cambodia / December 1991

Maurits and Ian and I meet about Sisophon. Maurits is fairly happy at the progress, confident we'll be getting more funding soon. After he leaves, I meet with the accountant, somebody from the central pharmacy, and an EC official, and then Ian and I start talking about MSF politics. I tell him about Jim Lanes letters, how he says the Dutch are tightly controlling everything, not prepared to let us run things freely. No green light like before. There is some nasty stuff going on back home. Ian says "Nah, can't be." We use the phone at headquarters to call Jim Lane but can't get a connection. No all-important update from Toronto.

People leave me alone at headquarters after the debriefings. Ian decides to go out to procure supplies for Sisophon while I hang around, making phone calls, writing home, walking. It isn't enough. I want luxury. I've been stuck up north for months with nothing in the way of extravagance and in a few short days Ian and I are going to be on a plane back up there. I need a greater rest. I need to "get Western."

I've a few hundred dollars with me, most of it left over from my fifty-dollar monthly stipend, which is hard to spend up in Sisophon, but I've other money too. People keep talking about the Cambodiana, the new luxury hotel built on the Mekong. Maurits says it isn't open yet and asks aloud why anyone would want to go to a Western type of hotel anyway. I'm twenty pounds underweight, haven't bothered to shave in a month, can't sleep because of the heat, and terrorized by loudspeaker noise everywhere I go. Why would I want to go to a five-star hotel?

The Cambodiana even rated a mention in one of the staff meetings. Aukeje from Holland told me about it. They said they would make the Cambodiana off-limits because people from MSF were the ones at the frontlines of the humanitarian crisis in Cambodia and shouldn't be seen staying in luxury hotels. It is bad form. Only problem is, the ones making the rules had never lived at the front. They could go to the French restaurants any night of the week. They could telephone home. They had plumbing, swimming pools, tennis. But still, it is important that I behave, look, and act the part. I remember Jacques de Milliano saying I had to like it.

So Maurits comes up to me in his sandals, not smoking this time but smiling. He is trying to be nice about it. He starts with, "No more motor scooter riding around Phnom Penh." It is too dangerous, he says. We will have to walk from now on. I note very carefully that he said no motor scooter riding "around Phnom Penh" and just nodded in agreement because with that mention of "around Phnom Penh" it meant, technically, we could still ride them in Sisophon. Rob will laugh when I tell him that.

Then Maurits says, "Did you really spend three hundred dollars on phone calls? Dat is echt obsceen. That's the record. I had Madame Leanne in the office check it because they hadn't ever seen a total so high before, but it was correct. Ah yah, you miss your girlfriend. I know. How did she get a nice Dutch name, anyway? I thought all you had over there were British and French people."

He mentions that there has been a new complaint about MSF people disturbing the neighbors by the Number Four House and did I know anything about it? No? Well then, he says, there is another thing. It is about accommodations. MSF will only pay for the Sokhalay-Aeroflot Hotel, which I know is the crappy one with the occasional rat in the elevator, and if I didn't like that I could stay at the Number Four house. But for sure, MSF isn't going to pay for the Cambodiana or even part of it. He says it was "contra to our sensibility."

Right there I see my plan. I could check in to the crappy Sokhalay-Aeroflot Hotel, leave messages about me being out around town for the day, and then out for the evening seeing friends, but in actuality I'd go directly to the Cambodiana. I was bent on it at that point. I needed to swim in its pool, indulge in a steak dinner and drink real coffee while reading the morning's *Herald Tribune*.

And one more thing from Maurits. People have been talking. He wants to know if I am "okay." That's precisely what he says. He doesn't mean physically sick with Dengue or Shigella; he means more like am I hanging together okay. Gerald and Caroline had said something and I hadn't been in touch in those last weeks from Sisophon. Aukeje said I had made fun of the radio communications. These are real security issues, he explains. The report I had given to him and Eric Goemaere is fine. More than fine. On the face of it everything looks like it is going well up in Sisophon—well, as good as to be expected in a partly massacred, Wild West kind of town surrounded by a few hundred thousand landmines.

He ends the monologue with, "Have you given any thought to extending?" He says there are remarkable opportunities opening up here. MSF is going to be the first into all the new zones and we are going to be having a huge role with the deplacée. He says Kratié in the east would be something I couldn't miss—all the refugees and deplacées returning. Cambodia is being reunited. Then he says, "We can find a job for your girlfriend. Think about it. You should consider continuing here. Come on," he cajoles. "I want to show you something."

We take his Land Cruiser down Norordom Boulevard past the National Museum and Royal Palace to the Sisowath Quay and arrive at an unfinished four-story-high white building. The neighbour to the right is the new German Embassy and on the left is the headquarters of a European construction conglomerate. Workers are coming and going, wheeling cement bags into the unfinished home. Others have six-by-twos under their arms. They disappear under an arch into a courtyard that looks grand, but empty. Everything is whitewashed and there are no fixtures in place, no art on the walls, nothing wired up. Up above on the first, second, and third floors are a total of about fifteen rooms, each with an entrance onto the hallway and a view either of the old city or the Mekong River and the Quay where there are some more embassies and other buildings under construction.

I am standing in the new MSF headquarters.

"I know it's overkill." He says it like the Dutch do—"Ooooverkill"—"but we are the biggest private medical charity in the country, biggest budget. I know it looks like a development headquarters, but we have the lead here. The country's in an emergency, a big one that won't go away."

He shows me where some of the permanent staff will sleep, where the reception and meeting rooms will be. And on the roof is an open space exposed to the scorching sun during the day and the stars at night. A perfect location for parties. Off to the corner there is a group of flow-erpots and some plants neatly positioned away from the wind. They are orchids and they are Maurits's, one of the pleasures he enjoyed to get away from all the planning and managing and complaining. The view of the city, well, I had only seen it like this from a plane. Two million Cambodians living in grey apartments and rickety homes. And off towards the Mekong, only two blocks away, is the Cambodiana, gleaming white with an Olympic-sized pool filled with blue, lightly chlorinated water, perfectly uniformed attendants at its edge, ready to serve.

The man's name escapes me. He works in the MSF office part time. I don't know what his job is but I had seen him around the supply area, by the trucks and in the administration area working with receipts. There is some creepy slickness about him and his English is pretty good. Everyone else parlez francais. He helps me load my silver Zero suitcase and Ortlieb waterproof bag into the truck and we start driving to the crappy Sokhalay-Aeroflot Hotel.

"You are staying at the Cambodiana, yes?"

"No, not me."

"Everyone says you are going to the great hotel. It's open now, yes."

"Is it?"

"Bat hoy! Greatest hotel in all of Kampuchea."

We are going down a residential street and he slows down by a house and some girls come out. They are giggling, speaking a dialect unfamiliar to me, and my driver is revving the engine to impress them, behaving like it's his truck. He says, "Last night I paid them two dollars and they took their clothes off. Yes, these ones." The girls are giggling, covering their mouths and then a man comes out of the house. My driver puts his sunglasses on and we are on our way.

He starts talking in a hushed tone. There is no one else in the car. He wants to know if I can keep a secret. Sure.

"I have some bones, yes."

"Bones?"

"Yes, I will sell them to you."

"Why?"

"Because I like you. You are my friend."

"Okay, you like me, but what are these bones?"

He looks around and lowers his voice further.

"US pilot remains."

"Huh?"

"They are real. They are the bones from a killed pilot. Shot down in the war."

"What the hell do I want with something like that?"

"Stop yelling. You could sell them. You have connections, I do not, yes?"

"No."

"Please keep it a secret."

"Whatever."

"Don't tell Maurits."

We go up to the steps of the crappy Sokhalay-Aeroflot Hotel. It's dark, the lobby walls are faced with cracked porcelain, and no one is there. My driver tells me to wait. The street around the hotel looks fairly safe. I sort of know where I am. Someone finally comes out. I wonder if she works for the hotel because she doesn't know how to give me a room key. No matter, she has me fill out the forms and checks my passport, riffles through all the accordion pages and visas, and eventually she finds my special visa from the Cambodian government. I have to show her the visa. That way she can bill the MSF account directly.

I ask my driver to leave. Normally an MSF driver charged with delivering an aid worker to a hotel will insist on staying until the paperwork is done and the bags are moved upstairs, but not this one. He sees an opportunity to go and play for an hour somewhere. Play hooky. So, I send him away and, yes, of course I won't tell anyone that he's not going straight back to headquarters. As soon as he's gone, I ask for a cyclo and a minute later I'm being taken along the back streets, the streets where the expats do not normally go, so I'm invisible. The driver extends the black canvas canopy over me, positions an umbrella to block the sun and passers-by and I disappear behind my knock-off Ray Bans. The only way I can be identified is by the silver suitcase, so I cover it with a newspaper and tell the driver "Cambodiana, svp."

I left a note at the front desk of the Sokhalay-Aeroflot Hotel saying I was going to be out all day sightseeing, back very late with some friends of friends from Sisophon. Such dedication by me. Meeting with Sisophon folks down in the capital just to further the good relations. I also left a note at the MSF office saying I was going to take advantage of my last three days in the capital. I said I'd be out there enjoying Phnom Penh and its restaurants. I made a joke about trying to put some weight back on before going up north. I reminded them that this was my holiday and I kind of made it seem like I was saying, "Can you please leave me alone for a few days of peace?" Everyone knew my request to stay at the Cambodiana had been declined, so I felt I would be given a free pass to do whatever else I wanted.

We arrive at the hotel, stop at the gates, and immediately people from inside the great hotel run out to me. I shake the cyclo driver's hand. He looks in his palm and then bows to me. Two people are carrying my bags and one is just walking with me pointing out several features about the new hotel, its amenities, and how far along the construction is. No, no, "absolutement," there is no problem, the east wing is fully functional and I will be one of the very first honored guests.

They all make way to spin open the revolving metal and glass door, a window to this bastion of luxury. There are uniformed attendants standing listlessly at different stations and some of them are sagging into a podium or slouching against a wicker chair. As we enter, we are hit by a gush of cold air and all the uniformed attendants straighten up. A customer has entered. Everyone is smiling and they're even greeting me in English. Of course they have rooms. Of course everything is fully functioning—the pool, the restaurant, the spa, and the smoking room. Yes, they have in-room dining, and, after a minute, the manager on duty is delighted to report that a junior suite has been made available for me. I hand over a magic plastic card, sign the register, offer up my passport, and the manager is smiling away.

The two who carried my bags into the lobby are nowhere to be seen. Now I've got two new helpers. A third one comes from behind a corner and presses the elevator button for me. Why trouble myself? It's really cold in the hotel but I'm not complaining. Still, maybe I should buy a new sweater in the boutique. As we go up, I peer out the elevator windows. Every window gives a steeper perspective on the Mekong River. "Saart," they say, it's very beautiful. And just down the hall on the eighth floor is my room. Double doors to get in. The luggage floats into the closet, the curtains slide apart, there are round light bulbs the size of melons lining the bathroom mirror, and the tub is oversized.

One of them opens a cabinet and the television glides out. He turns it on. I stare at it. I'm lost looking into it. The picture and sound are very clear. I had forgotten how it carries you along, mesmerizes you.

An announcer is describing a car race that just finished five thousand miles away at Hockenheim in Germany. There are words running along the bottom of the screen, something about the Olympics and how splendid it will be in Barcelona. That should make Olaf happy. And that is followed by two reports about the Soviet Union. One on somebody Yeltsin in Moscow and one on Reagan in Berlin. And then it flashes to a stock market report. My god, the markets have soared.

One of the bellhops coughs. Oh. Let's see, most Cambodians make about three hundred a year, divide by three-sixty-five. Call it a dollar. Two happy men.

The door shuts and I run a bath. I've got the TV on CNN nice and loud so I can hear it while the bath's filling and I've got the stereo even louder. I'm looking over the room service menu and can't believe the prices. "No," I'm told over the phone, "the prices are correct. You get a discount while the hotel is under construction."

The prices were so cheap I begin to paste the room service chits in one of my Grumbacher notebooks, the sixth one I've filled up to that point in Cambodia. The chits from that day show me starting off with a Heineken, the real ones from Holland, two crème caramels, then imported flank steak doused in wine, with Perrier and, I confess, ice cream, a cigar from the bar's humidor and another Heineken. I had a second bath right after dinner. The bill says I watched three movies that first day, back to back to back. Called everyone at home. My brothers couldn't believe it was me for a minute. For once I got to make calls without having the MSF receptionists in the same room. Just too interesting for them not to eavesdrop.

In the morning, around ten, I call the crappy Sokhalay-Aeroflot Hotel to see if there are any messages, but it is a bad connection and the receptionist doesn't understand French, English, or my Khmer, so I let it go. I have to repeat my name and recite all the words I know for "message" in all the languages, but nothing registers. After several minutes we hit upon "MSF." She gets MSF and says, "Ah, oui, MSF, les médecins docteurs, oui." But that is it. Not that helpful.

I don't care. What can they do, fire me? Then I wouldn't have to go back to Sisophon. I am a bargain at fifty dollars a month and besides, I had told one person where I am just in case everyone got stressed. That is Guy, the Belgian administrator-logistician, whom I trust. He is in and out of the office all day, and for sure he would have heard something if they were trying to locate me. He said, "I don't fucking care if you go to Cambodiana. No one should. It's your money."

I hit the Olympic pool to sun tan and add to my weight. Entire pool to myself. I pace myself with the desserts and beverages from the outdoor menu and I remember penning something in my journal about the Epicurean approach to luxury hotels. That as opposed to hedonism. The former leads to a sublime balance, the latter to overindulgence, like stuffed Romans. I wanted the sublime. And it's worth pointing out, if you took Phnom Penh, or Sisophon for that matter, vanquished the armies and put your room beside a tropical body of water like the Mekong or the South China Sea, you'd have a Caribbean kind of paradise.

The hotel is almost empty of patrons, yet there is a full complement of staff. Three of them attend to me at the pool. Soon a fourth shows up with my repast: fresh fruit, imported cheese, coffee, and the morning's *International Herald Tribune*. The paper must have been flown in on the early flight from Bangkok. The moment I feel hot, I dive in the pool. I keep diving in and out of the pool all morning until I've had more than enough sun and need to hide out indoors.

That afternoon there is a knock at the door, which is funny because I haven't ordered anything. I am in the middle of one of the five movies I had been watching up to that point. When I open the door it is Guy, all smiles, with his girlfriend, also smiling.

"What, is this your private palace?"

"Only friends allowed," I tell him as they saunter in.

"Are we allowed to smoke here?" asks Guy.

"I don't see why not. I'll just open a window. What shall I tell them to bring us to drink?"

"Oh, beer."

"Really? Better look at the menu. You can have those fancy drinks. The ones they put in a pineapple."

Her eyes light up. Guy says something about how long he's been waiting to watch that movie. They curl up on the one bed and I'm on the other. The delivery arrives and the steward doesn't care there's the sweet aroma of smoke in the room, but we give him an extra tip to make sure.

"US dollars okay?"

"Bat hoy!" says the smiling steward, there is no problem. None whatsoever.

25

Pochentong International Airport

Phnom Penh, Cambodia / December 1991

After forty-eight hours at the Cambodiana, I'm ready to step back into the swelter. I've put on a few pounds, far from ideal, but I'm recharged. I spend the next day running around the city getting things. Almost against my will, I am preparing to go back. Sisophon is tugging at me and I am dreading it. But I want to see them all again. Especially the kids.

I find Ian Small in one of the busy laneways under a canopy in the Russian market by the dry-goods area. He is leaning against some crates, smoking and adding up figures and supplies. All of our stuff is going up by truck tonight. We fly tomorrow.

"All of these crates can't be just for us?"

"Yeah, we need it."

There are about twenty crates full of hospital and building supplies.

"Does Rob know you bought so much stuff?"

"I don't know."

"Might have been a good idea to check with him."

"He told me to take care of it. So did Maurits. That's what I'm doing."

"Yeah, but we've never had anything like this. Nothing close. Why do we need two generators? And the paint?"

"Maurits wants us to quadruple everything. You saw the budget. We're going to be as big as ICRC."

"What's this?"

"Canned hams, cookies, pasta, cheese, some wine."

"That's all for us?"

"Sure."

"No way. We'll never eat that much. Never."

Ian laughs. "Don't worry, we can get refills in a month. I'll arrange to have it all sent up by truck."

"This is crazy."

"I'll take care of everything. You don't have to be a logistician any more."

Two men from the MSF office come by carrying a crate. They hoist it up and into the back of the truck and then in unison take out handkerchiefs to wipe their brows. One of them is the driver from the other day, the one who tried to sell me the US pilot bones. He waits until Ian and the other guy are busy talking.

"You didn't tell Maurits about the bones?"

"Never mind."

"I know you went to the Cambodiana," he whispers, as if it were a State secret.

"Get lost," I tell him. He smiles; he thinks I'm joking.

That market, the Russian, is by far the best in Phnom Penh. You can get anything you want here, still, in these dying days of the Soviet empire. Comecon is delivering the luxury goods but it's obvious the Soviet Union is either doomed or destined for a new era. I wander off to find what may be the last tins of caviar and boxes of Romeo y Juliettas or whatever Cuban cigars the shopkeepers have tucked away in some corner of the market.

Those Russians, they always had the best perks: little treasures mixed in with bags of flower and cans of crankshaft oil. Potato vodka from the Ukraine; red wine from the Boyar Estates in Bulgaria. We had found it with ease many other times at the beginning of the year, but where are they now? I make a full sweep of the place. The rows of stalls are confusing, so Ian and I start asking around. We hadn't missed anything. Our suspicions are confirmed: the Russian goods are all gone. The people tell us the Russians left a week ago. Our favorite stalls had disappeared. Rob was right. Comecon was fading away along with the Soviet Union.

Guy says he knows of a Comecon station out by the industrial park, the one that has cured meats and, we hope, caviar and cigars. When we arrive, though, the Russian butcher ignores us. The shelves are mostly empty up front. He has some butter tins and breads, stuff we can get anywhere, but Guy knows the cagey ways of this butcher and surmises he has other stuff tucked away out of sight.

"Where's the wine and fish?"

He shrugs, waiting. Guy shows him some US money and the butcher signals us to wait. He allows the other customers to leave on their own time.

"He's got wine. No cigars, no caviar. Why do you want that shit anyway? The fish eggs are probably bad."

"How many bottles of wine does he have?"

"He'll sell you six."

"Not a case?"

"He's saying six."

"All right, six, but ask him again about the cigars."

But this time, the man speaks directly to me. "No cigars. I smoke. I want cigars. Can't find."

We had struck out at the Russian market and at the butcher's shop, and next day we were to head up to Sisophon without cigars, but we did have all the other goodies. But that afternoon, Ian says in a triumphant tone, "Your package arrived." It is a fortuitous moment. He is hugging something the size of four loaves of bread dressed in clear plastic bubble wrap. There are stickers on the wrap detailing how the package had arrived in the Kingdom of Cambodia via Bangkok, Singapore, and the famous House of Hajenius smoke shop on the Rokinstraat in Amsterdam. The Indo-Swiss courier service had done it again, faithfully delivering four boxes of premium Cuban cigars, intact and properly humidified—at a price, of course.

Maurits doesn't show up at the airport to see Ian and me off. He typically sees people off at the airport, so I'm not sure what this lack of courtesy means. For the most part he was always considerate while having a tough job to do, but there were times, obviously, when he wasn't there for you. I figure the only way he'd be happy is if I told him I'd stay on another year. Then I thought, Maybe he found out about my stay at the Cambodiana.

It's always a bizarre scene at the airport. Planes late, late, late. People getting mad about it. People having to return home and come back the next morning. People's luggage being flown off and out of Cambodia although they're not even on board. Sometimes it's a carefully orchestrated system to get bribes out of people—and I don't mean an extra twenty US at the airport. It is more of a social relationship, as in, Get to know us, make us happy long in advance, you know, a kind of arrangement, and we'll make sure all your people get on board early, just fine.

All over Africa and Asia, airports are their own world. One day, I was at the International Airport in Maputo, Mozambique, along with a no-nonsense Dutch pediatrician. This was the leave I had taken from Harvard for a month to visit MSF programs. The pediatrician warned me about the pickpockets and fraud artists. You had to pay US $40 as a kind of departure tax, and, sure enough, there was a man at the departure gate on the tarmac waiting for passengers to filter through. He was leaning on a lectern. While my Dutch acquaintance was fumbling for the money in her money belt, the man took it from her and helped himself to about a hundred extra. She called him on it. He tried to make it seem like he had made a mistake. But there was no note of apology and it was no mistake. She erupted, and there was quite a scene. The supervisor arrived and the man tried to make it seem like he was just trying to help the lady find the correct change. So the supervisor motioned to us to be on our way as the man was only trying to be helpful. Then she went berserk, going on and on about how she was in *their* country trying to help *their* people, working for next to nothing, and this was the thanks she got. She said words that were meant to shame the official, trying to get everyone to notice, to get him in trouble, but I know the only thing the man was ashamed about was that he didn't actually get all her money.

So Ian and I have been waiting in the lounge of Pochentong International Airport in Phnom Penh for a couple of hours, waiting for the Tupolev Tu-134. It's hot outside, maybe a hundred, but inside we are roasting. Someone in their wisdom decided to keep out the heat by shutting all of the windows. The windows are up high and you needed a long pole to flip open the latch. No one knew where the pole was. But the lack of air conditioning was a boon for the soft-drink lady. She was selling soda pops by the dozens. Ian and I both thought collusion was at work to sell more soda pop. The way these things go, she may well have been paying a kind of tax or kickback to her co-conspirators.

The Tupolev arrives, its four rear-mounted jet engines thundering as it touches down. We watch through a window as the plane crawls to a halt. The pilots deplane but the passengers are kept onboard for a half hour. It's not clear why. Then the travelers are allowed to leave. Some of them kiss the ground. The plane remains on the tarmac for another two hours. No one comes or goes. No baggage is removed. No fuel truck drives up to replenish the tanks. Ian is adding up the hours. He says in another two hours, the trip would have been faster by car.

Finally we are all ushered out. Nice breeze. Our shirts dry. Some official does a head count as we go out on the hot asphalt. Ian and I try to find our designated seat. First problem: our tickets say 36-C and 36-D. Surprise, the last row is designated 28. We have to go back inside the terminal. Everyone does. The flight has been double-booked. We find ourselves back in the steaming lounge and the soft-drink stand is, of course, closed. No more cola, Fanta, or Viet Namese Heineken.

A little quicker this time, we are issued new seats and ushered out in single file. This time it's the pilot himself who checks our tickets and taps each of us on the shoulder as we go up the steps and into the Tu-134. It looks ancient inside. This plane is of Sixties vintage, and I'm wondering how well it's been passing regular maintenance checks.

"Nah, they've got to pass all the same international standards that planes all over the world do," says Ian. I am not convinced.

The stewardess comes along to make sure our seat belts are on. It isn't sufficient that they are buckled across our laps; she tests them and pulls them tight. She puts her back into it each time. The door is shut and soon a kind of fog fills the cabin. There is a problem with the air conditioning. After a couple of minutes I can't make out the passengers just a few rows ahead of me. The stewardesses run through the pre-flight announcements in French, Khmer, and Russian. We have no idea what they're saying but Ian's seat is broken and he is admonished by a stewardess for not putting it upright. But the hinge has fallen off. It's cracked into two pieces. So then there's a mad attempt to fix it before takeoff. He's got two stewardesses leaning over him, trying to right the seat. After a while they give up. We take off with Ian in a semi-reclined state and then the fog starts to abate. As Phnom Penh recedes into distance, Ian says he wants water or a beer. Oh, we both would love a beer. The man across the aisle from us is pouring his own Mekong brandy into a cup he brought. He drinks it, pours another and makes eye contact with Ian. "Chong?" he says.

"Chong hoy!" says Ian, accepting the shot of brandy.

Then he makes a very bad face. Mekong brandy is raw, like vitriol, and everyone complains about it. There's no beer on the plane. Everybody is given a plastic bag holding a stale ham sandwich. We drink from communal plastic cups, maybe ten of them. When one section has had enough to drink, the stewardesses gather the cups, splash them with a bit of water and then hand them out to the passengers in the next section.

I remember a flight from London to Blantyre, Malawi. It was a decent modern plane, a 747, and I was seated next to a sixteen-year-old girl who lived in Blantyre. We had filet mignon and a selection of reds, and two in-flight movies. She was a totally typical sixteen-year-old, smart, worldly enough, the jokes didn't skip over her. Two or three times a year she had traveled to the U.K. to see relatives. She could have passed for someone living out her youth in Manchester or in a suburb of Philadelphia. I was quite ignorant of the politics of Malawi at the time and the most I knew was that there was an eighty-year-old former physician running the country, Dr. Hastings Banda, so I asked her about him.

"Oh yes," she said, "he's a wonderful man. He's made the country great."

Well, that's nice, I thought. But later I found out all about Banda, and all of the innocents disappearing in Malawi and how this Banda may have been ninety already, not a real doctor but up to his ears in blood he'd spilled. You should have seen the piece Amnesty wrote about the good doctor. So I wondered about that sixteen-year-old and her comment about the "wonderful" Hastings Banda. Had to have been a coached line. Something her father taught her to spout when a conversation with a stranger turned to the politics of Malawi. Maybe she thought that I was an informant, someone ready to cosy up to her on the eleven-hour flight home to uncover any anti-Banda sentiment, make some notes and pass it along to some clandestine branch of the Malawi police.

But here in Cambodia we are speeding north in the Tu-134 and down below the country is green. Lush green from all the rain and sun. Even the lakes are green now, each one a soup of algae. We are gods flying at half the speed of sound a few miles above the ground. Kings in the temples below could not have imagined this. Up over the Tonle Sap we fly, due north to Siem Reap. Ian is excited to be going up north, away from the suffocating capital. He wants to see the ancient ruins and to meet Rob and see little Sisophon for the first time. We fly to the edge of a mile-high thundercloud. I think, Aren't you supposed to avoid such clouds because of the powerful updrafts and downdrafts, and the lightning?

The plane bounces through some rough air and suddenly an updraft sucks us up a few hundred feet. Everyone is glued to their seats until we level out. The passenger next to Ian gives a "Wow, I'm glad that's over" look and just as quickly we start plummeting down and our trays are floating in the air. We feel light and a dozen people are screaming. I look over at the Cambodian businessman, the one drinking the Mekong brandy. He's got two hands pushing the paperwork down on his lunch tray. The stewardess is hugging a headrest and has a leg coiled around a seat. In an instant where I actually fear for my life, I see Smiles.

But just as suddenly the plane steadies. The screams turn to relief laughter. The stewardess uncoils herself and marches off to get a tray of sandwiches and the businessman is back at his paperwork. When the plane lands, passengers—mostly Cambodians—again kiss the ground and then march off to find their luggage. The airport is so sleepy. The attendants couldn't care if you walked right through customs to where the Russian military helicopters are standing by an old Anotov AN-2—a plywood biplane still in service. We walk through the airport lounge to the entrance way, in expectation of finding a car waiting to pick us up. No car. "Who cares?" Ian says, throwing down a bag to use as a pillow. He has made it up north to a place where there is a new kind of peace to behold. He just wants to take it all in. The temples. The jungle. Pure nature.

We fall asleep and are woken by a horn. A muddy Land Cruiser careens around the corner. It's two hours late.

"Bad roads," says Rob. "We're going to have to spend the night in Siem Reap."

"Don't mind if we do."

And when we get there, Siem Reap is showing the signs of progress. The Grand Angkor Hotel was a wreck when we saw it half a year ago; now the lobby has been done up in gold paint and teak. A man in a uniform stands beside a concierge desk. The Grand Angkor is looking like a mini-Cambodiana with a pool and concierge desk. A concierge desk for what? For tours of the Temples, says Rob.

We couldn't stay at the MSF Siem Reap house; it is bursting with new nurses and doctors. It seems like their project grew and they got tired of everyone passing through and bunking down. These days everyone is taking time to tour Siem Reap, to see the temples—spooky, thousand-year-old Buddhist works of genius.

26

L'Hôpital Provincial de Banteay Meanchey

Sisophon, Cambodia / January 1992

There goes Ian. His first job is to build a latrine and wash stand for the hospital, out back where the tuberculosis patients convalesce. Rob is gone for the day to the Thamar Puok outpost where even he admitted the system was working, so Ian is in Sisophon calling his own shots. I watch as he leans on a spade, smoke in one hand, directing three workers. One to bring in the pipes, one to lay the tiles, and one to pour the cement. Cement? What's wrong with wood? The latrine he is building is so solid it's bomb-proof. It has a stainless steel pump and a clay shingled roof. The drain and a scrub-down area have grooves in the floor so that the waste water can be channeled neatly away to the river. I'd never seen one like this.

Rob let out an "Oy, yoy yoy" when he saw Ian's handiwork. "That's one month's construction budget gone in a day. Dit is een probleem!"

"Saart nas," replies Mogiath, saying how beautiful it is. He launches into a speech about the virtues of MSF. Ian is a very, very welcomed new member of the team. The next morning the cement has hardened and the families are washing their clothes. Everyone is smiling on this sunny day, putting their backs into the washing. Mogiath says we should photograph the latrine and wash stand. This, he declares, is an example of the great success and partnership for le Hôpital Provincial de la nouvelle provence Banteay Meanchey. Such a good-looking hospital now.

Mogiath is now directly discussing plans with Ian. Why trouble Rob? Mogiath and Ian can figure out how to spend all the new money themselves. They need a new entrance way and terrace for the administration office. This is for business purposes. Also, the pharmacy building is long overdue for its "promised" repairs. I see Ian and Mogiath in the middle of the compound. They're taking turns pointing to buildings. This one could use a better roof, that one needs a new cement foundation. The thing is Maurits wanted this. But I see something coming. Rob will be intervening, reasserting his control, and Mogiath and the others won't be liking it. Not one bit. They aren't about to get the fancy hospital they have all been fanaticizing about. It isn't going to be like the ICRC hospital complex in neighboring Mongkol Borei.

We gather at the hospital café. Ian promises to tone it down for a while. Rob says he's willing to open his thinking. We all agree to a new unified front. And what do we see from the café that day? A deplacée family. It is the first to come through Sisophon, likely the first of many thousands given the new Paris peace treaty. They are like refugee families, only they are living in camps inside the country. We never see them in town, but here is a family walking right past us at the café. A family of seven. The father and oldest son walk out in front, leading a mule hitched to a wooden cart. In the cart, stacked high, are boxes, all their possessions, some food, and water jugs. Children and one old woman, likely the matriarch of the family, are crammed among the possessions. I glance into the cart and see the kids but don't see a sign of their mother.

Rob yells, "Sok sa bay?"

"Bat, sok sa bay!" replies the man—he's well.

"Coming back from the camps? On your way back home?"

"Bat, we're going back to the Stung."

"Where's that? By the Tonle Sap?"

"By the Thom."

"Ho," says Rob. "Isn't there the Khmer Rouge over there?"

"All gone. They went to Pailin."

"How many more are coming?"

"Many more," says the man.

In Pailin, the Khmer Rouge are guarding the gem mines and cutting down all the hardwood forests for currency. With the hard currency they are buying weapons from the Chinese and using them on the

Khmer People's army and government troops. Officially the Chinese deny selling arms. But the jungle forests are undeniably being razed. All gone forever. Just like in Europe. An arboreal continent shaved clean.

I remember standing in the Jacmel River mouth in Haiti where it empties into the Caribbean Sea. Men were bathing upstream and some boys were working a net trying to catch tarpon and snook. I stood there knee-deep feeling the brown water tug at me. Same thing as here. The Haitians are cutting down all their trees. No longer anchored by the tree roots, the topsoil sloughs off easily and is washed into the sea. And without topsoil, there's nothing to soak up all that water. The flash floods come. Nothing can grow. People get sick with all those pockets of stagnant water and limited food. Bad thing, that deforestation.

Rob had disappeared for a couple of hours to meet with Sao Sim and the governor's representatives. He brings news that the border with Thailand is opening. In fact it was already opened to travelers with special visas. There was going to be a kind of parade with Thai and Khmer government types meeting at the border bridge for a joint crossing. We were invited—MSF was going to be one of the lead trucks going across the border. We'd have to put the flag on the back and fly it high. For a year we had been fifty kilometers from the border, close enough to smell what they were cooking for supper. Now we could go there and eat it. The only way to Thailand involved two days overland to Phnom Penh, wait for one of the biweekly flights to Bangkok, then drive southwest to Aranya Prathet, then Poipet. A week. All because the armies were in the way.

The convoy is fronted by three military jeeps, one with an antiaircraft cannon, and there are two troop carriers with us. Next in line is the government Land Rover, two private taxis of dignitaries, then us. Wi is driving, so Rob, Ian, and I just relax, have a beverage and start scheming about what wondrous things we are going to buy. Rob is the expert, having lived for several years in Thailand. He says he knows just where to find everything. "Just you wait," he says.

Over the border it is tranquil in Aranya Prathet. Just a tropical town, everything calm and easy. Life isn't hard here. Aranya Prathet is like Sisophon, except it has Western noises, neon lights, lots of cars, air conditioning. It is all plugged in and in color. And milk. Shops have milk and different kinds of ice creams. We haven't been able to get that in a year. Proper eggs, too, not the crunchy mysterious kind, and cheese, different kinds of fresh bread, canned ham, cereal, potato chips, and chocolate bars. They also display cassettes with recognizable music, newly released movies on VHS, international newspapers, and televisions. Everything for a modest price.

We make some phone calls home. It is lunch hour, so when we call everyone in North America we are waking everybody. Who cares? We had made it to Thailand. Still, we aren't able to reach Jim Lane. Too bad. A call from the field like that would have been fun. Instead, we fax him a message. Thailand is connected. Not like Sisophon. Cambodia remains another world.

You can tell a Thai from a Khmer at a hundred yards. The Thais are thicker and taller, lighter-skinned, and they dress differently, more cosmopolitan, like Japanese tourists with shopping bags and cameras around their shoulders. They come along in twos and threes. Their sense of magic and ghosts is strong, kind of like the English. But the Thais hate to be alone. They can't stand it. The other thing is they don't stare at us. Foreigners aren't that rare over here. We aren't a spectacle for once.

Each of us spends a month's salary on the new Thai bounty. The food alone fills seven Deluxe Superior coolers. We throw everything in the back of the Land Cruiser and, later that day, take it to the Blue House in Sisophon. Some stuff needs to be set up. Rob wires up the TV and the new stereo and I get the new shortwave hooked up to the speakers. The BBC Asia report fills our home. We discover we get one TV channel with the aerial, but still, we have videos, about twenty movies to feast on. Ian fires up the new generator that he built under a cinderblock bunker to keep it quiet. It gives off a gentle purr instead of the noise we had come to hate.

We played "Achtung Baby" so loud you couldn't hear the afternoon announcement. For once a small triumph over the haute-parleur. No noise complaints from the neighbors either. They loved the noise. Anything but silence and numbness. We swing open the gates and ten of the neighborhood kids—Smiles, Monster Man—all of them come up to the balcony and dance to our music, mouthing the words they don't understand. Little Genius was the best at it. Rob finds some soda, and we have ample ice for once, on account of Ian's organization. We don't have to worry about that stuff anymore. The party lasts for a couple of hours. We keep searching through the coolers and finding treasures. Every time we stumble upon something savoury and perishable, we remind each other that we'd better eat it up right away to avoid spoilage.

Bun Thoeun comes by. We don't know where he has been of late, and as he comes up the stairs, how about that, there is the reason in his arms. It's a baby girl: Toch Thoeun. Our lead doctor was a father. Well, we say, there'd be a special gift from Rob and me when we get to it. Come on up, we yell to all of our friends passing by on the road. Join the celebration. The border is open and our standard of living has gone up a few notches. The first movie we played that night was the spaghetti Western *The Good, the Bad and the Ugly*. It took us away. It resonated because Sisophon is a Wild West town.

Almost every night now we watch movies up there by the balcony. The kids come too, half a dozen at a time, stretching out on a pillow, blankets laid out on the smooth mahogany, and watch the cinema, calling for popcorn. Instant American kids.

I don't think any of the kids have ever watched a movie before, and maybe they've snuck a look at one of the TVs in town, but it was all Thai crap picked up from over the border, or some lousy propaganda film produced in Phnom Penh.

We have a library of forty or fifty movies now, some classic Hitchcock, Spielberg, and a twenty-fifth anniversary history of the Rolling Stones that we watch again and again. It's hilarious watching Keith's non-enunciation. Late at night we would throw on Coppola's *Apocalypse Now* with all its gore and heavy scenes, like the bull sacrifice and the head in Martin Sheen's lap. Ian's going, "Cool," and Rob's saying, "It's amazing," and in the background there was Madame Jewn, peaking up from the stairwell, eyes bugged out, riveted.

One movie night we were watching *Star Wars* with a handful of the kids on the floor, when we hear someone shouting up at us from the street. It's Monster Boy and as always he is naked and in a combative mood, skipping around in a circle to get our attention. He's taunting us for fun, wiggling his nose in disrespect, calling us bar rang. He's three.

So we shout down to him to come on up and, as soon as he's in the house, the others are making a face because of a bad odor. The other kids always made fun of how dirty he was. Monster Boy was filthy, dirt caked everywhere. So we thought, time for the bar rangs to wash away all of that Cambodian dirt. Give him a bath. Soap him up, wash his hair, and then pour scoopfuls of water from the ung pot, washing it all away until he's squeaky-clean. We give him a squirt of Madame Jewn's knock-off Chanel Number Five, tie a balloon to his wrist, and send him home, a bit bewildered and still completely naked to his family. He ambled down the mud road, now only managing a half-skip every few steps in between glances back at the bar rangs in the Blue House.

The thing was, his father was the town's water delivery man. He had been filling up our ung pot all year. But he wasn't just the water delivery man; he was the *blind* water delivery man. Blind for twenty years, he had never actually seen his kids, but he sure could smell them.

None of the new Thai stuff rivaled the old standby, the white and gold Frisbee, the one the kids went wild for. Better than balloons. Better than money or chocolate. They always want the supernatural Frisbee. We'd bring it out and, like dogs noticing a scent, half a dozen kids would come out of the bushes wanting to play. They would even keep their voices hushed so the others in town wouldn't hear. They wanted the Frisbee for themselves. Outside our door, we'd have ten kids and then twenty, then fifty. The first few times we had over a hundred children running after Ian and me as we launched the Frisbee back and forth over their heads, their hands waving at the disc as it floated by. Smiles loved the game, catching the Frisbee even with her baby brother on her hip—until she was too tired and I'd feel a tug on my shirt—Smiles passing her brother to me. The kids would be happy to play all day but after a while, the game always ended. There was a rice lake in the way, or the deplacée camp or the minefields.

Or one of us had to do rounds. That's what ended the fun for me. Rob was away overnight again in Siem Reap and Ian was out at the Thamar Puok outpost. We were finally making good progress there.

Not easy to have a success in the countryside. But it meant I was on my own again for a day. Had to pass by all the wards. See what was up and make sure no one was critically ill. All is okay on the maternity ward. A new one entered the world just as I arrived. It's a boy held by his tired, smiling mother. All is fine on the adult ward too. I am spooked for a second because the old man we had been helping all month was nowhere to be seen. I have been so used to seeing him in the corner bed, I assume something grave has happened. But there he is, leaning on a cane, standing all by himself for the first time. His eyes are saying, "Look at me." Well, he'll be going home soon.

But then Sok Samuth, the nurse, wants me. He's not looking so pleased. Even a little worried.

"What's the matter, Sok Samuth? Can't be that bad."

"Bat, bat, everything's fine," he says.

"That's good. You look like you saw a ghost."

He manages a half-smile and he's got my hand, taking me across the compound to the children's ward. As we cross the compound a fierce wind blasts us. It makes the corrugated tin roof rattle.

"What's the matter? A mine? Some kid step on a mine? A blessure?"

"No. Not a mine."

We walk in and there's a mother standing by her child. It's a little girl. She's a very beautiful girl with straight black hair, maybe six or eight, big eyes, a bit younger than Smiles and just as lovely. But she's lying too still under a white sheet on the bamboo bed and her mother is talking in a monotone, staring off to the corner asking for help from Buddha. The little girl is staring at me, tracking every move I make. She's so weak, all she can do is move her eyes.

Sok Samuth approaches the bed and takes down the sheets. It's very sad what we see. The girl is inhumanly thin and her skin is peeling off. He pulls the sheet up over the girl's body again and the mother keeps up her monotone plea for Buddha while the little girl follows me, eye to eye. She wants me to make her feel better.

I'm thinking, No, not this one. The whole thing was about this one. It was always about this one.

"What is it?" he asks me.

"I don't know. Is there a fever?"

"Non, pas de fièvre." She is cool to the touch and there isn't any shivering, no chills; it is just that she is so very thin and her skin is like that. All my team could tell me was that she'd been sick for a few weeks and that her appetite was poor for a week and that she became worse before the weekend. That's when they came here, but they couldn't come right away because the father was away working. They were from the countryside out by Thamar Pouk and they had waited before coming.

We did the tests, the usual ones, and nothing turned up. We gave her the medicines of choice and fluids and tried to get her to eat. It was hard for the mother to keep her daughter's head up while we tried to feed her.

I radioed the capital but could only get Aukeje in Phnom Penh. I tried twice that day, but no one else was around. Why couldn't they have a physician available to go over things when you had a difficult case? They did manage to patch me over to Siem Reap; I asked Monique, the head of mission there, about the girl. The reception was poor. It was always poor to the east but on that damn day it was impossible.

I checked the two pediatric textbooks we had at the Blue House. Nothing. It could be kwashiorkor, protein malnutrition, all by itself, but we weren't hearing about that out in the countryside. It was still lush and the harvests had been so good. Why would she be starving now? So maybe it is a cancer. I was thinking, What would Professor Jim Anderson do? How would my great mentor go after the diagnosis?

27

Sisophon

Cambodia / January 1992

Madame Somath comes to wake me. Someone has followed her up-stairs, and through the slight blur of the mosquito netting I can see a man smiling. She normally wouldn't have brought someone straight up like that while I was sleeping, but I suppose she sensed something about my old friend Andrew Thompson.

"Dr. Thompson. My favorite Kiwi doctor."

"You said to drop in if I'm ever passing through Sisophon."

"Man, it's good to see you."

"Last time I saw you, there was a lot less of you. I'm glad you're healthy again. Look at you. You're almost fat. And where's the beard?"

"I let them take care of me in the capital. They're way prettier than the barbers here in town."

"Yeah, you don't want these guys."

"How long are you here?"

"I need a bed tonight. And I haven't eaten since dawn. Is the Lotus still in business?"

"Oh, yeah, and that short woman Dee Ling will squawk right to your face if you don't order the min sup pau."

"I hate that."

"She'll squawk if you don't order it. I'm telling you."

That timing couldn't have been better. I liked that guy so much. Him and Coen Albers. Something about the way they moved through the space as doctors—total naturals. His driver got their Land Cruiser up on our tarmac beside the blue fence, and Madame Somath told

235

the driver where to put all their stuff for the night. She was mostly in charge now. Since Ian had arrived, we didn't need as much help in the house and around town. Madame Jewn showed up on weekends and during the weekdays when there was extra work.

Andrew and I eat at the Lotus restaurant. Dee Ling squawks at us from the kitchen, and Andrew twists his head around every few minutes to tell her the food is fine, to placate her. He says it honestly isn't that bad, which is quite a compliment because Andrew had been working up at Khao I Dang on the Thai border, where you can get Tom yam pla krop and Pla nung khing sai het along the palm-tree-lined boulevards.

We talk about everything, about how the peace is coming now and how the country is being reborn. He remarks that spending a year in Cambodia is a traumatic experience and that it can't help but change you. It changes everyone. He writes his address beside a sketch of the Blue House in my Grumbacher number six. It's his parents' address in New Zealand, a permanent address, because who knows where he'll be in a year or two, or in a decade. He tells me he's moving on. He's finished two years here, shaking his head as he says it. Time to go.

I ask him for one favor before he leaves.

"Andrew, there's a girl on the ward. Quite ill. I can't figure it out."

We're there in a few minutes. Andrew's driver has the Land Cruiser idling outside the compound gates. The mother's speaking less now and the little girl, I can't get over how beautiful she is and how her eyes are tracking me around the room.

Andrew is shaken when he sees her skin. "Has Rob seen her?"

"No. He's been away the whole time."

"What are the tests showing? Nothing? I'm not surprised."

He leans over the girl and hears her heart sounds with his stethoscope. The lungs are clear still. The stomach is still.

"It might be TB. Treating it's worth a try now."

Andrew looks over the chart and then leans over the girl and brushes a lock of black hair away from her eye.

In the morning I see the mother in the courtyard by one of the horse-drawn carts, and then I see what I don't want to see. A nurse is carrying the little girl, wrapped up in the white sheet, her face shrouded.

They place her tiny body in the back of the cart, and the mother isn't talking now. All she manages is a nod to the nurses when they lay her daughter in the back of the cart. And then they started moving along the High Road, I suppose up to Thamar Puok.

There is no need to do rounds right then. I tell them no tea today. All the other patients are stable, I suppose, and receiving the right care. At least there are diagnoses for everyone to work with. I slouch into the brown-thatched MSF office, and maybe ten minutes later I get the Grumbacher out and fail to write something. Such big white eleven-by-fourteen pages. I wait until eleven-thirty to walk home the back way, the way that takes me across to the Low Road immediately away from the hospital compound. Take the usual shower but no lunch. Look at all my cigars and music and videos and all the photos Rob had on the wall of our fabulous year in Sisophon. I crawl under the mosquito net but sleep does not come. I go out and sit downstairs on the cracked steps by the ung pot.

Little girls in Cambodia stay by their mothers until they can walk; then the siblings take turns holding them on hip as they run from one plaything to another. They live in a veritable paradise. When the child is heavy she learns to walk and then to run. Better hurry up or she might miss the game. You can hear them calling. Then comes school and all that wondrous learning, maybe the Bopha Lokey dance and ancient songs. Tao Rean, they call it, and it lasts until they enter young woman-hood. That's when the Bonzes offer welcome and the doors are opened for marriage and family. This latter blessing continues the never-ending cycle of life and how little girls give us more little girls and little boys, and on and on.

So you get to see life and death as a humanitarian, beautiful little girls dying, that kind of thing. They call it témoignage, witnessing.

A shadow moves across the fence. There is only one child who can stand in silence, without saying, "Om," or, "Balloon." The shade and sun catch her between the slats. She has her hand up, the fingers poking through a knot hole in the fence, wanting me to catch them before she runs away. It is the game we play.

"Not now, Smiles. Not today."

I can see she's beaming away, and her fingers are still there.

"Please, Smiles. Not this day."

But that little Smiles is persistent. She knows if she's patient, I'll come over to the fence to try and catch her fingers, and she will get to run away. She'll get to win the game. I'm looking around the Blue House. The stupid Blue House on the punishing Low Road, in god-abandoned Sisophon. Up I heave, heavier than I thought. Okay, Smiles, here I come. Out of habit, as I cross the tiny courtyard, I look in the great ung pot. The water's clear and there's that tiny silver fish, skittering around.

Smiles is looking right at me; her little pug nose is scrunched up and her eyes have got that glee in them. I reach up to touch her hand and I'm reaching up slowly because what's the point? I know she'll pull it away and win the game. The game always ends like that with the elusive thing going away.

But this time, she does not pull her hand away. She keeps it right there for me to touch. How about that little Smiles? She doesn't even try to move and I'm holding her tiny fingers, and they feel warm and very much alive.

"You're beautiful, little Smiles. Blessings on you. How do they say that here? Choom Reap Soo-ah?"

"Cha," she nods yes, "Choom Reap Soo-ah."

Ian has the Land Cruiser packed up, ready for the final run to Phnom Penh. He's got a small box in the back holding ten choice bootleg cassettes he picked up in Bangkok, a full complement of soda crackers, Edam cheese, and Swiss chocolate, plus a six-pack of beer we had newly discovered in our market: Stella Artois. There are vacation resorts on the Riviera with less selection. Finding luxury isn't much of a challenge anymore.

The weeks had somehow melted away until the new year festival arrived. This year a television news team showed up from Thailand to cover the event. The TV crew crammed their equipment into a four-by-four and drove over the border in a matter of hours. It used to take a week. Not the same old Sisophon anymore.

A week later, we had the first rain and, with it, the first ultra-hot weather. The skies were filled again with those massive mile-high rain clouds.

Things couldn't be going better in the hospital or out there in the outposts. As well as can be expected, anyway. Ian was staying on until summer when his year-long contract was done, and Rob—well, you kind of had the impression Rob wasn't going anywhere. His Cambodian adventure had started on the Thai side in the refugee camps and now he had seen the refugees start to come home. He was nearly fluent in Khmer, very much harmonized with the people and the place. My guess was he'd build a home somewhere closer to Siem Reap. And that was going to be some impressive home with all those lightly taxed Dutch Guilders the good doctor had socked away over the years.

It was time for me to get back home. Literally, time to cool off a bit, see what my girlfriend Carrie was up to. Maybe start something up with her. Maybe make our own little kouns.

Ian had been up early on this day. He told me a radio message came through from Maurits asking officially if I'd consider staying on another year. I could do a six-month contract, or even three. They were flexible at head office and were interested in discussing options when I arrived. They said I'd be in line for a two-hundred-percent raise. I'd be topping US $200 a month.

"Why not stay three more and then decide?" Ian asked.

But Rob didn't bother asking. He recognized when someone had had enough.

About twenty of the townspeople we knew came out to say goodbye.

Madame Boran appeared in an ankle-length purple sarong, smiling with her beetle-nut-stained teeth. Hard to believe she was fifty. Bun Thoeun and his wife had their baby with them, little Toch Thoeun, and everybody took turns peering into the wicker basket.

Mogiath had sent regrets that morning about not being able to attend, as he was feeling unwell. I tracked him down anyway in his private office across from the hospital wards. He was embarrassed as I walked in and he tried to get up off the bed where a private nurse was placing cups all over his naked back. This was a traditional therapy called cupping, a perfectly harmless healing they all did. The nurse put a flammable grease inside the cups, lit them, and while they burned, placed them on Mogiath's back. When the flame snuffed out, it caused a vacuum and the cup was suctioned to his back. I told him to rest. That it's no problem. Those cups, I'm sure were making him feel much better. I said I had come out of respect to thank him for his support all year and most importantly for being a friend.

Mogiath's chin was in full swing and out came the same old speech about the "historic co-operation" between the Hôpital Sisophon de District Banteay Meanchey and MSF. "Oui, oui, oui, MSF est la meilleure organization medical du monde." And, to ensure his bets were spread nicely around the craps table, he added a few kind words about the new physician, a Dutch national on his way to replace me. But the speech faded. And then he said nothing for a minute and his chin trembled. "Mork vijn. Come home to Sisophon soon, my friend."

As I walked over to the Land Cruiser, all the kids were patting me on the back, giving hugs. They had skipped school to see me off—how irresponsible of little Genius and Monster Man, and their friend Barbie. But where was Smiles? She was nowhere to be seen. Only yesterday I had tried to give her a gift and explain what was happening, that I wasn't coming back for a long time. "Ott mork vijn," I said. But when I reached out to hold her, she took a few steps into the bushes and after a minute ran away behind her house.

Then, as I heaved myself up into the Land Cruiser for the last time, I saw her. She was behind a dense patch of green, moving to hide herself as the wind jostled the leaves. I didn't think this part of it was going to be so hard. She was just a little girl. I wanted her to know that she was a very beautiful girl, "Saart nas" as they say, that she was the most precious thing I found in Cambodia. I had Madame Somath confirm my Khmer phrasing. But she didn't know the word "precious." No one knew it and then Bun Thoeun came over. I know he got it right because he said it first in French and next in English. That Bun Thoeun, always right up on everything. And I know Smiles heard it when I yelled out, calling her, for the first time, by her traditional Khmer name, Dee. Because when I said it, she stopped moving and the bushes no longer hid her, so I got to see her that one last time.

As Ian clambers in beside me, and gets the truck idling, I think of the day before, when he and I hiked up the Tun Kean volcanic mountain, up past the crazy Bonze lady walking in her circle trance, over the jagged volcanic rocks up the thin trail to where the wind was streaming, taking away our sweat and giving us a break from the heat. Our pant-legs were flapping in the wind. It was the same constant perfect breeze I had first felt up in the high country of Grenada and all over East Africa and even in the mountains of Peru.

Ian offered me the Frisbee.

"Your honor, man. You're the one leaving."

"I'm going to throw it into the wind and float it all the way out to the Tonle Sap."

We stepped out onto an outcrop. Ian kicked away some of the loose stones and started a countdown. When I launched the Frisbee, the wind up there, it was too strong, and the Frisbee took a crazy steep dive and crashed a few meters away.

"No, no, no," yelled Ian, as he scaled down the rocks to get it. "This is how you do it."

But the same thing happened. The wind was working against us and just as the Frisbee was airborne it took the same crazy dive. That wind wasn't letting us throw it away.

"We have to go over there. Where there's more of a sudden drop," I said.

"If we go over there, we won't see it go. The Frisbee is white, man. It'll be lost in the sun. The wind will just take it up into the sun and we'll never see where it comes down."

We began to crawl over to a better spot but Ian wanted to have a smoke first and get out of the wind. Last chance to celebrate, last chance to relax up there in the high country.

It's hard to hold a light in that wind, so he huddled behind a man-sized boulder. It reminded me of the famous "smoking hole" on the mountain edge of the Soudan Couloir ski run at Whistler-Blackcomb.

But there's no snow in Cambodia, none the Khmer culture has ever seen, just sugar palms and temples built by Suryavarman II. The view will never leave me. A thousand-foot-high black jagged mountain standing in the middle of a sea of green squares. Rice fields in every direction, disappearing in a fuzzy haze where there should be horizons.

I held the Frisbee, ready. The wind calmed for just an instant and I let it go.

"Did you see that?"

Ian nodded. He said it had to be the perfect shot. The Frisbee went out and up, straight into the white haze.

Endnotes

The following entries provide detail about people, places, and organizations mentioned in *Cambodia Calling*. The information has been sourced from encyclopedic sites, scholarly articles, annual and scientific reports, national and local newspapers, and magazines, as well as journal notes, travel logs, and conversations. A bibliography is attached.

CHAPTER 1

Milton Obote

Uganda became an independent nation in 1962 with Milton Obote as prime minister. After overthrowing the King in 1966, Obote changed the constitution and elevated himself to president. Coups and counter-coups occurred throughout the next twenty years. In 1971, Idi Amin took power, ruling the country militarily for the coming decade. It's estimated that 300,000 Ugandan lives were lost under Amin's rule. He forcibly removed the entrepreneurial Indian minority from Uganda, decimating the economy. His reign was ended after the Uganda–Tanzania War in 1979 in which Tanzanian forces, aided by Ugandan exiles, invaded Uganda, returning Obote to power. Two months after the author traveled through Uganda, Obote was deposed once more in July 1985 by General Tito Okello. Okello, in turn, was ousted after the so called "bush war" by the National Resistance Army (NRA) operating under the leadership of the current president, Yoweri Museveni.

CHAPTER 2

Jinja

Established in 1907, Jinja is the fourth largest city in Uganda. It is located approximately 90 kilometers northeast of the capital, Kampala, on the north shore of Lake Victoria, near the source of the White Nile River.

CHAPTER 3

Médecins Sans Frontières (MSF)/Doctors Without Borders

Médecins Sans Frontières/Doctors Without Borders is the world's largest independent, international medical relief organization, best known for providing humanitarian medical assistance in war-torn regions and developing countries. Working with local national staff, the organization currently provides medical care and education to populations in more than 70 countries, and is strictly neutral.

The organization was founded in 1971 by a small group of French physicians and journalists in the aftermath of the Nigerian Civil War. The group witnessed human rights abuses and public health disasters during the war but was unable to provide medical assistance due to political constraints. This, in effect, put them in the position of being complicit with the offending government. Upon their return, they were determined to find a new way to respond rapidly and effectively to public health emergencies, with complete independence from political, economic, and religious influences.

MSF is governed by an international board of directors, and is organized into 19 sections, including Canada. About 3,000 doctors, nurses, midwives, administrators, and logisticians run international projects, alongside thousands of national staff. Approximately 1,000 permanent staff recruit volunteers, manage finances and organize media relations for the twenty sections. Eighty percent of the organization's funding is from private donors, and the remainder comes from governmental and corporate sources. MSF's annual budget now approaches half a billion USD.

MSF was awarded the 1999 Nobel Peace Prize "in recognition of the organization's pioneering humanitarian work on several continents," according to the Nobel Committee.

CHAPTER 4

Makerere University

Makerere University was established as a technical school in 1922 and became the University of East Africa in 1963. Today, Makerere University enrolls about 30,000 undergraduates and 3,000 postgraduates and has a full compliment of academic courses and degrees. Mulago Hospital is the largest hospital in Uganda, and is affiliated with Makerere University. Many post-independence African leaders, including former Ugandan president Milton Obote and Tanzanian president Julius Nyerere, studied at Makerere.

Drs. Liz and Don Hillman

Elizabeth Hillman grew up in Northern Ontario and was educated in a railway car converted into a school and family home by her father who was the local teacher. She attended medical school at the University of Western Ontario (UWO class of 1951) and postgraduate training in pediatrics at UWO; McGill; Great Ormond St. Hospital in London, England; Harvard; and the Liverpool School of Tropical Health. While at Harvard, she married Donald Hillman (McGill medicine Class of 1951) and had five children in seven years. Based in Montreal, the Hillmans held various positions at McGill's Montreal Children's Hospital and McMaster University, and had many international placements together, including Malaysia, Bhutan, Laos, Viet Nam, South Africa, Zambia, Tanzania, Kenya, and Uganda. Both received awards from the Royal College and were named to the Order of Canada in 1994. Don Hillman died in July 2006.

Kenneth Mason

Kenneth Mason is an English thespian and movie actor who was based in Nairobi in the 1980s. He appeared in Sydney Pollack's 1985 Oscar-winning movie *Out of Africa* as the banker. The movie was based on Karen Blixen's true story about rural life in colonial East Africa.

CHAPTER 6

James E. Anderson

Professor James Anderson had a varied career as an anatomist, physical anthropologist, medical educator, and specialist in adolescent medicine. Born in Perth, Ontario, in 1926, he was orphaned while still young. He entered medical school at the University of Toronto, graduating in 1953, and worked with the well-known anatomy professor, J. C. B. Grant, later acting as editor of Grant's *Atlas of Anatomy*. As an archeologist he researched early human morphology and civilization in Canada, Mexico, and other places, and created a manual in 1962 called *The Human Skeleton*. Anderson left the University of Toronto in 1967 to become chair and professor of anatomy at the new medical school at McMaster University. As one of the original founders, he was a champion of the self-directed, problem-based, small-group learning approach at the school. He developed an interest in the social and educational issues particular to the adolescent population and created a unique alternative high school in the 1970s, called "Cool School," to provide a learning sanctuary for marginalized yet bright children challenged with learning disabilities. Famed for his brilliant and unconventional approach to academia and medicine, he was also well-known for his sense of humor, and his special connection with students was legion.

CHAPTER 7

McMaster University School of Medicine

In 1966 a group of innovative founding educators including Dr. James Anderson and Dr. John Evans, the school's first dean, created a non-conventional medical school. The hallmark of the educational style was self-directed learning, a problem-based curriculum, and self-evaluation. The resulting school initiated a revolution in healthcare training worldwide and the faculty has a strong reputation for excellence internationally.

Grenada

Christopher Columbus first sighted the island of Grenada in 1498, calling it Conception Island, and it was later named Grenada. The colony became a Crown Colony of the United Kingdom in 1877. Grenada became independent in 1974 under the leadership of Premier Sir Eric Matthew Gairy, the first Prime Minister of Grenada. Gairy's government became increasingly authoritarian and dictatorial, prompting a coup d'état in March 1979 by the charismatic and popular left-wing leader Maurice Bishop. Bishop's failure to allow elections, coupled with his left-leaning views and cooperation with communist Cuba, did not sit well with the country's neighbors, including the United States. A power struggle developed between Bishop and a majority of the ruling party. This led to Bishop's house arrest and eventual execution at Fort George on October 19, 1983. A new pro-Soviet/Cuban government under General Hudson Austin assumed power under a coup d'état. At that time there were about 50 Cuban military advisors and 700 armed construction workers on the island. Six days later, the island was invaded by United States forces during a military operation called Urgent Fury.

CHAPTER 8

MSF Canada

The Canadian section of Médecins Sans Frontières/Doctors Without Borders (MSF) was officially founded in 1991, but the movement in Canada started several years earlier, notably in 1988 when MSF Holland gave tacit approval for its development. Like each of the nineteen national chapters of MSF, Canada recruits medical and logistical personnel to work with national staff on overseas missions, improves public awareness of human rights issues, and raises funds from the general public and government agencies. MSF field projects respond to situations where human security is at risk, such as public health emergencies caused by armed conflict and poverty. The MSF Canada National Office is located in Toronto. Since 1991, Canadians have taken on close to 2,000 international field assignments in over 80 countries and have raised funds approaching $100 million (Canadian dollars). In 2006 MSF Canada directly managed healthcare projects in five countries: Colombia, Côte d'Ivoire, Haiti, Nigeria, and Republic of the Congo.

CHAPTER 9

Cambodia

The Kingdom of Cambodia is located in Southeast Asia and borders Thailand to its west and northwest, Viet Nam to the east, Laos in the northeast, and the South China Sea in the south. Phnom Penh is the capital city. Cambodia succeeded the Hindu and Buddhist Khmer Empire, which spanned the Indo-Chinese Peninsula between the 11th and 14th centuries.

Most of Cambodia's 13 million people are Theravada Buddhists and are of Khmer heritage. The nation also has a substantial number of ethnic Chinese, Viet Namese and Muslim Cham, as well as small animist hill tribes. The Mekong River cuts through the center of Cambodia. The Khmer refer to it as the Tonlé Thom or "the great river" and the Tonlé Sap, "the freshwater lake," an important source of fish for the nation. Much of Cambodia is near sea level, which allows for a phenomenon unique in the world: the Tonlé Sap River actually reverses direction in the wet season. The river flows backwards, carrying water from the Mekong back into the Tonlé Sap Lake and surrounding flood plain.

In 1863 King Norodom entered into an agreement with France whereby Cambodia would remain a protectorate. From 1863 to 1953 Cambodia was part of the French colony of Indo-China. After war-time Japanese occupation (1941 to 1945), Cambodia gained independence on November 9, 1953. Becoming a constitutional monarchy under King Norodom Sihanouk in 1955, Sihanouk abdicated, handing his father the throne. This allowed Sihanouk to be elected Prime Minister. When his father died in 1960, Sihanouk assumed the title of Prince and head of state. Sihanouk remained officially neutral as the Viet Nam War progressed; he was ousted in 1970 by a military coup led by Prime Minister General Lon Nol and Prince Sisowath Sirik Matak. While stationed in Beijing, Sihanouk realigned himself with the communist Khmer Rouge rebels who had been slowly gaining territory in the remote regions. He encouraged his followers to overthrow the pro-United States government of Lon Nol. This hastened the onset of civil war and the rise of the Khmer Rouge.

Secret B-52 bombing raids by the United States on purported Viet Cong bases within Cambodia occurred after Lon Nol assumed power. As the Cambodian Communists strengthened in Cambodia, the bombing escalated and eventually included strikes on suspected Khmer Rouge sites. There is wide variation to the estimates of the number of Cambodians killed during the bombing campaigns. As many as half a million civilians are believed to have died from the bombings and 2 million were made refugees. Such military action galvanized support for the Khmer Rouge, turning many thousands of young Cambodians against the US-backed Lon Nol regime. The Khmer Rouge reached Phnom Penh and took power in 1975, changing the official name of the country to Democratic Kampuchea, led by Pol Pot (Saloth Sar).

Cambodian specialist Michael Vickery indicated that about 750,000 deaths in excess of normal occurred during the Khmer Rouge regime and approximately half of these were due to executions. The "Finnish Inquiry Commission" gave a figure of roughly one million dead from killings, hunger, disease, and overwork; and of that 75,000 to 150,000 is a "realistic estimate" for outright executions. There are higher estimates of Khmer Rouge atrocities, and some estimates have been criticized as being politically motivated exaggerations. A figure of three million deaths between 1975 and 1979 was given by the Viet Namese-sponsored Phnom Penh regime, the PRK. Father Francois Ponchaud's research suggested 2.3 million; the Yale Cambodian Autogenocide Project estimated 1.7 million; Amnesty International estimated 1.4 million; and the United States Department of State, 1.2 million. Khieu Samphan and Pol Pot cited figures of 1 million and 800,000, respectively.

Part of the death toll under Pol Pot can be attributed to the conditions left by the war with the United States. Because of the destruction of infrastructure and general predicament of the population, rice planting for the next harvest would have to be done by laborers and farmers who were seriously malnourished. The final United States AID report predicted "widespread starvation" and "slave labor and starvation rations for half the nation's people" for the coming year, and "general deprivation and suffering ... over the next two or three years before Cambodia can get back to rice self-sufficiency." Cambodia scholar David Chandler commented that the bombing turned "thousands of young Cambodians into participating in an anti-American crusade," as it "destroyed a good deal of the fabric of prewar Cambodian society and provided the Khmer Rouge with the psychological ingredients of a violent, vengeful, and unrelenting social revolution." Philip Windsor opined that "French intransigence had turned nationalists into Communists," and "American ruthlessness now turned Communists into totalitarian fanatics."

Viet Nam invaded Cambodia in November 1978 to stop Khmer Rouge border transgressions, to end the genocide of Viet Namese people in Cambodia (who were persecuted out of proportion to the rest of the population), and to end the genocide in general. Warfare between the Viet Namese and the Khmer Rouge continued from 1978 to the late 1980s with almost no international arbitration or involvement. Beginning in Paris in 1989, peace efforts culminated two years later in October 1991, with the United Nations being given a mandate to deal with refugees, to secure disarmament, and to enforce a ceasefire. It was the first comprehensive peace settlement in Cambodia in over twenty years.

Only in recent years has political stability taken hold in Cambodia. In 1997, however, political stability in Cambodia was upset during a coup d'état, but the nation has remained stable otherwise. Cambodia has been a recipient of significant economic and humanitarian international aid (notably from developed nations such as Japan, France, Australia, and the United States) as well as from the NGO community. MSF continues to work in Cambodia.

CHAPTER 10

Angkor Wat

Angkor Wat is the holiest temple in Cambodia and was built for King Suryavarman II in the 12th century as his capital city. Located in Angkor, near Siem Reap, it is the largest temple at the site, and the only one to have remained intact and is a significant religious center. The temple is an example of the high classical style of Khmer architecture and has become a symbol of great national pride and the country's prime tourist attraction for visitors. In January 2003 riots erupted in Phnom Penh when a false rumor circulated that a Thai soap opera actress had claimed that Angkor Wat belonged to Thailand. Angkor Wat was over-grown with dense vegetation and required considerable work in the 20th century. Though the restoration slowed during the wars in the 1970s and 1980s, little damage was actually done to the temple.

CHAPTER 11

Sisophon

Sisophon is the main city of Banteay Meanchey, Cambodia, and is sepa-rated by Cambodia's National Road 5 and National Road 6. The largest hospital in the province is located in Sisophon.

Banteay Meanchey

Banteay (fort) Meanchey (victorious) is a new province in Cambodia cre-ated after the Viet Nam occupation. It is located in the northwest of the country, and its name indicates the furthest advance of the Viet Namese army during its invasion in early 1979. The forces had stopped at Stung Tuk Thlaa (Clear Water River) to the west of town, which was then serving as the dividing security line. During the Khmer Republic rule (1970–1975) and after the 1975 Democratic Kampuchea movement, the Khmer Republic used the region for key military recruitment and training but then in 1977, during the Khmer Rouge Northwestern Region purge, it was converted into one of the execution centers and prisons for the civil-ians and cadres who were accused of being enemies of Kampuchea. Fierce military activity ensued between Viet Nam, Democratic Kampuchea forces, and other factions afterwards and continued into 1991.

KPLNF

The pro-Western Khmer People's National Liberation Front (KPLNF) was created in October 1979 and was headed by former prime minister Son Sann. It came into existence to counter the Communist presence in Cambodia during the Viet Namese occupation and was the stron-gest of the country's non-Communist resistance forces. The KPLNF were sheltered in refugee camps such as "Site 2" inside Thailand near the Thai–Cambodian border not far from Sisophon.

About 160,000 civilians were controlled by the KPLNF. They were survivors of the Pol Pot era, therefore toughened, and a ready source of recruitment for the armed wing, the Khmer People's National Liberation Armed Forces (KPNLAF, commanded by General Dien Diel). Almost a third of their approximately 15,000 guerrillas were wiped out in a 1984–85 Viet Namese counterinsurgency offensive. Their soldiers lacked the military strength of the Chinese-trained and -supplied Khmer Rouge.

Despite prior atrocities by the Khmer Rouge, the KPLNF formed a tripartite political alliance in 1982 known as the Coalition Government of Democratic Kampuchea (CGDK), which included the Khmer Rouge. It also included Sihanouk's FUNCINPEC, an abbreviation of Front Uni National pour un Cambodge Indépendant, Neutre, Pacifique, et Coopératif, or "National United Front for an Independent, Neutral, Peaceful, and Cooperative Cambodia."

CHAPTER 24

Phnom Penh

Phnom Penh is the capital city of Cambodia and is a significant tourist destination for Cambodia. Phnom Penh is known for its traditional Khmer and French-colonial architecture. It is the most populous city in Cambodia and serves as the commercial and political hub. Of 13 million Cambodians, more than one million live in Phnom Penh. In 1866, under the reign of King Norodom I, Phnom Penh became the permanent seat of government. The Royal Palace was built at this time and remains a defining element of Cambodian society, as does the role of the King. Phnom Penh was known as the Pearl of Asia from the 1920s and over the next four decades the city and nation continued to experience growth and prosperity until the civil wars that began in the 1970s.

References for the Endnotes

CHAPTER 1
Adhola,Yoga, "The Roots, Emergence, and Growth of the Uganda Peoples Congress, 1600–1985," Uganda Peoples Congress. http://www.upcparty.net/upcparty/index.htm.
Agence France-Presse, "Milton Obote Dies at 80; Strongman in Uganda, Twice Overthrown," *New York Times*, October 11, 2005.
"I Come from Royal Ancestry," *The Monitor*, part of series, October 2005.
Marshall, Julian, Milton Obote reference, *The Guardian*, October 12, 2005.

CHAPTER 2
Wikipedia, s.v. "Jinja, Uganda," http://en.wikipedia.org/wiki/Jinja%2C_Uganda (accessed September 5, 2007).

CHAPTER 3
Médecins Sans Frontières International Homepage, www.msf.org (accessed August 15, 2007).

CHAPTER 4
Makerere University, "Historical Background," http://mak.ac.ug/makerere/index.php?option=com_content&task=view&id=17&Itemid=71 (accessed September 16, 2007).
University of Ottawa, Dr. Elizabeth Hillman (biography), http://www.medecine.uottawa.ca/epid/eng/hillmanbio.html (accessed October 1, 2007).

CHAPTER 7

McMaster University, Faculty of Health Sciences (description), http://fhs.mcmaster.ca/main/index.html (accessed September 16, 2007).

Wikipedia, s.v. "Grenada-History 1958-1984: Independence and Revolution," http://en.wikipedia.org/wiki/Grenada#History_1958–1984:_Independence_and_Revolution (accessed September 20, 2007).

CHAPTER 8

Médecins Sans Frontières Canada Homepage, "The Work of MSF," www.msf.ca.

CHAPTER 9

Cambodian Genocide Group, "A Brief History of the Cambodian Genocide." http://www.cambodiangenocide.org/genocide.htm (accessed July 25, 2006).

Encyclopaedia Britannica Online, s.v. Britannica.com: "History of Cambodia," http://www.britannica.com/eb/article-129475/Cambodia (accessed July 25, 2006).

Etcheson, Craig, "Documentation Centre of Cambodia," Mekong Network, www.mekong.net (accessed October 5, 2007).

U.S. Department of State, "Country Profile of Cambodia," http://www.state.gov/r/pa/ei/bgn/2732.htm (accessed July 26, 2006).

Wikipedia, s.v. "Cambodia, History of Cambodia, Khmer Rouge," http://en.wikipedia.org/wiki/Cambodia_under_Pol_Pot_%281975-1979%29 (accessed August 20, 2007).

CHAPTER 10

"Editor Didn't Check Rumour," *The Nation*, http://www.nationmultimedia.com/search/page.arcview.php?clid=2&id=73303&usrsess=(accessed January 31, 2003).

Wikipedia, s.v. "Angkor Wat." http://en.wikipedia.org/wiki/Angkor_Wat (accessed October 5, 2007).

CHAPTER 11

Country Studies, "Cambodia Country Studies," http://www.countrystudies.com/cambodia/ (accessed October 20, 2007).

Wikipedia, s.v. "KPLNF/Banteay Meanchey" (accessed October 4, 2007).

CHAPTER 24

National Institute of Statistics, Ministry of Planning, Phnom Penh, Cambodia. 2004. *Cambodia Inter-Censal Population Survey 2004.*
National Institute of Statistics, Ministry of Planning, Phnom Penh, Cambodia. 1998. *General Population Census of Cambodia 1998.*
Peace of Angkor, "Phnom Penh," http://www.peaceofangkorweb.com/ PhnomPenh.htm (accessed October 5, 2007).

Selected Bibliography for the Endnotes

Adkin, Mark. 1989. *Urgent Fury: The Battle for Grenada: The Truth Behind the Largest U.S. Military Operation Since Vietnam.* Trans-Atlantic Publications. ISBN 0-85052-023-1

Beck, Robert J. 1993. *The Grenada Invasion: Politics, Law, and Foreign Policy Decisionmaking.* Boulder: Westview Press. ISBN 0-8133-8709-4

Chandler, D.P. 1993. *A History of Cambodia* (2nd ed.). Boulder, CO: Westview Press

Jerkic, Sonja M. May 2001. "The Influence of James E. Anderson on Canadian Physical Anthropology," in *Out of the Past: The History of Human Osteology at the University of Toronto,* edited by Larry Sawchuk and Susan Pfeiffer. CITD Press: University of Toronto at Scarborough

Shawcross, William. Revised edition (October 25, 2002). *Sideshow: Kissinger, Nixon and the Destruction of Cambodia.* United States: Cooper Square Press. ISBN 0-8154-1224-X

Sihanouk, Norodom 1973. *My War with the CIA, The Memoirs of Prince Norodom Sihanouk, as Related to Wilfred Burchett.* Pantheon Books

Steele, Beverley A. 2003. *Grenada: A History of Its* People (Island Histories). MacMillan Caribbean. ISBN 0-333-93053-3

A Note on MSF Canada

While the founder of MSF Canada is no longer officially representing the organization, I would like to express my immense gratitude to my colleagues, here and abroad, for the friendships that grew out of this journey with Doctors Without Borders. Many people deserve acknowledgment for founding and building MSF Canada and it is impossible to mention everyone. Beyond the seminal contributions of Jim Lane who now practices law in Toronto and Marilyn McHarg who amassed incredible international field experience with MSF and is now MSF Canada's current general director, Ben Chapman, an administrator, continues to guide MSF Canada for these many years. He worked closely with Jos Nolle to establish our organization in the beginning. Dr. Michael Schull was President when MSF was awarded the Nobel Peace Prize in 1999 and Dr. James Orbiniski was International President at that time. Peter Dalglish contributed greatly in the early days as did Kathleen Dennis, Chris Dowry, Jeni Mastin, Steve O'Malley. Alfred Page, and Vanessa Van School. Chris Doll, a lawyer, was on the board for numerous years, and led the development of MSF in the west of Canada, and Dr. Joni Guptil, a current board member, led the development of MSF in the east. Ian Small went on to work many years in the field with MSF and now Oxfam.

International field work is most highly respected in our organization. So too are the local national staff, colleagues such as Dr. Bun Thoeun in Sisophon, who make tremendous contributions, endure great risk, and most often go unrecognized. But it is those we seek to serve that MSF values above all else; the countless remarkable yet nameless innocent people who get caught up in the madness of poverty and war. They are independent of the causes of this peril and they deserve better in our world. As Jacques de Milliano once told me, there are no good or bad victims in war—there are just victims.

Acknowledgments

I have specific debts to acknowledge to two people. They are David Lawson from Burlington, who offered keen literary guidance on all aspects of *Cambodia Calling*; and Don Coles, a great poet, who read my first draft, kept me on track and shared a path to writing.

I owe thanks to other people for their friendship and advice. Sam Hiyate of the Rights Factory who deftly guided *Cambodia Calling* as literary agent and Don Loney who astutely edited this book, conceived of the title and kept the process fun. Several people read early drafts and offered insight: Nikki Barrett, Michaela Cornell, Susan Lawson, and Sarah Lawson. Kanha Chan Say helped with the Khmer translation.

Many people provided encouragement to me: my brothers John and Mark Heinzl, and my parents Jane and Rudy Heinzl who are always behind me no matter what unconventional direction life is taking. (This book is the trip around the world I always promised.)

And to my wonderful family: my sons Ryan and Carson, already great travelers, and my wife Carrie, who was there when I returned.